DEFENDING
POLITICS

DEFENDING POLITICS

POLITICS

Why Democracy Matters in the
Twenty-First Century

MATTHEW FLINDERS

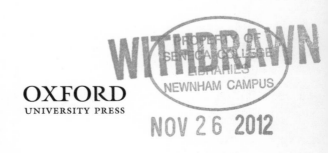

OXFORD
UNIVERSITY PRESS

OXFORD
UNIVERSITY PRESS

Great Clarendon Street, Oxford OX2 6DP

Oxford University Press is a department of the University of Oxford.
It furthers the University's objective of excellence in research, scholarship,
and education by publishing worldwide in

Oxford New York

Auckland Cape Town Dar es Salaam Hong Kong Karachi
Kuala Lumpur Madrid Melbourne Mexico City Nairobi
New Delhi Shanghai Taipei Toronto

With offices in

Argentina Austria Brazil Chile Czech Republic France Greece
Guatemala Hungary Italy Japan Poland Portugal Singapore
South Korea Switzerland Thailand Turkey Ukraine Vietnam

Oxford is a registered trade mark of Oxford University Press
in the UK and in certain other countries

Published in the United States
by Oxford University Press Inc., New York

British Library Cataloguing in Publication Data

Data available

Library of Congress Cataloging in Publication Data

Library of Congress Control Number: 2011942655

Typeset by SPI Publisher Services, Pondicherry, India
Printed in Great Britain
on acid-free paper by
Clays Ltd, St Ives plc

ISBN 978-0-19-964442-1

Politicians seldom if ever get [into power] by merit alone, at least in democratic states. Sometimes, to be sure, it happens, but only by a kind of miracle. They are chosen normally for quite different reasons, the chief of which is simply their power to impress and enchant the intellectually underprivileged... Will any of them venture to tell the plain truth, the whole truth and nothing but the truth about the situation of the country, foreign or domestic? Will any of them refrain from promises that he knows he can't fulfil—that no human being could fulfil? Will any of them utter a word, however obvious, that will alarm and alienate any of the huge pack of morons who cluster at the public trough, wallowing in the gap that grows thinner and thinner, hoping against hope? Answer: maybe for a few weeks at the start... but not after the issue is fairly joined, and the struggle is on in earnest... they will divest themselves from their character as sensible, candid and truthful men, and become simply candidates for office, bent only on collaring votes.

H. L.Mencken, *A Mencken Chrestomathy* (1948)

We fought our battle of words and did not see that the familiar words had lost their bearing and pointed in the wrong directions. We said 'democracy' solemnly as in prayer, and soon afterwards the greatest nation of Europe voted, by perfectly democratic methods, its assassins into power. We worshipped the will of the masses, and their will turned out to be death and self-destruction... The social progress for which we fought became a progress towards the slave labour camp; our liberalism made us accomplices of tyrants and oppressors; our love for peace invited aggression and led to war.

Arthur Koestler, *Arrow in the Blue* (1952)

[T]oday, public life has become a matter of formal obligation. Most citizens approach their dealings with the state in a spirit of resigned acquiescence, but this public enervation is in its scope much broader than political affairs. Manners and ritual interchanges with strangers are looked on as at best formal and dry, at worst as phony. The stranger himself is a threatening figure, and few people can take pleasure in that world of strangers, the cosmopolitan city. A res publica stands in general for those bonds of association and mutual commitment which exist between people who are not joined together by ties of family or intimate association; it is the bond of a crowd, of a 'people', of a polity, rather than bonds of family and friends.

Richard Sennet, *The Fall of Public Man* (1978)

Modern civilization, in all of its aspects and everywhere on the planet, is plunging ever deeper into a multiplicity of crises that call into question its governing principles, practices and institutions. In this 'crisis of crises' there is one that is yet to receive the attention it deserves: the impending failure of the liberal polity, the modern system of politics founded on the tenets of classical liberalism and the rationalistic philosophy of the

Enlightenment. Liberal polity is based on intrinsically self-destructive and potentially dangerous principles. It has already failed in its collectivist form and, contrary to the view of many, is now moribund in its individualist form as well... Thus the three main components of modern civilization—liberal polity, exploitative economy and purposive rationality—are riddled with inner contradictions. Civilization is therefore collapsing. As a result the latent totalitarianism of modern politics is likely to manifest itself with increasing force in the years to come. In short, without a major advance in civilization, we confront a political debacle.

William Ophuls, Requiem for Modern Politics (1997)

The majority of politicians on the evidence available to us are interested not in the truth but in power and in the maintenance of that power. To maintain that power it is essential that people remain in ignorance, that they live in ignorance of the truth, even the truth of their own lives. What surrounds us therefore is a vast tapestry of lies, upon which we feed.

Harold Pinter Art, Truth & Politics (2005)

FOREWORD

We live in strange and troubled times. Across North Africa and the Middle East people are fighting and dying in the name of democracy. And yet within the long-established democracies of North America, Western Europe, and Australasia public opinion surveys suggest that large sections of the public are more distrustful, disengaged, sceptical, and disillusioned with democratic politics than ever before. 'Politics', for the many rather than just a few, has become a dirty word conjuring up notions of sleaze, corruption, greed, and inefficiency. Let me be the person who dares to put his head above the parapet and speak in defence of politics. Let me stand up and argue against the current anti-political sentiment and state in no uncertain terms that the vast majority of politicians are over-worked and under-paid, that public servants generally do a fantastic job in the face of huge pressures, and that, most broadly, democratic politics delivers far more than most people acknowledge or understand. Across the developed world we reap the fruits of fundamentally honest political systems and the time has come to stand up and fight back in the name of democracy.

We must not allow our political systems to become synonymous with failure because public apathy and distrust places a mighty weight on those who have stepped forward on behalf of society in order to attempt to deal with the wave after wave of crises (social, economic, environmental, etc.) that crash upon the shore of politics with ever-increasing frequency. Let me be even bolder. In the United Kingdom a cost-benefit analysis of the *Telegraph*'s exposure of the MPs' expenses system in 2009 would probably reveal a negative balance sheet. The sensational drip-drip-drip approach to covering the issue was the political equivalent of napalm or carpet-bombing and appears to have left all politicians as weak and cowering aspects of a rather dejected political landscape. In the United States the great expectations that propelled Obama into office, the promises of change and new beginnings, now weigh heavily upon not only the President as an individual but on the political system more widely. Our confidence in democratic politics is low and our collective self-belief is shaken. The 'bad faith model of politics' in which all politicians are viewed as incompetent, selfish, or corrupt has become the dominant lens through which everything is viewed and understood. Read much of the media, in print or on-line, and that's how it is: malaise, decline, corruption, challenges unmet, promises unfulfilled. My message to politicians and citizens alike is simple: democracy is not broken, it delivers far more than many people realize but we need to develop a new set of authentic political relationships that harness the potential of informed and engaged citizens.

I am not arguing that democratic politics as we know it is perfect. Politicians too often promise too much and deliver too little and some have abused their positions for personal gain but I will not let the behaviour of a few destroy the achievements of the many. Although imperfect, we can do much worse than honour 'mere politics'. Indeed we must examine very carefully the claims of those who would do better or who would apparently turn their backs on politics completely. We must also challenge those who bemoan politics but in the next breath demand that the institutions of the state do more and more. Politics can and does make a positive difference to people's lives. It delivers far more than most people in the United States, the United Kingdom, and other 'disaffected democracies' realize. I want to argue that while those who carp and criticize from the sidelines about the failure and limitations of democratic politics have shown a genius for demolition, there are still those who can undertake the far riskier business of reconstruction.

The twenty-first century will belong to those individuals, communities, and countries who are willing to respond to the world as it changes, to modernize and adapt and see the loss of once fixed reference points as an opportunity rather than a threat. Put slightly differently, the twenty-first century will deliver most to those who are able to rebuff the 'politics of pessimism' and in its place cultivate a more buoyant and vibrant 'politics of optimism'. But this transition will only occur if we are willing to ask some very hard questions about the balance between *rights* and *responsibilities*, about the meaning of democracy, and about the limits of politics.

In tackling these questions I want to provoke you by daring to suggest that large sections of the public have become politically decadent in their expectations about what politics should deliver, how politicians should behave and their own responsibilities within society. I want to suggest that people 'hate politics' because they simply do not understand the central essence of democracy and that the contemporary climate of anti-politics is arguably rooted in a generation that has become complacent and parochial, and in doing so have forgotten the alternatives to democratic politics, by which I mean the human cost, the pain, and the suffering that occurs when democratic politics truly fails. Those individuals who remember the two world wars that stained the first half of the twentieth century might well possess a far more urgent and personal understanding of why politics matters and why it is sometimes necessary to speak up in its defence. Politics succeeds because it generally ensures stability and order: it avoids anarchy or arbitrary rule. Those who argue that democratic politics is broken would do well to read Tim Butcher's *Blood River*. Its account of a recent journey across Africa reveals the raw violence, manipulation, poverty, and extortion—the politics of fear—that democratic politics generally prevents. However, as part of this fight-back politicians urgently need to rediscover the moral nerve and capacity to speak with the authority and weight of their predecessors. At the heart of this rediscovery must be the acceptance that 'the first business of government is to govern', as Churchill put it, 'which may at times call for the deliberate endurance of unpopularity'. Yet it is this paradox, let us call it 'the governing paradox'—the need for politicians to garner and sustain popular support versus the more basic need for politicians to sometimes deny the public, reject demands, or make unpopular decisions—that I want to put at the heart of this book.

It could be argued that this governing paradox is not as extreme as one might think: the public are not stupid. They understand that in the wake of the global economic crisis the financial situation is not good and that around the world significant cuts within the public sector will have to be made; just as they are aware that responding to climate change is likely to require significant lifestyle changes. But politicians need to offer strong political leadership that demonstrates courage and an appetite to speak with emotion, clarity, and direction. They need to be confident about what they believe is true, set out their agenda, and not be buffeted by the next day's headlines or focus groups. Political leadership: nothing more, nothing less. In the end politicians have to make really difficult decisions and they have to live with the consequences. My concern is that the contemporary negativity, the very big gap that has emerged between the governors and the governed, has made us lose our sense of what might be. Not everybody will agree with my argument. I would be disappointed if they did. But I do hope this book might be read widely, particularly beyond the universities, and that it might provoke a little honest reflection and an understanding that democracies are actually more fragile (and more beautiful) than most people realize.

Just as Bernard Crick's original *In Defence of Politics* was written 'in one deep breath at a particular time', so was this book. It was conceived and for the most part written some months ago during a ten-and-a-half-hour train journey from Exeter to Sheffield. Since then I have sought to refine and develop my arguments but my ambition has not been to write a sequel to Crick's classic text but instead to pen a complementary text that projects and amplifies his argument into the twenty-first century. This is because his simple quest to restore confidence in politics and pierce the skin of the anti-political climate remains more important today than it did almost half a century ago. However, if imitation is the highest form of praise then I am happy to admit that I have sought to imitate Crick's seminal book in terms of structure and style. Sequels, as film lovers will generally attest, are rarely as good as the original and in this sense I write this book anticipating that many people will criticize me for attempting to build so directly upon Crick's work, let alone daring to speak in praise of politics and in defence of politicians. But that is exactly what this book does and in developing my thoughts, ideas, and arguments I have become indebted to a huge number of people; although they are too numerous to mention individually I owe them all an immense debt of gratitude.

Speaking in defence of politics is not easy. The anti-political climate has reached such a level that anyone daring to stand up for politicians or political processes risks being immediately labelled as irrational or (even worse) harbouring political ambitions themselves. I harbour no ambitions within party politics but can no longer stand on the sidelines and watch a noble profession—public service interwoven with a belief in the capacity of collective endeavour—be the constant focus of ridicule and derision, especially when anti-political arguments are commonly deployed as a Trojan horse for market-based solutions that risk deconstructing a public sphere that we have spent a century building. Almost half a century ago Bernard Crick wrote *In Defence of Politics* as a sharp and thoughtful rejoinder to those who would decry the achievements and principles of democratic politics. His argument is even more relevant today. Sing out in praise of politics!

Matthew Flinders
University of Sheffield

PREFACE

In 1962 Bernard Crick penned a seminal essay that attempted to justify politics in plain words. It attempted to respond to the 'brittle cynicism' that had emerged about the activities of politicians and the capacities of the state by arguing that politics remained the only tested alternative to government by outright coercion. *In Defence of Politics* was written to make a particular argument at a particular point in political history. Throughout the world less than a third of countries were functioning democracies in the early 1960s, while other types of regime, notably authoritarianism and dictatorships, were apparently flourishing. By the end of the twentieth century, however, the situation had changed significantly as democracy flourished in Eastern Europe, Southern Europe, and large parts of South America. Yet at the very same period in history public confidence in democratic politics and public trust in politicians was declining rapidly within most established democracies. Politics, it would appear, was and is increasingly interpreted as failing.

Crick was one of the first academics to identify the emergence of a growing gap between the governors and the governed and he sought to close this gap through a plea for common sense. He was the first to admit that politics was not perfect but it was vastly superior to any of the alternative regimes that were to be found around the world. *In Defence of Politics* therefore made a bold and forthright argument that challenged the social climate of the time. This short book (Crick described it as little more than 'an essay') was without doubt a defining and profound literary contribution to the debate about the evolving nature of politics. Without dissecting his text in too much detail it is worth highlighting three critical elements of Crick's work before reflecting on its contemporary relevance.

First, the book provided a bold polemic that was willing to challenge established viewpoints. For Crick 'politics' was not an activity to be continually derided and attacked but was for the most part an element of human behaviour that should be cherished and protected from idealized notions and unrealistic expectations (issues that form key pillars of this book). Politics was and remained, for Crick, a virtuous form of collective engagement that was understandably limited by the weaknesses of the human condition, the 'muddle and uncertainty' arising from increasing inter-dependency across and within nations, and the vicissitudes of fate. 'The reality is that any system of representation, however ramshackle, incomplete, and at times even corrupt', Crick argued, 'is better than none; and is better than one that will represent only an alleged single interest of the governed'.

In this regard (and secondly), the book was as much about how to study and understand politics as it was about politics itself. For Crick the role of a scholar was about more than attempting to produce robust social scientific 'data' or 'evidence' but was equally concerned with being willing to make and develop bold and provocative arguments unencumbered by the need to support each point or theme with a range of supporting references. Crick therefore wrote on a wide canvas and this often necessitated the use of a fairly broad brush but the result was a portrait of politics that could be accessed by a broad range of individuals. Indeed, possibly the most important element of *In Defence of Politics* was its simple accessibility. It was and remains a book that can be read and appreciated by everyone. Crick was, then, a writer as well as a scholar. This might sound an odd comment but what I mean was that Crick not only wrote in a clear and accessible manner, but he also wrote with a broader social purpose. His aim was not to communicate solely with like-minded scholars but to engage with and stimulate the wider public. Few contemporary political scientists appear to share such concerns. Even fewer appear to have read more broadly on the nature of political language, why it matters, and on 'the mere joy of words'. To adopt this quote from George Orwell is apt not only because his essays 'Why I Write' and 'Politics and the English Language' have much to teach the modern student of politics (professors included) but also because Crick dedicated almost a decade of his life to writing *George Orwell: A Life* (1982).

Crick's *Defence* remains a book that is eminently readable. It is packed full of energy, emotion, prescience, and not a little wit. It is true that Crick's narrow definition of politics was the subject of some debate and a number of intellectual contortions and it is also true that, at first glance, some of his themes appear badly dated. And yet his central argument stands out: politics was not perfect, it could not 'make every sad heart glad' but it offered a form of collective social engagement through which tensions, debates, and arguments could be heard and mediated in order to provide a largely safe and stable environment. Modern democratic politics succeeds because it generally ensures stability and order: it avoids anarchy or arbitrary rule. Politics can and does affect and shape people's lives. It saves lives. It forges a sense of collective endeavour, social support, and a sense of humility. Just as Orwell was content to praise 'mere words' so too was Crick content to praise 'mere politics'.

Third and finally, if a defence of politics was needed during the middle of the twentieth century, then it is undoubtedly required with even greater verve and articulation at the dawn of the twenty-first century. There is now an urgent and pressing need to be a little brave—to risk inevitable misunderstanding and deliberate criticism—in order to defend politics from those who seek to narrow and subvert the political realm and against those who have become politically decadent. Let me simply say that democratic politics matters more than most people understand and acknowledge. It matters because on the whole it delivers. Here then is a simple book about the nature of politics and governing in the twenty-first century. It is 'occasioned'—in the words of Hobbes—'by the disorders of the present time' and is an attempt to justify politics in plain words by saying what it is, what it is not, and what it can never be. It rejects the profound and deep pessimism that surrounds politics in the twenty-first century by dismissing the shallow nihilism of the anti-political climate and in its place emphasizing the positive achievements of politics. It is not a systematic or evidence-based treatise. But it is an attempt to respond to contemporary political disenchantment by (in turn) defending politics against *itself*, against *the market*, against *denial*, against *crises*, and lastly (but certainly not least) against *the media*. It seeks to recast Crick's argument within the contours of contemporary debates and themes by remaining true to the intellectual thrust and style of *In Defence of Politics*. At the same time it forges a distinct line of argument regarding the limits of politics, and the need to reflect on the emergence of an expectations gap between what is promised by politicians, what is demanded by the public, and what can realistically be delivered by the state.

What makes this argument particularly timely in the second decade of the twenty-first century is the existence of a clear mismatch or gap between *capacity* and *demand* across a wide range of fields (financial, social, environmental, institutional, etc.).

The demands of numerous severe and complex political challenges loom large and the public's expectations regarding the standards of services it expects democratic politics to deliver have never been higher and yet the capacity of politicians to respond is arguably constrained by a lack of capital in all its various forms. In order to explore what can be termed the politics of public expectations and use it to foster a more constructive and positive defence of politics this book adopts Crick's original structure but adapts it to the themes of governing in the twenty-first century (see Box 1).

This is clearly a wide-ranging book and, like painting on a large canvas, this will require the use of a fairly broad brush, in both analytical and empirical terms. It is also a book that cannot avoid the use of certain terms and phrases that might at first appear alien to the reader. I have attempted to avoid the use of academic jargon wherever possible but at the end of the day politics is a complex business and to some extent this book has to reflect this fact in order to provide an honest account. Let me warn you from the start therefore that this book is not intended to provide the political equivalent of painting-by-numbers

---

Box 1 In Defence of Politics: Then and Now

IN DEFENCE OF POLITICS, BERNARD CRICK 1962	DEFENDING POLITICS, MATTHEW FLINDERS 2012
1. The Nature of Political Rule in the Twentieth Century	1. The Nature of Political Rule in the Twenty-First Century
2. A Defence of Politics against Ideology	2. A Defence of Politics against Itself
3. A Defence of Politics against Democracy	3. A Defence of Politics against the Market
4. A Defence of Politics against Nationalism	4. A Defence of Politics against Denial
5. A Defence of Politics against Technology	5. A Defence of Politics against Crises
6. A Defence of Politics against its Friends	6. A Defence of Politics against the Media
7. In Praise of Politics	7. In Praise of Politics

and does instead place expectations on the shoulders of its readers—expectations in the sense of a commitment to engaging with arguments or themes that demand a little mental energy, a commitment to read and reread those sections that are inevitably challenging, and finally a commitment not simply to completing the book but also to why the arguments I have sought to make actually matter to each and every one of us. Take your time when reading this book.

Overall I hope that by emphasizing some of the achievements of politics and daring to swim against the tide of popular opinion, I might provoke some reflection on whether political institutions, political processes, and politicians really deserve to be the focus of such extreme public ridicule and derision. My only request to you, the reader, is that you approach this book with an open and enquiring frame of mind and that you devote a little thought to two interconnected ideas that challenge the anti-political and anti-politician street populism that currently holds sway. Firstly, if politics is failing, its failings are undoubtedly systemic in nature. Have you ever wondered if it is just a little too easy to blame politicians? If politics is viewed as failing, the challenge lies in promoting understanding, education, and communication. It also lies in turning passive consumers into active citizens and in understanding that democratic politics is not a spectator sport. Secondly, with this in mind, beware of anyone or any party that tries to sell you a perfect formula for all the world's ills—there isn't one. Democratic politics is messy, cumbersome, and at times frustrating because life and the world are themselves generally messy, cumbersome, and at times frustrating. There are no simple solutions to the challenges we face but there *is* great reason to cherish and celebrate our democratic achievements and democratic potential.

CONTENTS

I

THE NATURE OF POLITICAL RULE IN THE TWENTY-FIRST CENTURY

To renounce or destroy politics is to destroy the very thing which gives order to the pluralism and variety of civilised society, the thing that enables us to enjoy variety without either suffering either anarchy or the tyranny of single truths.

Bernard Crick, *In Defence of Politics* (1962)

Government is accepted as, at best, a necessary evil, one we must put up with while resenting the necessity. We want as little of it as possible, since anything beyond that necessary minimum instantly cancels one or another liberty.

Garry Wills, *A Necessary Evil* (1999)

'Politics' is a dirty word, a term that has come to acquire a whole array of almost entirely negative associations and connotations in contemporary discourse. Politics is synonymous with sleaze, corruption and duplicity, greed, self-interest and self-importance, interference, inefficiency and intransigence. It is at best, a necessary evil, at worst an entirely malevolent force that needs to be kept in check.

Colin Hay, *Why We Hate Politics* (2007)

If the twentieth century witnessed the triumph of democracy, something appears to have gone seriously wrong. Citizens around the world appear to have become distrustful of politicians, sceptical about democratic institutions, and disillusioned about the capacity of democratic politics to resolve pressing social concerns. Some might argue that a degree of suspicion amongst citizens about the motivation and behaviour of politicians is an important and generally healthy component of a vigorous democracy. And yet there is a vast difference between *healthy scepticism* and *corrosive cynicism*. The former suggests a belief in the nature of a regime alongside a large dose of caution about the risk that some individuals may be tempted to abuse the system for their own benefit rather than the public's. The latter, by contrast, suggests fatalism about the intrinsic qualities of a regime that is tied to an almost inevitable sense of failure. This book argues that the millennium was marked by an almost global shift in public attitudes from one of healthy scepticism to corrosive cynicism. This is reflected in a vast body of survey evidence, declining electoral turnouts, the collapse of political party membership lists, and an array of other indicators. A great number of scholars have already mined this rich seam of material in order to reveal and attempt to understand the existence of 'disaffected democracies' and why we apparently 'hate politics'.

This book does not review the research and data in any great detail or seek to devise new pseudo-scientific theories of citizen disengagement but it does seek to make an argument of almost primitive simplicity: democratic politics delivers far more than most members of the public appear to acknowledge and understand. If more and more people are disappointed with what politics delivers then maybe the fault lies with those who demand too much and fail to acknowledge the essence of democratic engagement and the complexities of governing in the twenty-first century rather than in democratic politics itself. This argument matters because democracy is a fragile system of rule and by constantly deriding its achievements and demonizing politicians we risk destroying what is in reality a quite beautiful reflection of the channelling of private interests for the public good. Put simply, therefore, my argument is that democratic politics may not be perfect but it remains vastly superior to any other form of regime. Let me go even further; most politicians are actually just and only a very few are *just* awful. Most politicians enter public life in order to make a positive difference to people's lives, their motivations are altruistic, and in making this choice they generally forgo the benefits of a permanent job and a higher salary while also accepting the significant pressure that holding political office places on an individual and his or her family.

You should by now have gathered that this book is both exploring a major political issue while at the same time making a very strong argument about the need to challenge and reject the current anti-political sentiment that seems to have invaded the public consciousness. Like Bernard Crick half a century before me I want to respond and reject the public cynicism surrounding politics and by offering a bold defence of politics, construct a more balanced account of the benefits and strengths that our political system has to offer. This is not a very fashionable argument to make but it is far from meaningless to believe that the most important task for students of politics, both intellectually and morally, is to provide a defence of democratic politics against those who would seek to destroy its achievements. Moreover, at a time when academics are frequently criticized for saying more and more about less and less and even blamed, to some extent, for fuelling public disenchantment with politics, I prefer to risk error, and to some degree even ridicule, rather than to suffer boredom. This book is therefore a plea in favour of a paradigm shift in the way we view and understand politics. This shift is based on a rejection of the 'bad faith model of politics'—the view of politics as a malevolent force and politicians as by definition greedy, corrupt, self-interested, and incompetent—and an attempt to replace 'the politics of pessimism' with a more buoyant 'politics of optimism' that adopts a more balanced and proportionate view of politics (and therefore politicians).

As such I want to make some very bold statements in order to challenge established stereotypes. I want to provide a frank account of politics, of why politicians behave in the manner they do, and I want to cast the light of public scrutiny on a range of hitherto invisible political actors who wield great power within our democracies but arguably exhibit little responsibility. In a sense what I am arguing is that if we face a problem of political disconnection, we need to rebuild a set of *authentic* political relationships that focus not just on the responsibilities and behaviour of politicians but also involve expectations of all social actors, including the public. At the heart of this authentic relationship must also be a large dose of realism about the limits of democratic politics: limits in the sense of what we can expect politics to deliver; limits in the sense of acknowledging that democracy involves both costs and benefits; limits in the sense of giving as well as taking; and limits in the sense of how our popular culture reinforces the idea that politics is disreputable when in fact we should celebrate 'mere politics' at every opportunity because the alternatives are too horrible to contemplate.

This was in a sense the core argument of Crick's original *Defence* that was penned exactly fifty years ago and in this context the role of this chapter is to build a clear relationship with Crick's book while also acknowledging how the nature of politics and the challenges of governing have altered. In order to demonstrate and build upon Crick's intellectual legacy this chapter seeks to engage with four main sets of questions:

1. What does democracy mean? What is the essence of democratic politics? Are we defining as 'failings' those aspects of politics that actually deliver so much?

2. What evidence is there that politics has become a 'dirty' word? Does the public 'love' democracy but 'hate' politics? What puzzles does the available evidence present to those committed to speaking in praise of politics?

3. How has the nature of political rule changed in the last fifty years? What do these changes suggest about the challenges of governing? Is it possible to identify a general pattern or trend with broader social implications?

4. So what? Why does any of this matter? Why should the reader or the broader public at large actually care?

Engaging with these four sets of questions provides us with a starting point from which to evaluate the performance of democratic politics. By the end of this chapter I want you to understand that the manner in which many political debates are presented and commonly understood are too simplistic and as a result tend to produce more heat than light. In doing so I make no apology for the fact that at times I will make demands on the reader, due to the simple fact that politics is a complex activity and therefore revealing why it sometimes works and sometimes fails, why politicians behave the way they do, or why the distinction between 'consumers' and 'citizens' actually matters. I will from time to time have to take you on a journey into a rather abstract world. I cannot help this but I will try and make this journey as comfortable as I can. If you sometimes get a little frustrated with the pace or nature of my argument and are tempted to terminate this journey early, please be reminded of Thomas Paine's belief that 'Those who expect to reap the blessings of freedom must undergo the fatigue of supporting it'.

Indeed, all that I really ask of the reader is that you let go of everything you know and instead study this book with an open mind for it is only by stripping away a number of false assumptions and oversimplifications about politics and by returning to a very basic but honest account of democratic engagement that we will be able to expose why politics matters, what it delivers, what it offers, and why politicians behave the way they do. This chapter therefore matters not just because it provides the basic foundations for the rest of this book but because it reveals just how difficult governing has become. Politics is a hard, worldly, and (sometimes) dirty game. It is by no means perfect. But it is generally successful in avoiding war, preventing authoritarian rule, responding to public pressure, delivering social goods, and preventing poverty and disease. It cannot, however, deliver simple solutions to complex problems and its capacity to deliver positive change and respond to social challenges is undermined if its citizens forget the simple essence of politics.

A Politics of Understanding

In order to demonstrate the distinctiveness or value of a particular object or manner of behaving, it is useful to provide some reference points or markers against which judgements concerning qualities, both positive and negative, can be made. This section seeks to draw out the simple essence of politics—a commitment to stability and compromise through social dialogue—through a brief exploration of the core tenets of other regime types. This process exposes why democratic politics matters and why those who argue against politics or agitate for a different form of regime must be challenged. Democratic politics is a form of social engagement. It is a moral activity and it provides a way of taking control of our lives by cultivating mutual understanding, engineering collective endeavours, and taking collective decisions about the allocation of scarce resources. Democratic politics can therefore be viewed as a counterweight to the vicissitudes of fate and to the individualizing and competitive forces of the market. Laws and regulations are needed to restrain the predatory and protect the weak.

In order to understand the role of politics as a *counterweight* and to understand how the issue of *rationing* flows into broader debates concerning the boundary between the public and private spheres, it is useful to draw upon the insights of Albert Hirschman's influential book *Exit, Voice and Loyalty* (1980). The distribution of any finite resources can be, as Hirschman's book explained, based on a system of either *externalized* or *internalized* rationing. In the former method decisions about how to distribute (or to collect) resources are not taken by individuals but are instead taken by politicians (or officials working on behalf of politicians), who in turn are accountable to the public through various processes and elections. In systems based upon internalized rationing, decisions over how to allocate resources is a matter for individuals rather than the state. Anti-political, anti-government groups, like the Tea Party movement in the United States, generally advocate a shift from externalized to internalized rationing (i.e. lower taxes, lower public spending, etc.), due to a desire to maximize the freedom of the individual, combined with a deep distrust of 'the state'.

Although any system of externalized rationing can at times appear overly centralized, controlling, and even unfair, its position at the core of democratic politics occurred not by accident but by design. Put slightly differently, democratic politics is founded on the basis of collective endeavour. It seeks to avoid a violent and arbitrary state of nature in which the politics of fear rules, and instead attempts to construct a shared public sphere in which everyone enjoys *rights* and *responsibilities*. Taking this focus on externalized rationing one step further, by which I simply mean the imposition of decisions about the collection and distribution of resources (e.g. money, aid, jobs, support, benefits, protection, etc.), allows us to introduce three themes that will reappear at various points in this book. The first theme is the notion of a 'collective action problem'. This is simply the fact that at times some form of externalized rationing is necessary to prevent the over-exploitation of certain shared resources. From fish in the sea through to wood in the forests and pollution in the atmosphere there are a number of contemporary political challenges that suggest that multiple individuals acting independently in their own self-interest can ultimately destroy a shared resource. Following on from this (and our second theme), it is necessary to understand that freedom and constraint are not opposites but frequently serve as both sides of the same coin.

The imposition of restraints through laws, tax policies, limits, regulations, etc. (i.e. forms of externalized rationing) avoids inferior social outcomes and therefore protects certain individual *and* collective freedoms. The idea of politics as a counterweight or equalizing force flows into our third theme: that politics reflects shared social values about the need to protect sections of society from the vagaries of a pure market economy. This generally involves the provision of a social safety net (state benefits, public education, healthcare, etc.) alongside a

broader commitment to supporting, protecting, and retraining disadvantaged social groups. It is for exactly this reason that Aristotle argued
that politics was, at base, a moral and noble activity and that Crick
wrote of politics as a 'great and civilising human activity'. These three
tenets—let us call them (1) shared resource planning, (2) realizing positive social outcomes, and (3) protecting the vulnerable—coalesce to
reveal a rich form of political morality that is very different, some
might say inherently opposed, to the logic of free competition, with its
preference for internalized rationing and market-based allocation. The
central ambition of a democratic political regime is therefore not to
deliver some idealized notion of a perfect society but a more basic and
grubbier form of governing that is generally stable and broadly acceptable to *all* citizens (i.e. not perfection but a workable and more modest
version of an integrated, mutually respectful, and above all stable system of rule).

Understanding this basic point provides a bridge between Bernard
Crick's *In Defence of Politics* (1962) and the political scientist Gerry
Stoker's more recent account of *Why Politics Matters* (2006). Both
books explain how democratic engagement provides the institutional
and cultural mainframe that shapes social attitudes and mediates social
conflict. There will always be winners and losers but the process of
politics should foster a degree of mutual respect and humility. The *polis*
is, as Aristotle emphasized, the aggregate of many members and it is for
exactly this reason that politics remains the 'master science': the social
foundation that allows legal, social, and economic structures to operate.
Yet it is rarely acknowledged as representing the paradigm of collective
engagement and endeavour, or for embodying an ethic and a con-
scious purpose that cannot be reduced to the market. Is it possible that
we 'hate' politics because we have forgotten its specific and limited
nature, its overwhelming value, and also its innate fragility? Could it be
that our expectations are so high that politics appears almost destined
to disappoint? Democratic politics cannot make 'every sad heart glad',
as Crick argued, nor did it ever promise to do so. But not always
getting what you want, an awareness that public governance is often
slow and bureaucratic, a frustration that some decisions are hard to
understand or have to be made in secret, disbelief and anger at the self-
interested behaviour of a small number of politicians, and an acceptance that some people will always take out more from the system than
they put in—these are the prices you pay for living in a democracy.

And remember it is a democracy that on the whole does deliver, does protect the vulnerable, does deliver a range of public goods, does save lives, does allow citizens to speak out, does respond to public opinion, and does manage the peaceful transition of power at elections.

One way of reconsidering the value of democratic politics is to consider the main alternatives to democratic rule and through this achieve a new vantage point. Tyranny remains, as Crick so powerfully argued, the most obvious alternative to democratic politics. In this regard Hannah Arendt's *The Origins of Totalitarianism* (1951) remains a powerful counterpoint from which to understand how the birth of a stable democratic regime (in which differing opinions can be expressed, tolerated, and to some extent mediated) is founded on the 'rule of law', the protection of basic freedoms, and the existence of trust in a state system. The democratic method of rule is to listen to groups so as to conciliate them as far as possible, give them legal and political recognition, the tools of political literacy, and a sense of security within a safe and reasonably effective form of articulation. This method of organizing the general process of politics and government can take a variety of forms but irrespective of the specific manner in which political engagement and deliberation takes place within a democracy, it is forged on a radically different mode of governing than tyranny, oligarchy, monarchy, dictatorship, theocracy, totalitarianism, or authoritarianism.

For those born in North America or Western Europe since the Second World War the notions of 'authoritarianism' and alternative regimes may be viewed as faintly quaint and incredibly outdated. And yet, as the international monitor 'Freedom House' makes clear in its 2011 report, there is a very real authoritarian challenge to democracy. According to the organization's findings, 2010 was the fifth consecutive year in which global democratic standards suffered a decline—the longest continued decline in the nearly forty-year history of the organization's reporting. The increasing truculence of the world's most powerful authoritarian regimes, notably China and Russia, has coincided with either an unwillingness or inability of some of the world's fledgling democracies, in Latin America, Africa, and Asia, to meet the authoritarian challenge. In 2010 the number of full democratic regimes in the world stood at 87, representing 45 per cent of the world's 194 countries and just under 3 billion people (43 per cent of the global population). The number of partial democracies in which there is limited respect for political rights stood at 60 (31 per cent of all countries assessed by the survey and home to 22 per cent of the world's population). A total of 47 countries were deemed undemocratic in the sense that basic political rights are simply absent.

Put slightly differently, nearly two and a half billion people, 35 per cent of the global population, live in authoritarian regimes, and if a democracy is defined as a country that exhibits open political competition, respect for civil liberties and the rule of law, and an independent media, then democracy is the exception rather than the rule. More worrying is the long-term trend, which suggests that democracy's forward march peaked in 2000 and has since then retreated as a number of democratic indicators have deteriorated. Large sections of the world exist through regimes based upon brute force, where the rule of the tyrant and the oligarch is quite simple—to clobber, coerce, and overawe all or most other groups in the interest of their own. This 'Big Man, Small Man' mode of governing is inherently unstable and too often leaves the masses trapped between civil war, social unrest, and 'the politics of the belly'. Democratic politics succeeds because it generally ensures stability and order. It avoids anarchy or arbitrary rule, which is why thousands of people from non-democratic regimes in Eastern Europe, the Middle East, South-East Asia, and Africa risk their lives to get into Western Europe, North America, or Australia. Compared with them the 'disaffected democrats' of the developed world have lives of unimaginable good fortune. The Arab Spring adds a new dimension to this debate.

What can I say about the Middle East apart from the fact that the public in this region appear far more optimistic about democratic politics than those who have arguably become complacent about why politics matters. The fact that a young unemployed man felt he had no choice but to set himself on fire in order to protest against the authoritarianism of the Tunisian regime underlines the alternative to democratic politics. However, the Arab Spring also raises a number of questions about the public's expectations of politics, whether democratic regimes have a responsibility and duty to support and protect those fighting for democracy, and how to entrench democratic values within a post-revolution context. This book is about the Middle East only in so far as it seeks to defend and promote democratic politics, but even the most cursory analysis of the Arab Spring underlines the fact that political leadership is about taking decisions in the face of disparate opinions. The fact is that someone has to make a decision on the basis of imperfect information and then live with the consequences of that decision. Whether it is about the allocation of resources between schools, whether to increase taxes, or whether to send troops into war, someone has to weigh up the evidence and come down on one side or another. In this context indecision simply becomes a more hesitant and weak form of decision-making. But in a democracy political decisions are ultimately resolved at the ballot box rather than by violence. One side wins; one side loses; but at least the losers live to fight another day.

Democratic politics thus arises from recognizing the need for *restraint* alongside *opportunity*. It is a social activity, a social relationship, which serves an anthropological function in terms of preserving a community that has become too large to be governed via traditional customs or pure arbitrary rule. Charles Darwin's observation that 'it is not the strongest of the species that survives nor the most intelligent but the one most responsive to change' shares much with Edmund Burke's famous aphorism about the need to 'reform in order to preserve', and reminds us that politics is a complex activity and not simply an end point or the grasping of an ideal. History did not, despite Francis Fukayama's arguments to the contrary, end in 1989 and those who look back on the various waves of democratization risk overlooking not only the existence of counter-trends but also disregarding the intrinsic fragility of democracy that this book seeks to bring to the fore. The first decade of the twenty-first century is not the first time that democracy has been said to be 'in crisis' but the broader global pattern, alongside the cynicism and negativism that increasingly pervades social attitudes in Western Europe and North America, underlines the need for a bold restatement of the nature and virtues of democracy.

Once this bigger picture is painted it may appear odd that politicians appear unable to articulate a coherent defence of their role or capacity. This may be because the dominant and aggressive anti-political climate has sapped their moral nerve and capacity to speak with the authority and weight of their predecessors. It might, on the other hand, reflect a number of what might be termed democratic paradoxes that actually make it very difficult for elected politicians to make unpopular statements or decisions. Although the journalist and critic of American life Henry Mencken (1880–1956) was possibly correct when he wrote that 'The men the American public admire most extravagantly are the most daring liars; the men they detest most violently are those who try to tell them the truth', the time may have come for politicians to be a little brave. This section has attempted to be a little brave. It has attempted to sketch out the basic essence of politics and be honest about the fact that democratic politics can be a messy and frustrating business, for all concerned, because it is about producing collective decisions from multiple and competing arguments and opinions. When the public demands that politicians 'listen to the people' they need to understand that the public rarely, if ever, share the same demands, desires, or interests. Understanding what the public want and what will best serve the 'public interest' is therefore more difficult than is commonly understood, which in turn leads us into a discussion of the politics of public expectations. Before focusing on that topic, however, it is necessary to explore the issue of political disenchantment in a little more detail.

Democratic Challenges, Democratic Choices

From Gabriel Almond and Sidney Verba's seminal *The Civic Culture* (1963) through to Colin Hay's equally influential *Why We Hate Politics* (2007) scholars have identified and debated the apparent erosion of political support for political institutions, political processes, and politicians in established democracies consistently since Crick's *Defence* was published fifty years ago.★ For those readers who desire a more detailed account of the available research, Pippa Norris's *Democratic Deficits* (2011) is undoubtedly the most sophisticated and state-of-the-art book on this topic. The aim of this section is not to review the vast body of work on this topic in any detail but simply to draw upon this earlier research in order to make three basic but interrelated arguments, which

---

★ With Michael Crozier, Samuel Huntington, and Joji Watanuki's *The Crisis of Democracy* (1975), Seymour Martin Lipset and William Schneider's *The Confidence Gap* (1983), Hans-Dieter Klingemann and Dieter Fuchs's *Citizens and the State* (1995), and Joseph Nye, Philip Zelikow, and David King's *Why People Don't Trust Government* (1997), Susan Pharr and Robert Putnam's *Disaffected Democracies* (2000), Russell Dalton's *Democratic Challenges, Democratic Choices* (2004), Mariano Torcal and José Montero's *Political Disaffection in Contemporary Democracies* (2006) providing important stepping stones in between.

each in their own ways weave together to form the backcloth against which this book's defence of politics can be located and understood. These can be summarized as follows:

(1) It is possible to identify a democratic paradox that focuses attention on the way in which the purported 'triumph of democracy' in the final quarter of the twentieth century appears to have led to growing levels of public disenchantment and distrust of all things 'political'.

(2) Public opinion and social survey data actually reveal high levels of public support for the concept of 'democracy' but low levels of confidence or support for day-to-day politics.

(3) The public can be a selfish and fickle master to serve.

The final decades of the twentieth century undoubtedly witnessed a global shift in the balance between democratic and non-democratic regimes as a mixture of factors (the dissolution of colonial frameworks, the fall of certain regimes, the collapse of the Soviet Union, the resurgence of democracy in Latin America, the forces of globalization, etc.) combined to create what can now, with the benefit of hindsight, be viewed as a historical spike in the number of democracies. It is too early to understand how the Arab Spring might play out in terms of post-revolution politics but, irrespective of what happens in the Middle East, it is possible to identify a global *democratic paradox*. This paradox reflects an apparent disconnection between democratic performance and public attitudes whereby at the historical point at which established democratic regimes are actually delivering more for their citizens (in terms of educational provision, welfare benefits, social housing, safety, and stability, etc.) than ever before, the public's levels of confidence in political institutions, political processes, and their trust in politicians has declined significantly.

Of course, the situation should not be exaggerated; public confidence in democratic politics has historically been subject to fluctuations and the erosion of public support varies within and between countries (for example, in social demographic or cultural terms or in relation to specific political institutions). Despite this, the overall picture painted by the available data is undoubtedly gloomy. Political disaffection has increased in recent years to the point at which phrases such as 'the life and death of politics', 'post-democratic politics', 'the end of politics', and the emergence of a 'global democratic recession' form an increasing focus of public and scholarly debates. Russell Dalton reviewed all the available data in his book *Democratic Challenges, Democratic Choices* (2004) and concluded, 'regardless of recent trends in the economy, in large and small nations, in presidential and parliamentary systems, in countries with few parties and many, in federal and unitary states, the direction of change is the same [downwards]'. A cross-national European survey by ICM in March 2011 found that only 6 per cent of people trust politicians and only 9 per cent believe that politicians act with honesty or integrity. Some degree of public scepticism of politicians is a healthy element of democratic life but scepticism seems to have slipped into corrosive cynicism. Simply stated, the social survey data suggests that something is wrong: that democratic politics is either under-performing or that citizens are expecting too much (possibly both).

Even in democratic regimes, however, all is not lost. A majority of people echo the view first articulated by David Riesman in *The Lonely Crowd* that those 'who profess to hate politicians would insist they only really hate *bad* or *corrupt* politicians'. Beneath the shallow or visible veneer of public disenchantment there lurks a more solid social commitment to democracy that provides grounds not only for optimism but also grounds for piercing the thin veneer of anti-political sentiment that has become so fashionable. The public's *specific attitudes* towards politicians, parties, or governments are generally negative, as revealed in numerous social surveys in a vast range of established democracies but when public attitudes are assessed at a more *general* or *systemic* level it is overwhelmingly clear that public support for the concept of democracy remains very high. What this points us toward is a disconnection. The public retain a high attachment to the principles of democratic governance but at the same time appear to have lost faith in the practical application of those principles. This attachment to the principles of democracy was noted by David Easton in his *Framework for Political Analysis* (1965) and specifically through his distinction between *specific support* for political institutions (which appears to be in short supply, especially amongst certain sections of the political community) and *diffuse support* (which for the time being appears strong).

The existence of apparently rich reserves of 'diffuse support' is critical to this book's broader defence of politics, due to the manner in which it acts as a buffer against the cruder forms of anti-political street populism. Although the public may have lost confidence in specific political institutions or politicians, they have not lost faith in the general values or philosophy of democratic politics. Although it is pushing simplification a little too far to suggest that the public 'hate' politics but 'love' democracy, it is equally important not to overlook the importance and value of this diffused support. Diffuse support provides the foundation through which day-to-day fluctuations in the popularity of specific politicians or governments can be anchored to a broader social structure. It provides a form of social capital that can be accumulated and spent as required and it is an absence of diffuse support that explains why democratizing states are so susceptible to crises and the re-emergence of authoritarian forms of governing. The existence of relatively healthy levels of diffuse support also provides an entry point for a broader discussion about the complexity of public attitudes that may help us to understand the challenges of governing and the behaviour of politicians. More specifically, it is possible to suggest that the public is frequently a rather fickle and selfish master to serve and in order to illustrate this point I want to focus very briefly on three issues: the *perception gap*; the *demand gap*; and the *social gap*.

The *perception gap* highlights an interesting feature of social attitudes to politicians. When asked about their *general* opinion of politicians, members of the public will almost always respond negatively with pejorative terms such as 'liars', 'crooks', 'creeps', or 'wasters'. However, when the public are asked about their own specific politician, in the sense of who represents their community, they are generally very positive. Survey after survey in country after country therefore reveals a strange perception gap between the public's general view of politicians (very negative) and their view of specific politicians with whom they have had some personal contact (generally fairly positive). A perception gap is also visible if we examine the survey data on corruption. Over and over again the data reveals that the public believe that politicians and public servants are corrupt when in fact their personal experience of interacting with politicians and bureaucrats provides very little basis for this viewpoint. In the United Kingdom, for example, Eurobarometer data suggests that around 65 per cent of the public believe that 'the giving and taking of bribes, and the abuse of positions of power for personal gain' is 'widespread' amongst politicians. This belief was not, however, based on personal experience: the same data reveals that less than 3 per cent of the public claim to have ever been asked to pay a bribe. More broadly, Transparency International's analysis of levels of corruption around the world (defined as 'the abuse of entrusted power for private gain') reveals that levels of corruption are actually very low in many of those countries where public concern about standards of propriety amongst politicians is high.

If the perception gap provides grounds for at least some optimism, the *demand gap* begins to expose the manner in which the public frequently demand one thing but then react against it when politicians seek to fulfil those demands. Put slightly differently, if politicians are frequently duplicitous (which they frequently are), this may well stem from the public's own penchant for duplicity. What the public say they want and what they are willing to allow politicians to do are, therefore, two quite separate issues—and it is politicians who must somehow square the circle. During the May 2011 Congressional elections, for instance, the Republicans lost a previously safe seat as a result of their commitment to spend less on Medicare (i.e. healthcare for the elderly). And yet in 2010 the Republican Party had won victories across the United States based on the message that government spending was simply too high. On the other side of the world the Australian government was trying to square a similar circle. In June 2011 the Australian Prime Minister, Julia Gillard, received a report from the Climate Commission, entitled *The Critical Decade,* summarizing climate change science and just a month later her government published its response in the form of a new Clean Energy Future plan. The fact that this plan attempts to achieve targets that remain far lower than the scientific advice suggests is necessary reveals the dilemma of trying to reconcile incompatible goals. The paradox of the situation in Australia is that there is bipartisan public support for protecting the Great Barrier Reef at the same time as there is bipartisan public support for allowing carbon pollution to exceed levels that will destroy the Great Barrier Reef.

It would appear that the voters agreed with the general message in principle but were less willing to take tough decisions when the debate moved to the level of specifics. If we want to attack politics and politicians for failing to deliver, we need to be aware that the public are also capable of creating rhetoric–reality gaps. The public demand better services but are not willing to pay higher taxes. The public want to address climate change but they don't want to give up their energy-intensive lifestyles. They want to eat cake but not get fat. They care about dwindling fish stocks, just not enough to make them stop eating fish. It is in this vein that the political philosopher Slavoj Žižek uses an advert on American TV for a chocolate laxative—'Do you have constipation? Eat more of this chocolate'—to mock the modern public's constant demand for results without ever having to suffer unpleasant side-effects. The simple fact of life is that there are no simple solutions to complex problems and politicians cannot deliver meaningful change without public support and understanding. In the absence of public support and when faced with contradictory demands that mean 'as soon as you decide you divide', is it really surprising that politicians sometimes base their statecraft on what Bob Goodin calls 'a veil of ambiguity' that allows for different understandings of the processes and outcomes being available?

This focus on public understanding and support flows into a discussion of the final 'gap': what we might term the *social gap*. People often say to me that they want politicians to be 'normal' and for them to act like 'a regular guy'. Yet we place demands and expectations upon them that only a superhuman could ever fulfil. We slate politicians who appear unkempt or exhausted but equally condemn them for being on holiday if a crisis erupts. We want our politicians to be strong and determined yet passionate and flexible; a statesman while also relaxed; authoritative but not condescending; word perfect but not scripted; self-confident but not smug; confident but not arrogant; intelligent but not nerdy; handsome but not vain; family friendly but not work-shy. Although the political historian Peter Hennessy was writing about the office of the British Prime Minister when he wrote that 'The job requires the energy of Gladstone, the flair of Disraeli, the balls of Lloyd George, the administrative gifts of Attlee, the style of Macmillan and the sleeping patterns of Thatcher . . . human beings don't come like that', his sentiment is equally applicable to the American presidency, the German Chancellorship, or any modern leading political office, and in this regard Barack Obama's jibe in February 2011 that the worst part of being President was the fact that he was 'the only man wearing a jacket on Super Bowl Sunday' arguably encapsulates a much broader tension arising from the contradictory demands we place on politicians.

Let me tell you in no uncertain terms that most politicians are normal human beings like you and me. They laugh and they cry; they worry and they make mistakes; they will fail in some aspects of their work but succeed in others; they forgo personal gain in the name of public service; and they possess all the human frailties and weaknesses of any other person. It's hard to lie as a politician because everything they say is subject to enormous scrutiny. Even if they wanted to lie in the first place they would soon get found out. The life of a politician is rarely a glamorous one. Politics as a profession can undoubtedly be rewarding but rarely in financial terms. For most politicians, irrespective of whether they hold office at the local, regional, or national level, their role revolves around the minutiae of day-to-day politics in the sense of dealing with damp social housing, dog dirt in parks, public petitions, missing benefit payments, and those who want just one thing (and those who want another). Notwithstanding all that, what unites those who hold political office is a willingness to step into the arena in order to try and make a positive difference to society and people's lives. So when all is said and done, politics does make a positive difference to people's lives. It provides healthcare, education, and social protections; it protects basic human rights and freedoms; it provides clean water, electricity, and sanitation; it allows us to talk and to challenge and to protest, and most of all it provides a way of negotiating between our different viewpoints and demands without resorting to violence and fear.

The puzzles presented by the available data therefore take the form of a set of 'gaps' in relation to perceptions, demands, and society. Each in their own way converge to present a set of questions about *why* such a gap has apparently emerged between the governors and the governed. If most politicians are in fact honest and hard-working, why are they held in such low esteem? If corruption and scandal are the exception rather than the rule, why has politics become such a 'dirty' word? If politics is generally working, why do so many people associate it with failure?

In order to answer these questions and arrive at a more balanced and optimistic account of modern politics, we undoubtedly need to focus on the attitudes and behaviour of politicians—but we also need to take a rather harsh and honest look at ourselves. Democratic politics is not a spectator sport. Whether we like it or not, we are all political actors and within a democracy this brings with it rights and responsibilities; carping from the sidelines and blaming politicians for failing to deliver painless solutions to painful questions is simply too easy. We also need to cast the light of public scrutiny away from the public and politicians and towards those hitherto largely invisible political actors who play a role in shaping the way we interpret and understand the world around us. This brings us back to Crick's original *Defence* and particularly his willingness to defend politics from a range of foes, because the public's anxieties and frustrations with politics that Crick was amongst the first to identify and challenge have increased significantly despite his valiant defence; healthy scepticism has mutated into corrosive cynicism and as a result the gap between the governors and the governed has widened. I would suggest, however, that looking back to Crick's work in order to understand the *present* and possibly influence the *future* risks overlooking the manner in which the nature of political rule has altered. By this I mean that the basic challenges of governing, the role and capacity of politicians, and the position of the public vis-à-vis politics has changed.

In order to examine the changing nature of political rule and close the fifty-year gap between Crick's original *Defence* and this attempt to revisit and update his arguments, I want to employ the metaphor of a storm. Politics is a hard business. It has never been a profession for the faint-hearted because at times it demands a form of statecraft that some might call 'aggressive diplomacy' but others 'raw skulduggery'. However in today's politics the pressures are so intense, the criticism so brutal, the targeting so arbitrary, the challenges so great, the control levers so weak, that it is like operating in the middle of a mighty storm that allows little room for reflection and views politics as little more than a contagion to be demonized at every turn. If we really want to understand what drives this storm and why politicians frequently adopt self-protection strategies that infuriate the public then we need to focus on the changing dynamics of democratic politics, in terms of its demands, challenges, and opportunities, in the twenty-first century.

Fifty Years On

At the heart of this book is the belief that the public do not 'hate' politics but that it is closer to the truth to suggest that they expect too much from it and do not understand it. We should not therefore jump too high when scholars write of the 'end of politics' or the emergence of 'post-democracy' but we should be very aware of the manner in which the 'bad faith model of politics' risks destroying a beautiful and civilizing activity. The widespread perception that politics is failing matters because it plays into the hands of extremists who proffer simple solutions to complex problems. I'm always amazed when the World Values Survey reveals that most people think of 'politics' as 'not at all important' in their lives. The fruits of democratic politics are all around us—in the schools that educate our children, the clerks that administrate various benefits, the hospitals that tend the sick, the teams that build and maintain highways, the gardeners who tend the parks, the officers that imprison the dangerous, etc.—in a manner that illustrates the collective essence of democratic politics and underpins the notion of 'everyday politics' as a useful shorthand tool for revealing the positive day-to-day impact of politics on people's lives. And yet the nature of politics and the challenges of governing are almost unrecognizable when compared to the situation fifty years ago. Governing has become far more difficult, the demands on politicians are far greater, and the storm is raging with increasing intensity.

The argument of this section, and indeed this book, is to try to calm the storm by explaining that if democratic politics is deemed to be broken or failing, the reasons for this are *systemic* in nature. The great danger of the rise of anti-political sentiment is that it may generate a shift away from collective action and externalized rationing (discussed above) towards a more individualized structure that is simply ill-equipped to deal with the major social, economic, and environmental challenges that will shape the twenty-first century—less equipped in the sense that we will have lost those levers of social trust and social engagement, direction, and mutual support that politics delivers. Democratic politics is the politics of life chances, of opportunity, and constant renewal. 'Life politics', by contrast, revolves around individualized responses to social problems that can only ever fail. The 'bad faith model of politics' is therefore not only wrong but it also belittles our collective achievements and potential. It glamorizes those who heckle from the sidelines and encourages us to despise the very people we vote for. With this in mind let me outline the challenges that now face those who are foolish enough to enter the political arena by identifying eight ways in which the nature of political rule has altered during the past fifty years.

1. The Decline of Deference
2. The Growth of Overload
3. The Transition from Government to Governance

4. The Growth of Globalization
5. The Impact of Technology
6. The Accountability Explosion
7. The Ideological Blur
8. The Flight from Reality

My aim is not to explore each of these issues in great detail but simply to provide a flavour of how the challenges of governing have become more difficult because of them.

The Decline of Deference

One of the most important and most striking changes in the nature of political rule has to be the decline in deference amongst the public across advanced industrialized countries. This has complex and contested roots but is related to increased levels of educational attainment, the gradual erosion of religious practices and values, growing material security, and the progressive elimination of traditional risks to life (disease, starvation, poverty, etc.), the evolution of political rights that allowed the public to question those in authority, and the spread of new forms of knowledge and communication. Ironically, what this suggests is that political and economic development has facilitated the development of a more questioning citizenry that is increasingly willing to complain, criticize, or protest. Inter-generational value change has, as Ronald Inglehart argued in his path-breaking *The Silent Revolution* (1977), cultivated a shift from a public focus on material needs (like food, shelter, and protection) towards post-materialism (like human rights, sexual equality, and quality of life issues) which has in turn led to new political conflicts, rising public expectations, and an expansion of the responsibilities of the state.

The Growth of Overload

The second key change in the nature of political rule is that the boundaries of 'the political' appear to have expanded to the point at which politicians are expected to take responsibility for almost every aspect of modern life. This was a change in the nature of politics that first surfaced as part of the debate about the 'crisis of democracy' in the 1970s and led to a flurry of interest in the concepts of delegitimation, ungovernability, political overload, and political bankruptcy. As Anthony King and Michael Crozier argued in relation to the United Kingdom and United States (respectively), the 1950s and 1960s witnessed a massive growth in public expectations about what benefits could be provided by politics and politicians in Western democracies. Unrealistic expectations followed by dashed hopes had, in this argument, resulted in a serious decline in public confidence. King captured the point with an eloquence rarely found within modern scholarship: 'Once upon a time man looked to God to order the world. Then he looked to the market. Now he looks to government. And when things go wrong people blame not "Him" or "it" but "them" [i.e. politicians].'

One crucial element of the changing nature of politics since the 1960s and 1970s is that the public's expectations of politics have grown even greater, as have the range of issues for which politicians are expected to shoulder responsibilities. Science, to take just one example, has raised social anxieties and placed new demands at the door of politics that simply did not exist fifty years ago (human embryology, regenerative stem cell technology, xenotransplantation, nanotechnology, etc.). More broadly, it is possible to suggest that the concepts of 'fate' or 'bad luck' have lost any meaning in a world that expects politicians to prevent, manage, and respond within seconds to natural disasters, and as a result politicians are increasingly expected to alleviate both the likelihood and consequences of events (tsunamis, floods, volcanoes, earthquakes, tornados, extreme weather, etc.), which would for most of the twentieth century have existed beyond the realm of democratic politics. At a more basic level it is possible to suggest that the nature of many of the social challenges facing politics have grown in complexity in the sense that they appear messy, often intractable, and socially divisive (e.g. teenage pregnancy, mental health, obesity, etc.). What are often termed 'wicked issues' have always existed but their range and multifaceted characteristics have arguably augmented. This focus on growth and complexity flows into a third change in the nature of political rule—the shift from govern*ment* to govern*ance*.

The Transition from Government to Governance

Put very simply, the institutional framework through which public policies are designed and implemented has grown more complicated in recent decades. This reflects the impact of managerialist reforms that were implemented across the world during the 1980s and 1990s that sought to inject markets or market-style relationships into the public sector. This pattern of state reform was to some extent driven through a recognition that a gap was emerging between what was being demanded by the public and what could be realistically delivered by politics and politicians on the basis of available financial resources. More and more people expected European levels of public services but American levels of taxation. Increasing the standard of public services without increasing taxes could only be achieved by somehow engineering far higher levels of organizational efficiency (i.e. 'more bang for each buck'). 'New' public management therefore emphasized the 'unbundling' or 'unravelling' of traditionally large multi-purpose bureaucratic structures through privatization, contracting-out, and establishing semi-autonomous single-purpose bodies that were expected to operate under market-like conditions (targets, customer driven, performance-related pay, etc.).

The shift towards a 'hub model of governance' in which a small policy-making core led by elected politicians oversees the implementation of policies (i.e. steering but not rowing) through a network of public, private, and third-sector contractors may have been designed to reduce political overload and allow ministers to focus on long-term strategic planning. However, one of its unintended consequences has been an increasingly congested state. The issue of congestion takes us to the heart of the matter. If democratic politics is increasingly judged to be failing and if governing is getting harder, as it undoubtedly is, this is almost certainly due to the manner in which the number of organizations that are involved in the delivery of public services have increased substantially. Students of public policy have therefore traced the emergence of an increasingly dense and complex administrative landscape in which politicians have very few direct powers but must seek somehow to steer a vast range of organizations, like a conductor directing an orchestra, towards an agreed goal. It is for exactly this reason that ministers increasingly complain about the existence of 'rubber levers', by which they mean that the decisions they make in Washington, London, Paris, or Canberra appear to have been quashed or amended into something quite different by the time they reach the service delivery end of the supply chain. Focusing concern on the increasingly complex architecture of the state is by no means new but in the twenty-first century Anthony Downs's 'laws of bureaucracy' (first developed in *Inside*

Bureaucracy, 1967)—imperfect control, lessening control, diminishing control, and counter control—have taken on added meaning in the context of a broad concern regarding the 'hollowing out of the state'. The transition from relatively simple and straightforward governmental structures towards the more complex networks that underpin the concept of governance feeds into our fourth theme—globalization.

The Growth of Globalization

The geopolitics of the globe has altered in many ways over the past fifty years and as a result the role and capacity of national politicians has been transformed. Global flows and supranational agreements now mean that nation states are enmeshed within new frameworks of multi-level governance. The nation state has not yet been eclipsed but the manner in which it must now exercise its powers has been transformed. Developments in one country will now have knock-on consequences in other countries in a manner that was simply not true in the post-war decades, and the geopolitics of the twenty-first century will be unlike anything the modern world has seen before. The world is simply more economically, politically, and socially connected.

The world is also more unstable in terms of where power lies and how people expect to be governed. From Latin America, to Eastern Europe and now across North Africa and the Middle East, whatever democracy *is* the people seem to want it. The position, role, and capacity of the United States has also clearly changed in recent years. Crick wrote at a time when the United States was leading the free world and acting as a counterweight to authoritarian expansionism. With the collapse of the Soviet Union the world entered a period of uni-polarity as the United States was *the* superpower, but more recently the rise of Brazil, Russia, India, and most notably China, has opened a new era of international politics. Yet if power has shifted 'horizontally' across and between states there is also what could be termed a 'vertical' dimension to the growth of globalization. As Jonathan Koppell's *World Rule* (2011) illustrates, a network of global governance organizations, from the World Trade Organization to the Forest Stewardship Council, now plays a prominent role in the management of international affairs. These organizations tend to exist to some extent beyond the reach of national democratic frameworks but must somehow maintain a level of legitimacy through which they can satisfy the demands of key constituencies whose support is essential to the global regime. As a result, the democratization of global governance will undoubtedly emerge as a defining feature of the twenty-first century, as the fact that urgent global challenges demand global solutions (i.e. global reach and power) becomes increasingly obvious. The uprisings in the Middle East are a critical example of the power of globalization, not just in terms of changing public expectations about the way they expect to be governed, but also in terms of the mobility of information and the power of global reaction. The new social media's ability to pass information within and beyond a country through grainy images of protest, violence, and repression provides a new tool in the fight to fuel and shape change, which leads us to consider our fifth theme—technology.

The Impact of Technology

If the themes of deference, overload, governance, and globalization form four ways in which the nature of political rule has changed since the first publication of *In Defence of Politics* in 1962, the fifth topic focuses on changes in relation to information communication technology (ICT). The internet, twitter, and the emergence of the blogosphere add a new dimension to political engagement, which facilitates a sharper and more direct link between politicians and the public. President Obama's use of ICT in the 2008 presidential race, for example, exploited new forms of technological leverage, including electronic billboards, YouTube, websites, podcasts, email, social networking, text-messaging mobile phone activism, facebook, micro-sites—even buying advertising space on video games—not only to control the agenda but also to carefully tailor messages to target audiences and rebut the negative campaigning of his opponents. It revealed for the first time the power of the internet to shape electoral politics. As Claire Cain Miller wrote in the *New York Times*: 'one of the many ways that the election of Barack Obama as president has echoed that of John F. Kennedy is his use of a new medium that will forever change politics. For Mr Kennedy, it was television. For Mr Obama, it is the internet.'

The same technological forces have also delivered new opportunities for countries that crave to make the transition *to* democracy. Aung San Suu Kyi, the leader of the National League for Democracy in Burma, used the 2011 BBC Reith Lectures to outline the impact of technology in the Tunisian revolution and across North Africa and the

Middle East. Not only did new forms of technology allow the protestors to better organize and coordinate their movements but it kept the attention of the whole world firmly focused on them.

Not just every single death—but even every single wounded—can be made known to the world within minutes. In Libya, in Syria, and in Yemen the revolutionaries keep the world informed of the atrocities of those in power. The picture of a thirteen-year-old boy tortured to death in Syria aroused such anger and indignation that world leaders had to raise their voices in condemnation. Communications means contact and, in the context of the Middle Eastern revolutions, it was a freedom contact.

And yet although there are undoubtedly lessons for those interested in promoting democracy that can be learned from recent American political history, there is also a darker side to ICT that cannot be ignored. Lazy cyber-utopianism risks overlooking three basic concerns. First, authoritarian regimes (like China, Russia, and Iran) have utilized the internet as a tool of control and repression to spread propaganda and identify dissidents rather than promote democratic values. Secondly, the rise of the networked society risks undermining grassroots activism because active citizens and paid organizers door-stepping, persuading, and promoting candidates on the ground are simply less vital in an age of wired, networked, and connected people. As a result, the nature of campaigning and party politics is changing away from a focus on direct face-to-face citizen engagement. And finally, the on-line multi-mediated world in which various viewpoints and perspectives are voiced does not seem to apply to political discourse. On-line political comment in the blogosphere is overwhelmingly anti-political and generally imbued with the 'bad faith model of politics'. Changes in the nature of modern technology have, and still are, transforming the nature of politics in many ways but we are arguably on the cusp of a tipping-point in terms of whether they act as a force for the good of democracy or are simply used as tools to promote a crude version of political cynicism.

The Accountability Explosion

One way of teasing apart this issue is by focusing on the topic of accountability (our sixth issue), due to the manner in which the internet has delivered levels of information about politics that was simply unimaginable fifty years ago. The nature of political rule in the twenty-first century therefore appears to harbour little sympathy for the view that even in a democracy there is a legitimate role for some degree of secrecy. Instead, accountability has emerged as the *über*-concept of modern times. What is interesting, however, is that increasing levels of accountability, transparency, openness, and freedom of information have not restored public confidence in politics but have instead led to the creation of what John Keane has termed a 'monitory democracy' in which a vast range of agencies, boards, and commissions monitor the behaviour of politicians and public servants due to a belief that they are simply not to be trusted. Although Keane welcomes monitory democracy for the manner in which it can 'greatly complicate, and sometimes wrong-foot, the lives of politicians, parties, legislatures and governments', my sense is that life for most politicians and public servants is already complicated enough. Moreover, governing capacity is a requirement of any political system and we cannot bind the hands of politicians by placing more and more limits on their governing capacity, or by subjecting their every decision to forensic analysis, and then attack them for failing to govern with conviction or take decisive action.

To blend the issue of technological change with a focus on accountability, can we really believe that WikiLeaks is a positive addition to the political landscape? The organization and those individuals around it might claim to be 'promoting a climate of transparency and accountability necessary for an authentically liberal democracy', but since when was complete transparency ever held as either possible or desirable?

What political scientist Bob Goodin has described as a 'veil of ambiguity' reflects not some dastardly fact about politics but simply that it is part of human communication to say different things to a different audience. There are perfectly good reasons why we don't tell the same story to our husband or wife, our boss, our friends, or our children and there is nothing innately wrong with this. When the same logic is transferred to the political sphere the morally troubling elements of duplicity become more obvious but that does not hide the fact that sometimes a degree of moral duplicity is necessary to secure the common good. WikiLeaks therefore risks promoting a preciously naive anti-political vision of moral purity against which any system of politics is guaranteed to fail. In making this argument I am not in any way seeking to defend politicians or officials who abuse power, tell lies, or engage in corrupt (or morally dubious) practices but I am trying to put things in perspective. Attacking 'politics', in general, and 'politicians', in particular, is becoming something of a national blood sport in many countries. Very few politicians or public servants abuse power, tell lies, or engage in corrupt practices, at least not in those countries that seem to have lost most faith in politics, but by treating them as if they do we risk allowing ourselves to sink into a 'politics of pessimism' which is dangerously blinkered to the achievements and potential of democratic engagement. This brings me to a further and particularly significant change in the nature of politics: the role and influence of ideology.

The Ideological Blur

During the first two-thirds of the twentieth century politicians undoubtedly faced complex challenges and difficult decisions but they did at least possess a relatively clear and more stable ideological foundation. The politics of 'the left' or 'the right' provided a form of moral compass or anchorage through which politicians could rationalize their responses to social challenges and offer a relatively coherent governing narrative. I am not for one minute arguing, like some, that we exist in a 'post-ideological' historical phase but I am suggesting that politicians appear to have lost their political safety blankets, by which I mean recourse to a fairly clear and coherent ideological position, be it liberalism, socialism, or any other variant that provided a sense of direction. The traditional left–right divide still hangs in the atmosphere of contemporary politics but it lacks a certain sense of meaning and appears increasingly redundant.

'Left' versus 'Right', or more recently the progressive/conservative divide, may still animate political debate and language but they are essentially twentieth-century constructs whose capacity to inspire and renew has waned. It could be argued that the ideological foundations of mainstream politics have not waned but have, in fact, *narrowed* as political parties have clustered increasingly around a rather restricted acceptance of a market economy, in which the legitimate and appropriate role of the state vis-à-vis the market has been, at least until the global financial crisis, relatively uncontested. At the very least it would appear that as the ideological battleground has narrowed, politicians, the media, and social commentators have been forced to construct even more artificial boundaries. This may explain the rise of celebrity culture, the increasing focus on personality politics, and an approach to political debate that has become increasingly framed in terms of 'them' (i.e. politicians—untrustworthy, greedy, and corrupt) and 'us' (i.e. anyone who is not a politician and must therefore be generally above suspicion). Would it be too much to suggest that if the ideological spectrum narrowed towards the end of the twentieth century then the vacuum that this process created has been filled by a shallow, flawed, but very dangerous anti-political paradigm?

The reason why the blurring of ideological boundaries matters is because it offers such great potential for renewal and renaissance. The twenty-first century will belong to those who are willing to challenge dominant assumptions, take risks, and most of all think anew. The future, put slightly differently, will reward those who are both optimistic and open-minded, and see opportunities where others see threats. My concern is that too many people appear depressed, defeated, and closed-minded when our need for a vibrant marketplace of ideas is greater than ever. This notion of a marketplace of ideas leads us to consider our final theme and the changed role of academics.

The Flight from Reality

In reflecting on the contemporary relevance of academics my intention is not to bite those intellectual hands that have nourished me over the years but simply to suggest that when it comes to understanding public disengagement from politics, scholars may well be part of the problem—and also part of the cure. Bernard Crick was an exceptional man in many ways but he was also part of a generation of 'University Professors of Politics' that acknowledged that the acceptance of a Chair in Politics came with certain public and professional obligations. The role of a professor was not therefore to think great thoughts and write long books but to work alongside practitioners in a way that ensured academic knowledge and research informed the day-to-day operation of democratic politics. It was therefore common for professors to hold academic positions alongside senior positions in local or central government. There was also a very clear expectation that professors would engage in public debates more broadly and in a way that would to some extent counterbalance the promotion of over-simplistic arguments or untruths. The social responsibilities of professors were therefore taken seriously and played a role in lifting overall levels of public understanding and political literacy.

The more recent failure of academics to play a role in bridging the gap between the governors and the governed is possibly most obvious in relation to the dominant style of writing. If one returns to works like Sidney Low's *The Governance of England* (1903), Frederic Ogg and Perley Ray's *American Government* (1922), C. Wright Mill's *The Power Elite*, or Anthony Birch's *Representative and Responsible Government* (1964), they share a common trait in that all made fairly complex arguments but in a way that ordinary people could understand. The art of communication has, however, been lost in the twenty-first century as academics increasingly say more and more about less and less and in a manner that is frequently impenetrable to all but a handful of other professors. Academic writing has increasingly become associated with self-interested turf wars rather than public engagement. In *The Flight from Reality in the Human Sciences* (2005) Ian Shapiro, himself a professor of politics at Yale, exposes the manner in which academic scholarship tends to focus on 'manufacturing esoteric discourses with high entry costs for outsiders...all the better if they involve inside-the-cranium exercises that never require one to leave one's computer screen'. In his book *In Defence of Politicians* (2010), journalist Peter Riddell makes a similar point and suggests that 'To read many political science journals is to enter an enclosed and often narcissistic world of academics writing for each other. It is self-referential as well as self-reverential, and often unreadable to anyone but a specialist.'

Critics will respond—I can almost hear them sharpening their quills as I write—that they are victims of a system that pressurizes them to 'publish or perish' within an increasingly contract-based environment; that adopts an instrumental approach to knowledge that equates value with serving a practical purpose; that involves teaching ever higher numbers of increasingly demanding students and which still views the publication of peer-reviewed research-based scholarship in academic outlets as the main criteria for promotion. This de-limiting of the academic domain, which Frank Furedi's *Where Have All the Intellectuals Gone?* (2004) dissects with such precision, simply adds further weight to my concern that the politics professoriate increasingly resembles an academy of sleep walkers whose moral vigour has been sapped, their profession narrowed such that they no longer know where they are heading or why. Why is it that the introduction to Dante's *Inferno*

springs to mind? 'Midway upon this life on which we're bound I woke
to find myself in some dark wood, where the right way could not be
found.' My sense is that the discipline of political science (or 'political
studies') has to some degree lost its way and might therefore benefit
from reflecting upon its own professional responsibilities to the public
at large and particularly in relation to the ways in which it might
bridge the gap, through the provision of careful comment, balanced
analysis, and accessible works, which has emerged between the governors and the governed.

This section has, like all writing, posed a challenge in terms of balancing breadth and depth. My aim has been to paint a picture of how and
why the nature of political rule has changed in the last half-century
and particularly why the challenges of governing have become, if anything, harder. The storm is raging with an intensity that was hardly
imaginable fifty years ago. The question with which this leaves us at the
end of this section is whether it is possible to look across these eight
issues and deduce any general patterns or trends? My answer to this can
be summed up in three words: aggression, distance, and fluidity.

Aggression is meant in the sense that political competition is increasingly interpreted as little more than a form of warfare in which the
role of political actors is to 'attack' anyone who disagrees with them. As
Emmett Buell and Lee Sigelman outline in their book *Attack Politics*
(2008), the language, discourse, and tactics of politics is generally
focused on negative campaigning, personal slurs, and a view of politics
that defines any willingness to engage in serious debate, offer to nego-
tiate, or change your mind as evidence of weakness. It is bitter, short-
tempered, and its ambition is to sneer and jibe mercilessly.

Distance in the sense that arguing a gap has emerged between the
governors and the governed veils the fact that, in many ways, the traditional distance between politicians and the public has all but disappeared. We now know more about our politicians, their interests, their
families, and almost all aspects of their lives than we ever have in the
past. One of the defining features of modern politics is that the idea of
a politician enjoying a 'private life' appears almost laughable. The
demands of 24/7 rolling news, combined with a sense of public
entitlement to know everything about those they elect, conspire to
ensure that political life is incredibly intense: too close, yet in many
ways too distant.

Fluidity is meant in the simple sense that many of the social anchor points that gave meaning and direction to political life have become less tangible, less clear. The old debates about 'left and right' or 'big state versus small state' appear increasingly meaningless in a world driven by interdependency and the emergence of 'new' risks.

Disentangling all of this and putting it in some order is a hugely difficult task, made much more difficult by the fact that challenging the 'bad faith model of politics' can only bring with it a fair degree of criticism since it is a conventional wisdom that is so entrenched. However, we cannot avoid the fact that we seem to have lost our faith, our confidence in politics, and as a result urgently need to come to a better and more considered view of why politics matters. It is time to begin to fire back at those who would do without 'mere politics'.

Firing Back

The main aim of the previous section was to explore how the pace, direction, and intensity of modern democratic politics, in essence the very nature of political rule, has changed during the last fifty years. The public may conclude that politicians today are lesser people than those who held office in decades past—but they are wrong. What has changed is not so much the politicians, although we are at risk of creating a system that ensures that only the manically ambitious dare stand for office as 'normal' people refuse to submit to the abuse, pressure, hounding, and misrepresentation that becoming a politician generally involves. What is different is that the challenges are greater, the solutions more complex, the transparency that is demanded is of an utterly different nature to when Crick was writing his *Defence*. The hysteria that surrounds any attempt to discuss a serious issue is shrill, the opponents of any reform (and there are always opponents) will shout louder and to a wider audience, and even the smallest molehill will be amplified into the largest mountain.

The people are the same but the environment in which politics takes places is a planet away from the situation fifty years ago. As a result, although the list of topics and themes examined in the previous section might at first glance look like the random spoils of a political hunter-gatherer, they all combine to focus attention on the fact that the art of governing has grown far harder since Crick's *Defence* was first published.

So what? Why does any of this matter in terms of defending politics? How can any of this help cultivate a shift from 'the politics of pessimism' to 'the politics of optimism'? Let me answer these questions and conclude this chapter by focusing on three distinct levels. At the micro-political level the themes of *aggression*, *distance*, and *fluidity*, as already discussed, provide strands of thinking that will weave their way throughout this book to provide a continuous thread. Similarly, but at a mid-range level, this chapter's focus provides both the context and an entry point for the five specific foes against which democracy in the twenty-first century needs to be defended:

1. The decline of deference and the issue of overload force us to consider the management of public expectations and the need to defend politics *from itself* (Chapter 2). This turn of phrase is intended to expose the internal contradictions and inflationary pressures that are inherent in a system of governing that rests on popular consent and popular control.

2. A focus on governance and globalization highlights the need to defend the public sphere from the encroachment of *the market* (Chapter 3), not simply in the sense of seeking to reinstate an artificial divide between the public and private sphere but more subtly in the sense of understanding the individualizing logic of markets and how this eats away at collective values. 'Life politics', in the sense of individual responses to social problems, will always fail, just as any system founded on mass consumption and non-stop economic development must at some point confront the fact that the limits to growth are finite.

3. The themes of overload, governance, technological development, and accountability, by contrast, combine to focus our attention on the politics *of denial* (Chapter 4). The politics of denial is a shorthand phrase for the global trend towards the depoliticization of democratic politics by transferring functions and responsibilities to independent agencies, boards, and commissions, staffed by scientists, technocrats, accountants, bankers, ethicists, or judges, that are insulated from direct political control. As a result the sphere of democratic politics has been subject to a process of narrowing or 'infolding' that, in itself, reflects a naive faith in experts, the impact of anti-political arguments that tell us that politicians should never be trusted, and, most importantly, epitomizes a failure in our own collective confidence.

4. The fact that our confidence is low and our self-belief has been shaken is most evident in the manner in which wave after wave of crises fall upon the shores of politics. Defending politics against *crises* (Chapter 5) is therefore concerned with explaining why at a point in history when we are generally safer than we have ever been, we are so gripped by panic, anxiety, and worry to the point that we feel so weak, depressed, at times almost listless. Appreciating the impact of globalization, acknowledging the risks of new technology, understanding that the public need help in turning raw information into useful knowledge, being honest about the erosion of social institutions and ideological positions that helped us make sense of the world, and (critically) exposing the fact that many market actors actively conspire to keep the public in a constant state of fear provokes fresh questions about the changing nature of politics and the distribution of blame for its perceived failings. In a sense we know who is to blame—those evil politicians who are not be trusted. We know this is true because the media never stops telling us so.

5. In the twenty-first century no defence of politics could be complete without a frank and forceful account of the destructive role of the media (Chapter 6) and I make no apology for the force of my argument. Critics of my position will undoubtedly hide behind Enoch Powell's famous jibe that 'politicians who complain about the media are like sailors who complain about the sea' but in doing so they defend possibly the most destructive and insidious force within modern politics.

At the broadest macro-political level, however, this is a book about the management of public expectations. It is exactly this focus on public expectations that forms the hook on which this whole work hangs. Is it possible that we expect too much from politics (and to some extent are encouraged to do so) rather than receive too little? Might it be that more realistic recalibration of our expectations, based on a more secure understanding of the aims and ambitions of democracy, might prevent democracy from failing so often? Could it be that if the public genuinely believe that politics (and therefore politicians) are failing them, this may well tell us more about the public's (over-)expectations, than about the failure of our politicians?

The link between unrealistic public expectations and why we 'hate' politics has possibly been clearest in the United States since the election of Barack Obama. His campaign was based on the promise of radical and distinctive change: nothing more, nothing less. As the campaign came towards an end, and particularly as public opinion surveys suggested an Obama victory was likely, his campaign team's focus shifted to an emphasis on lowering public expectations about what he would be able to achieve if elected. The sudden financial crisis and the prospect of a deep and painful recession increased the urgency inside Obama's campaign team to bring people down to earth, after a campaign in which his soaring rhetoric and promises of 'hope' and 'change' were suddenly confronted with the reality of a stricken economy. Seeking to dampen down public expectations continued throughout the transition period following the election in an attempt to prevent 'a vast mood swing from exhilaration and euphoria to despair', as one of Obama's senior advisers noted. In response to questions about his immediate priorities on taking office Mr Obama repeatedly told the world's media that 'the first hundred days is going to be important, but it's probably the first thousand days that makes the difference . . . I won't stand here and pretend that any of this will be easy—especially now.'

It clearly has not been easy for Obama as the challenges of getting into office seem to have paled into insignificance against the challenges of governing. 'Yes we can' has in relation to many commitments turned into 'I'm still hoping we can at some point', and his approval ratings have fallen accordingly. And yet I'm personally quite relieved that Obama is not Superman. Too many people sidestep their own individual responsibilities as a citizen by looking for a superhero to take control. The election of Obama still demonstrates the capacity of democratic politics to renew itself, to reconnect with sections of the political community that had effectively become disenfranchised, and to secure agreements on ambitious policies that many thought could never be achieved. Viewed in this way, I put it to you that maybe the fabric of democratic politics is not quite as threadbare as many think. Hence my plea for a focus not on the 'bad faith model of politics' but on a new politics of optimism based on the argument that by demanding too much, holding unrealistic expectations about what politics can deliver, and failing to accept that the challenges of governing have become more difficult, we risk losing sight of democracy's basic achievements and its potential for renewal. My argument is not that politics is perfect. It is that when compared to alternative regimes its positive attributes become more obvious than is generally acknowledged and that the challenges that will define the twenty-first century will demand a collective response that can only be accommodated through democratic politics—not, however, politics as it has been practised in the past but a richer and deeper form of politics that can support a transition from *fear* societies to *free* societies.

The current public and intellectual climate is not obviously amenable to an argument that seeks to defend politics and speak in praise of politicians but that is exactly why this book is so important. The brave (or the foolish) individuals who dare to challenge public opinion frequently find themselves ploughing a rather lonely furrow, but by writing in praise of democratic politics I will actually be following a line of argument that has already been made in recent years, in slightly different ways and from varying perspectives, by a number of people. In this book I want to make the furrow slightly wider and deeper and want to stick my neck out even further and suggest that the public have become politically decadent in their expectations about what politics should deliver, how politicians should behave, and about their own responsibilities within society. I want to challenge the 'bad faith model of politics' by showing that democratic politics matters, because on the whole it delivers far more than most people recognize, and the alternatives are far worse. Let me provide you with a reference point: 'A vast, chaotic, misgoverned, dysfunctional morass; its rulers historically preoccupied with looting rather than governing. The armed forces bloated, parasitic, disloyal and generally useless except in so far as they threaten the lives and welfare of the much put upon civilian population.' Reflecting upon this recent description of an African state in the twenty-first century might encourage some of the critics who bemoan what democratic politics delivers to pause for thought.

I want to suggest that the roots of social disengagement within established democracies lie in a lack of political literacy and political understanding rather than any true or empirically borne 'hatred'. There may also be a demographic factor at play: this contemporary climate of anti-politics is arguably rooted in a generation that has become complacent and parochial, and in doing so has forgotten the alternatives to democratic politics. Those individuals who remember the two world wars that stained the first half of the twentieth century might well possess a far more urgent and personal understanding of why politics matters and why it is sometimes necessary to speak up in its defence. The experience of living through or losing loved ones forged a great collective belief in both democratic politics and the capacity of the state. It also taught many people never to take things for granted. My concern is that, despite the pain and suffering of two world wars, we seem to have forgotten this basic wisdom and in its place have created little more than a political marketplace in which there are very few incentives for politicians to actually tell the truth, and too many people who take for granted democratic politics and what it delivers.

In essence my argument is one of almost primitive simplicity: at the root of political disengagement is an 'expectations gap'. Closing this gap is as much to do with reducing 'demand' as with increasing 'supply'. But in order to reduce demand we must rediscover and treasure the basic spirit of politics and broker a meaningful debate about our collective future. Therefore, having examined the essence of democratic politics and how the nature of governing has altered since Bernard Crick first penned his defence of politics, I want to offer my first defence. It may at first appear quite an odd point of departure—a defence of politics against *itself*.

2

A DEFENCE OF POLITICS
AGAINST ITSELF

Democracy is perhaps the most promiscuous word in the world of public affairs. She is everybody's mistress and yet somehow retains her magic
even when a lover sees that her favours are being, in his light, illicitly
shared by many another. Indeed, even amid our pain at being denied her
exclusive fidelity, we are proud of her adaptability to all sorts of circumstances, to all sorts of company.

Bernard Crick, *In Defence of Politics* (1962)

In the free world the competition of ideas and of parties flourishes, and
allegiances are based on a single common principle or purpose that strug-
gles against a competing point of view. Though generally healthy for a
society, this competition can be quite dangerous if we lose sight of the fact
that there is a far greater divide between the world of freedom and the
world of fear than there is between competing factions within a free society.
If we fail to recognize this, we lose moral clarity. The legitimate differences
between us, the shades of gray in a free society, will be wrongly perceived
as black and white. Then the real black-and-white line that divides free
societies from fear societies, the real line that divides good from evil, will no
longer be distinguishable.

Natan Sharansky, *The Case for Democracy* (2004)

Double discourse on democracy is certainly nothing new. We are accus-
tomed to hearing that democracy is the worst of governments with the
exception of all others. But the new anti-democratic sentiment gives the
general formula a more troubling expression.

Jacques Rancière, *Hatred of Democracy* (2006)

Death and ambivalence; fear and hatred; limits and contradictions:
these may not be the most encouraging themes with which to
begin a chapter that seeks to defend and praise the achievements of

democratic politics, but it is only by being honest about the ambitions and limitations of politics that we can begin to develop a more optimistic account of its value, what it provides, and its future. Democracy is a crude but incredibly effective way of engineering a degree of civility between competing groups—crude in the sense that the democratic promise provides a right to participate, a right to be listened to, and a right to express your opinion about whether the current government should continue in office; but the realities of collective decision-making emphasize *voice* over *choice* and therefore conspire to ensure that not everyone will get what they want all of the time. It cannot 'make every sad heart glad', but it delivers far more than many people seem to appreciate.

In most of the developed world democracy has fulfilled the majority of our demands. It has delivered clean water and food, universal education and healthcare, old-age pensions, and social protections in the form of sickness cover, redundancy pay, employee rights, and a minimum wage. Democracy has broken the link between *politics* and *fear* that still plagues large parts of the world. Democracy (and therefore 'politics' and 'politicians') has brought us many of those things that we take for granted as essential elements of a civilized life. Despite this, large sections of the public in Western Europe and North America, and elsewhere, seem increasingly disappointed with what democratic politics delivers, how it operates, and believe that in some sense it is failing. It is undoubtedly true that democratic politics is not perfect, but my warning is simply that politics matters far more than most people realize and that democracy is far more fragile than many people appreciate. Its achievements and what it delivers are frequently lost in the vibrancy of day-to-day life, or what I have called 'everyday politics', which can only exist against the backdrop of a stable democratic regime.

Defending politics against *itself* therefore hinges on being honest about its imperfections. It also rests on posing some rather awkward questions about the responsibilities of the public vis-à-vis democratic politics—awkward in the sense that democracy rests on a relationship (or in reality a set of relationship*s*) between the governors and the governed, and this is a reciprocal relationship that brings with it rights and responsibilities for both sides. My concern is that the governing relationship has become one-sided. The expectations and demands placed upon the political system and politicians by the public have become so intense, immediate, and unrealistic that democracy is almost guaranteed to fail. No politics has the magic to satisfy a world of greater and greater expectations. Democracy, in its true and active form, rests upon the existence of active citizens, not passive critics, but my sense is that too many people possess a highly developed sense of their rights but an underdeveloped sense of their responsibilities. It is always easier to follow the path of least resistance and blame the wrongs of the world, our failings, or our situation on those loathsome politicians instead of acknowledging our own share of responsibility and acting accordingly. Political cynicism, disengagement, democratic decadence—call it what you will—is too often an excuse for physical and intellectual laziness.

If we are to lift the collective depression that appears to have fallen over large sections of society and put in its place a more optimistic and forward-looking account of politics, we (individuals, pressure groups, academics, journalists, politicians, political parties, etc.) all need to grow up and adopt a far more honest account of politics. We live in countries where a peaceful transition of power is the norm; where poverty is now understood in relative as opposed to absolute terms; where we are not short of choice (in relation to political opinions, consumer goods, etc.); and where the political system is responsive to public opinion. Democracy delivers because democracies do not go to war with each other. Their leaders don't want it and their people won't allow it.

A system in which ideas, conflicts, and interests are openly articulated and peacefully resolved may often, for understandable reasons, be a rather slow and complex one. It is also a system that is likely to contain contradictions and be quite fragile, due to the manner in which it must control, manage, and vent a vast number of competing pressures. This is a critical point. Democratic politics is to some extent 'volcanic' in the sense that political institutions, political processes, and politicians must accommodate a huge number of stresses and strains within the system. The external face of democratic politics may well appear calm but within this fragile shell exists a deep hot molten core of competing demands and pressures that all must somehow be contained and managed. Politics is therefore a constant balancing act that seeks to manage the day-to-day ebb and flow of transformational pressures arising from new demands, events, and challenges. Sometimes the pressures are too great and the volcano will erupt in the form of social protests, the defeat of a government, or a major period of national soul-searching, but in many ways even occasional volcanic eruptions can be viewed as part of a healthy democratic landscape.

Ironically, the most dangerous and challenging internal pressure that any democratic regime must manage is not corruption, economic failure, or the threat of natural disasters but public pressures and demands. It is the link between *democracy* and *populism* that creates the most fault-lines. It is exactly this tension between democracy and populism, by which I mean the need to channel and restrain public pressures and demands, that lies at the very heart of this chapter because the successful functioning of a democracy revolves around the establishment and maintenance of a very delicate equilibrium between the governors and the governed. This tension is rarely the subject of public discussion but needs to be brought to the fore in order to cultivate a more balanced and mature debate about the achievements, limits, and contradictions of democracy. This is a tension that reveals itself in a number of ways: in the need to balance governing capacity with democratic accountability; in the nurturing of social optimism and ambition while not over-inflating public expectations; in allowing public protest and dissent while protecting public safety and preventing the incitement of racial hatred or violence; and in allowing politicians to make tough decisions but also expecting them to retain public support. Democracy therefore rests on the imposition of some forms of restraint over popular engagement in the decision-making process. But its foundation *on* popular support makes it exceedingly difficult for politicians to reject demands or make necessary but unpopular decisions. The simple argument I am making here is that in the absence of any broad public understanding of the simple aims, limits, and costs of democracy, modern politics will inevitably contain the seeds of its own ruin because at the root of democratic politics lies a set of hard truths, which we ignore at out peril. Let me set these out very clearly.

1. Democratic politics revolves around putting collective interests above individual wants and desires.

2. A stable democracy must impose some form of limits on public engagement in politics and resist the insatiable growth of public demands.

3. It cannot therefore satisfy every person all of the time because it lacks the resources—and many individuals or groups seek to put their self-interest before the public interest.

4. In reality the notion of the 'public interest' is flawed, due to the existence of competing and frequently diametrically opposed demands, and the role of a politician is therefore inherently invidious.

5. The nature of a system in which politicians depend upon popular support makes it very difficult for them to make unpopular decisions, no matter how necessary they might be.

6. Politicians do not have a monopoly on duplicity. The public's rhetorical commitment to many issues often evaporates when it comes to the imposition of tough choices.

7. Political competition also creates incentives for politicians to over-inflate public expectations to the extent that some degree of failure and disappointment seems almost inevitable.

8. Politicians, like everyone else, will have to make commitments and decisions against a background of uncertainty and sometimes they will have to change their mind or will be unable to implement their promises.

9. The world can be a cruel place and democratic politics will from time to time demand that politicians engage in morally dubious practices in an attempt to secure the safety and well-being of society.

10. Politicians are human. They will make mistakes. They will have to live with the consequences of their decisions.

I make no apology for the fact that stating these truths may well disappoint and enrage the reader but my intention is exactly to animate a sense of passion, a feeling of responsibility, and most of all a sense of proportion. Democratic politics is by its very nature a messy game; it can also be a very dirty game, but naive and idealistic notions of democracy, taken alone and without any true and honest understanding of its core emphasis, tend to represent little more than the destruction of politics. Some people might believe democratic politics to be the 'least worst' system of rule but Crick was closer to the truth when he described it as 'a great and civilising human activity, something to be valued almost as a pearl beyond price in the history of the human condition'. Defending politics from itself is therefore fairly brutal in terms of seeking to forge a more honest and pragmatic account of politics. It revolves around a focus on politics as *it is* rather than how we might like it to be in some perfect world. Defending politics revolves around the rejection of naive assumptions and promoting an understanding of the internal contradictions and external challenges that attempting to govern through consensus bring with it. It also dares to suggest that too many citizens simply expect too much from politics. Put slightly differently, my defence of politics against itself demands a change in the perspective from which politics is understood and assessed: from that of a *political infant* to that of a *political adult*.

Defending politics from itself therefore rests on understanding exactly why it so often seems to promise more than it delivers and for this reason the simple hook on which this chapter (and indeed this book) hangs is the notion of an 'expectations gap'. I want to use the idea of an 'expectations gap' to explore the internal contradictions of democracy, to build a more realistic appreciation of the pressures and challenges of governing and also to consider how this gap might be closed. The great value of focusing on the existence, extent, and drivers of an 'expectations gap' is that not only does it translate complex questions into an accessible framework but it also presents interesting questions about the distinction between *supply* and *demand*, which in themselves help us further understand some of the internal contradictions of democracy and the pressures under which politicians operate. The aim of this chapter is to make us *think*, and all that I ask is that you read the following pages with an open and enquiring frame of mind. By the end of the chapter you may feel that you have judged politicians a little too harshly in the past. You may feel you understand better why political processes can so often be slow, frustrating, and cumbersome. You may feel that the behaviour of politicians that you loathe with such intensity is a reflection more of the demands and pressures of the system than of the individuals themselves. You might even feel, although you may not admit it, that in their situation you would probably behave exactly the same way.

In order to unpack the concept of democracy and defend politics from itself this chapter is divided into four sections which gradually take my argument from the very broadest level to a very specific focus on the existence and dilemmas of an 'expectations gap'. The first section focuses on the issue of realism. At the same time it provides a historical account of change by drawing upon John Keane's magisterial *The Life and Death of Democracy* (2009). This book and particularly its triumphant analysis of the role of new mechanisms of publicly controlling and monitoring the exercise of power (ethical watchdogs, regulators, audit processes, sleaze-busters, accountability commissions, etc.) reinforces this chapter's emphasis on the need for proportionality and balance. My argument is that democratic politics appears to have lost its capacity for limiting what Jacques Rancière describes in his book *Hatred of Democracy* (2006) as the 'disorder of passions eager for satisfaction'. Whereas Keane welcomes and rejoices in the explosion of power-monitoring and power-controlling devices, I interpret this development rather less positively—as *the death* of politics.

Having used Keane's work as a critical reference point, or more accurately as a *counter* point, the second section then focuses on the tension between democracy and populism and the inevitable need for some balance to be achieved between public participation and governing capacity. It therefore attempts to provide a candid account of the real-world dilemmas of governing and also dares to return to the point made in the previous chapter that the public can sometimes be a very harsh and selfish master to serve. Each of these themes contributes to a more mature and accurate understanding of some of the internal contradictions of democracy and the practical parameters within which politicians operate. These themes reveal a picture of democratic politics that is not black or white, that is not clear or consistent, that cannot produce simple solutions to complex challenges, and that cannot please everybody all of the time. Above all, they focus attention on *the politics of public expectations* and the need to judge the outputs and outcomes of democracy by a more realistic set of indicators.

To develop this line of thought, the third section then drills down still further, exploring the topic of public expectations in more detail. It outlines a very simple model of the 'expectations gap' and considers what this model tells us about closing the gap that has apparently emerged between the governors and the governed. Most importantly, the notion of an 'expectations gap' underlines the fact that democracy is essentially a two-way relationship that hinges not just on what the government and the state can deliver for individuals but also on what individuals can do for themselves, for each other, and for future generations. The broader implications of this approach, and particularly the manner in which the notion of an 'expectations gap' provides a weapon with which to defend politics against the *market, denial, crises,* and the *media* (the focus of Chapters 3, 4, 5, and 6, respectively), and how it presents new opportunities in the sense of a shift from the 'politics of pessimism' to the 'politics of optimism', are examined in the final section.

Life and Death

This section locates my argument about defending politics against itself within the broad sweep of history by drawing upon and critiquing John Keane's *The Life and Death of Democracy* (2009). This book traces the lineage and underlying ideals of democratic politics from early forms of assembly democracy, to representative democracy and then, from the middle of the twentieth century to the present day, a new stage in the history of democracy: 'monitory democracy'. This latest democratic stage posited by Keane is one in which the spirit, language, and institutions of politics are gradually transforming. If *representative* democracy reflects an (*external*) preoccupation with delivering social goods, then *monitory* democracy implies a partial shift to a more *internalized* focus: on controlling, monitoring, and scrutinizing politicians and decision-makers, based upon the assumed 'self-evident truth' that politicians are not to be trusted. This has led, Keane argues, to a now exponential system of 'checking-on, goading and humbling' those elected to power:

[p]ower-monitoring and power-controlling devices have begun to extend sideways and downwards through the whole political order. They penetrate the corridors of government and occupy the nooks and crannies of civil society, and in so doing they greatly complicate, and sometimes wrong-foot, the lives of politicians, parties, legislatures and governments. (p.12)

Monitory democracy is therefore focused on the multiple and overlapping means citizens now have to scrutinize, complain about, and resist their governments. This includes traditional forms of parliamentary and judicial accountability but also the increasing role of watchdogs, regulatory agencies, complaints mechanisms, audit processes, and the mechanisms of 'communicative abundance' like twitter, blogs, and mobile phones that ensures that everything that happens not only in the corridors of power but also in any actor's private life is frequently a matter for public debate. This situation resonates with my earlier focus on aggression, fluidity, and distance. Monitory democracy is driven by aggression and rejoices in the taking of political scalps. Monitory democracy is fluid in the sense that it rejects any boundary between public and private lives and draws its legitimacy on a fatuous sense of entitlement that suggests that everyone knows, or is entitled to know, what everyone else is up to all of the time. As a result monitory democracy appears to reject any sense of respectable or necessary distance between politicians and their duties or politicians and their publics. Keane celebrates the emergence of monitory democracy and particularly the manner in which the balance of power between the governors and the governed appears to have shifted as new forms of accountability and transparency make it much harder for politicians to keep things hidden or indulge in self-interested behaviour. The mantra that 'those whose actions adversely affect others should be held publicly accountable for the sake of everybody's wellbeing' is—like apple pie and motherhood—fairly hard to argue against. Yet there is no apparent awareness of the simple fact that governing is difficult, complex, messy, and that politicians cannot please everyone all of the time. Monitory democracy is therefore imbued not only with an essentially negative view of politics (an idea of politics in which 'nobody should rule'—a toxic brand) but also with the 'bad faith model of politics' that views politicians with contempt.

In writing *The Life and Death of Democracy* Keane has filled a wide gap in our knowledge with a 900-page tour de force about the evolution of democratic politics. His dissection of history and his description of the emergence of institutions of monitory democracy are almost beyond critique. However, it is in his normative preference for monitory democracy, to the extent of bordering on deification, that a major fault-line occurs. That my defence of politics, on the other hand, interprets the emergence of monitory democracy as something to *fear* rather than to *celebrate* should not by now surprise the reader. This is because monitory democracy represents not a new stage of democratic evolution but the collapse of democracy for the reason that, at base, it has lost all sense of *proportionality* and *realism*. The deeper tension between democracy and populism sits in the background but is never brought to the fore in order to explain the worldly art of politics, let alone suggest that politicians may be the victims of the system in which they are expected to operate. Monitory democracy has, by adopting 'the continuous public chastening of those who exercise power' as its founding principle, lost all sense of the fact that the notion of democracy is forged on the existence of a reciprocal relationship.

Put very simply, too much accountability can be as problematic as too little. There are many studies, like Robert Behn's *Rethinking Democratic Accountability* (2001), that reveal the manner in which dense accountability demands can undermine organizational effectiveness and thereby further undermine the public's confidence in politics to deliver. The need for a focus on proportionality is accompanied by the need for realism. We need to recognize that accountability mechanisms are rarely used to deliver a balanced and mature review of the available information with the aim of distributing either sanctions or rewards. Neither do they draw out the lesson-learning or 'best-practice' opportunities. Accountability is generally an element of 'attack politics' (i.e. an aggressive focus on failure over success, the exploitation of perceived personal or organizational vulnerabilities, with any willingness to listen or compromise interpreted as a sign of weakness, etc.) and is therefore most commonly of the 'gotcha!' variety. As a result, monitory democracy appears imbued with the 'bad faith model of politics' and tied to a view that accountability is always a 'good thing' that is naive and ironically outdated.

Monitory democracy may well be the most energetic and dynamic, the widest and deepest form of democracy ever known, but we need to retain just a little caution. It may be true that the institutions of monitory democracy put 'politicians, parties and elected governments permanently on their toes, they complicate their lives, question their authority and force them to change their agendas—and sometimes smother them in disgrace', but this may not necessarily be a positive development. Is it possible that 'the continuous public chastening' and 'public humbling' might have gone too far at exactly the point in history when the challenges of governing had already grown far harder? It is possible that monitory democracy contains self-fulfilling impulses, as the creation of more and more 'sleaze-busting' and 'muckraking' organizations applying simplistic assumptions to complex issues (and therefore justifying their existence) produce claims that are immediately seized upon by the media and sectional interests as evidence of systemic collapse and failure? Might it be possible that monitory democracy has lost all sense of balance and proportionality and is simply too populist? Keane himself acknowledges these risks and calls for an 'honest public recognition of the dysfunctions of monitory democracy'. Let us start this discussion by being honest about politics.

The Honest Broker

Any piece of writing inevitably represents a balance between breadth and depth and this section is no exception. In this section I want to explore the tension between democracy and populism in order to set out a more honest account of the challenges of governing through democratic processes. I want to suggest that some of the things that politicians do which frustrates and annoys the public, like promising more than they subsequently deliver or never giving a straight answer, often reflect systemic failings rather than self-serving or dishonest behaviour. There are no simple solutions to complex challenges. Politicians often don't tell the truth for the simple reason that there is no simple truth to be told; they are pulled like human wishbones by competing social forces that are impossible to reconcile and yet they know that the public is a harsh and capricious master to serve.

Preventing the disillusionment that flows from 'unreal ideals' can only come from being honest about the limits of democratic politics. The aim of this section is to expose the existence of multiple, diverse, and frequently contradictory pressures on politicians, political institutions, and political processes. As a result any mature understanding of democracy must acknowledge the need for restraint. Here lies the rub: it can be very hard for politicians to reject the demands of society, no matter how selfish or irrational, due to their need to generate and sustain a high degree of popular support. It is only by being very candid about the link between democracy and populism, challenging certain dominant assumptions about the role and behaviour of politicians and asking some very pointed questions about the responsibilities of the public vis-à-vis democratic governance, that we might craft a more optimistic account of exactly how much democracy does deliver and why it matters. At the root of any honest account of modern politics has to be an acceptance that mass democracy brings *order* as well as *disorder*. Democracy in modern societies is not the idyll of government 'of the people, by the people, for the people'. It is in reality an attempt to corral the disorder of (numerous and frequently irreconcilable) passions eager for satisfaction. It provides a mechanism or process through which to approach social challenges but it does not provide simple solutions or answers to complex problems. Therefore 'a good democratic government', Jacques Rancière suggests, 'is one capable of controlling the evil quite simply called democratic life'. Democratic life is not 'evil' (just as very few members of the public 'hate' politics) but the adoption of such powerful phraseology does at least encourage us to pause for thought and reflect more closely on the point that Rancière is making about democratic statecraft.

To associate the concept of 'democracy' with hatred is certainly nothing new. As John Lukacs's *Democracy and Populism: Fear and Hatred* (2005) reveals, 'democracy' was originally used in Ancient Greece as an insult by those who saw in the involvement of the masses the inevitable ruin of any legitimate system of rule. The history of democracy has for this reason been tied up with compromise as aristocratic legislators and experts strove to achieve a balance between popular control and stable government. It is this balance between popular control or 'the sovereignty of the people' and the basic need to empower decision-makers and their officials with an adequate degree of governing capacity which forms the crux of the issue. Understood in this manner the concept of 'democracy' would appear to have two adversaries—one external and one internal. The *external* enemy is visible and tangible and takes the form of tyranny, dictatorship, totalitarianism, or any system based upon arbitrary government or government without limits. As the American-led military campaigns in Iraq and Afghanistan and the more recent popular uprisings across North Africa and the Middle East demonstrate, non-democratic regimes can be overthrown or destabilized by a number of different processes.

The Arab Spring of 2011 forces us to confront a rather more subtle and insidious *internal* threat to democracy. This is that democracy can be too easily equated with freedom, with the passion for simple satisfaction, and as a result brings with it a risk of anarchy based around 'the power of the people'. The concept of democracy is wracked by inflationary pressure and without any acceptance of the need for restraint these can fuel the irresistible growth of public demands to the point at which they become unrealistic. The result is a decline in authority for politicians and the political system. This gradual but constant erosion of public belief, trust, and faith in political institutions, political processes, and politicians leads to the collapse of any broad commitment to the public interest. This is reflected in the amplification of self-interested demands by individuals and sectional groups alongside a general decline in the discipline and sacrifices required for the common good. Democracy therefore rests upon the need to achieve a delicate equilibrium between governing capacity and populism. The danger is that without any honest appreciation of the nature and limits of democracy—by which I mean the simple facts that (1) it cannot please everyone all of the time, (2) that some unpopular decisions may have to be imposed, and (3) that democracy and freedom are not synonymous—a situation will occur in which, as Crick warned in his original *Defence*, politics encourages 'people to expect too much—and the disillusionment of unreal ideals is an occupational hazard of free politics'. To place the 'disillusionment of unreal ideals' at the centre of an account of how we might understand political disaffection is by no means novel.

In the mid-1970s Samuel Brittan wrote of the 'economic contradictions of democracy' and based his analysis on what he called the 'two endemic threats to liberal representative democracy: the generation of excessive expectations and the disruptive effects of the pursuit of group self-interest in the market place'. Samuel Huntington's controversial book *American Politics: The Promise of Disharmony* (1981) approached the same topic from a different angle by arguing that there was an inevitable gap between the ideals of moral perfection that are often incorporated into democratic theory, on the one hand, and public criticism and the inbuilt imperfections of institutions, complex societies, and human frailty on the other. Like Reinhold Niebuhr, who said much the same thing in *Moral Man and Immoral Society* (1932), Huntington believed that a nation that refuses to understand this gap would destroy itself.

At the root of any honest account of politics is therefore a need to admit the gap between *theory* and *practice* or between *ideals* and *reality*. In making this point I am not arguing that we should stop striving for certain ideals or stop thinking of society as we would like it to be, but I am attempting to inject a degree of realism into debates about contemporary politics in order to stop us constantly deriding what is in reality a civilizing and hugely beneficial activity. Let me develop this point by focusing on three theories or 'ideals' in order to show how their real-world manifestation reinforces the tension between populism and democracy that this chapter is seeking to bring to the fore. These are:

(1) The idealized notion of 'the people'.

(2) The theory of limited government.

(3) The quest for consistency in how politicians operate.

Examining these three topics will also support my argument that we are all to some degree complicit in the failings and imperfections of democracy and may need to judge politicians a little less harshly.

'The People'

Possibly the most unhelpful idealized notion that hinders sensible debate relates to the existence of 'the people' or the 'public interest'. In reality societies increasingly consist of a heterogeneous mix of social groups with radically different demands. The role of a politician is therefore invidious and messy, as politicians are frequently forced to rob Peter to pay Paul, and must decide which particular constituencies to represent, protect, or assail at any given time. 'The real problem with politics', Gerry Stoker suggests in his book *Why Politics Matters* (2006), 'is that it is inevitably destined to disappoint because it is about the tough process of squeezing collective decisions out of multiple and competing interests and opinions'. Let me burnish this point with a little example. The Mississippi River Commission is responsible for fostering navigation, promoting commerce, and preventing destructive floods. In undertaking these tasks it is responsible for a drainage basin that covers 41 per cent of the United States and parts of two Canadian provinces. In *The Control of Nature* (1989) John McPhee notes how, 'In years gone by when there were no control structures, there were no complaints. The water went where it pleased. People took it as it came. The delta was in a state of nature,' but now the American state has attempted to impose some form of control mechanism, there are several million 'potential complainers, very few of whom are reluctant to present a grievance'. McPhee's point provides a neat bridge between the theme of overload that was discussed in the previous chapter and the argument about the scale and incompatible nature of the demands placed upon politicians and public officials that I am trying to make. Let me develop this example in a little more detail by recounting how in the late 1980s the President of the Mississippi River Commission, then Major General Thomas Sands, would each autumn take an inspection trip along the length of the river and as part of his duties would hold public meetings at various points.

General Sands cheerfully remarks that every time he makes one of these trips he gets 'beaten on the head and shoulders ... the crawfisherman and the shrimper come up within five minutes and ask for opposite things'. The craw-fishermen say 'Put more water in, the water is low'. Shrimpers don't want more water. They are benefitted by low water. In the high water season farmers say 'Get the water off us quicker' but folks downstream don't want it quicker. We divert some fresh water into marshes, because the marshes need it for the nutrients and the sedimentation, but oyster fishermen complain. The variety of competing interests is phenomenal. (pp.22–3)

Although highlighting the trials and tribulations of the Mississippi River Commission may appear a rather queer case study, it provides a very simple and accessible example of a basic challenge of modern governance because the demands placed upon this organization are by no means unique. They represent very much the rule rather than the exception as politicians and their officials in almost every field of policy are subject to a wide variety of competing interests, each seeking a specific political response and demanding certain outputs for its members. As such, politics and 'public service' is generally a profession based around negotiation, compromise, and the acceptance of what economists would call 'sub-optimal' decisions simply because that is the price we pay for sharing power. Max Weber's description of democratic politics as the 'slow boring through hard boards' captures perfectly the day-to-day reality of governing. Apart from times of crisis, politics works around the slow and careful accretion of marginal gains and this feature, although frequently creating frustration and attracting complaint, is the beauty of politics—not its failure. Indeed the theory of limited government (our second topic of discussion) explicitly chides politicians and the state for trying to do too much and tries to impose constraints on them to limit their power. Liberal democracy is therefore infused with a libertarian distrust of democratic politics and seeks to ensure that the private sphere takes priority over the public realm. And yet even here there is a gap between the public's stated wishes and its actual demands.

Limited Government

A key assumption of modern democratic politics is that 'we' the public should be left alone to live as we want without fear of being nagged or morally judged. 'Freedom has in this sense become', the philosopher Alain de Botton has noted, 'the supreme moral virtue'. Instructing individuals about how much they should drink, what car they drive, or how they bring up their children is not seen as a role for politicians or the state. Modern politics on both the 'left' and the 'right' (to employ two outdated terms) is dominated by a libertarian ideology in which the realm of politics is generally treated with suspicion (and derision) and the public reacts in a hostile way if 'the state' attempts to encourage a change in the public's behaviour. As a result, policies that might try and get individuals to take a little more exercise, curb their drinking, or engage in more voluntary activity are generally greeted with howls of anti-political and anti-government protest. It is in exactly this climate that governments have focused their attention on developing more modest and subtle ways of encouraging us to place collective goods above individual desire. It was for exactly this reason that Richard Thaler and Cass Sunstein's book *Nudge* (2008) achieved best-seller status and was so avidly devoured by politicians around the world. This concern with freedom can be traced back to thinkers like John Stuart Mill who in his famous book *On Liberty* (1859) outlined the limits of legitimate state action and the dangers of what would come to be known as 'the nanny state'. As a result, very few politicians dare to exhort us to have the 'nobility of spirit', as Aristotle called it, which takes the form of generosity, temperance, and courage because libertarian political philosophy, like Robert Wolff's *In Defence of Anarchism* (1998), arguably adopts an unhelpfully sophisticated view of individuals that denies the need for regular reminders of the fact that we all form one small part of a collective whole.

This emphasis on individuality and freedom can be challenged from both an empirical and theoretical position, the sum of which provides a more honest account of the trials and tribulations of democratic politics. From a practical point of view, although the public may well have a rather jaded view of politicians and an ideological commitment to limited government, they are rather less prepared to apply this position to the real world and as a result politicians are expected to take responsibility for an ever-expanding range of topics. It was only half in jest that President Sarkozy quipped in 2010 that when snow blocks the roads, swine flu closes a school, or volcanic ash closes the airports 'c'est le faute à Sarko'. However, public pressure generally ensures that politicians and political processes *do* respond (as a provider, facilitator, information provider, rescuer, funder, regulator, or guarantor of last resort) and with a level of force and professionalism that is simply absent when natural disasters or crises occur in non-democratic regimes.

The theory of *limited* government is therefore quite distinct from the *realities* of democratic governance and this in itself reveals a puzzle of contemporary politics: for all the anti-government, anti-political ranting, and social anxiety about the 'failure' of politics, democratic politics still provides a form of social-political or social-psychological safety blanket in times of heightened public concern. This in turn allows us to develop some pointed questions about the behaviour of individuals and the responsibilities we all possess as members of a civilized society. Might it be that we revile politicians with such intensity because deep down we lack the strength to resist certain forms of behaviour and resent the fact when they try and make us take our obligations more seriously? The directions we need are rarely complex—eat less fat, walk more, recycle plastics and glass, etc.—but as individuals we generally react against external attempts to encourage us to do what, deep down, we actually believe *is* necessary.

The true risks to ourselves therefore turn out to be very different from those conceived of by libertarians. It is rarely the case that we find ourselves in the hands of some sinister external rule-maker and too often the real danger runs in an opposite direction. We face temptations and compulsions that we revile but that we lack the strength and encouragement to resist, much to our eventual disappointment. The aim here is not to return to Rousseau's arguments about 'forcing people to be free' but simply to acknowledge that democratic systems must involve some element of restraint. Democracy is not a synonym for freedom or individual choice, and sometimes politicians will have to make unpopular decisions. This leads into a discussion of our third ideal—consistency.

The Quest for Consistency

Demands for a more open, honest, and consistent model of politics are completely understandable and well founded but my aim here is to dare to suggest that if the public really want politicians to be honest with them then they need to understand that they will not always like what they hear. Politics has limits. It is messy, frequently unpredictable, and therefore in some areas inconsistent. Politics is about reconciling the irreconcilable, bashing square pegs into round holes, and squaring circles while at the same time achieving a degree of consent and minimizing injury. As a result it is not often pretty to watch. It is a form of rule that emphasizes listening (to others) and accepting (decisions you may not like) as much as talking (at others) and demanding (from others). It demands a small amount of secrecy on the part of politicians and a large element of self-control on the part of individuals, interest groups, and journalists. Freedom of speech, freedom of movement, freedom of information does not simply therefore confer responsibilities on politicians and public servants. It also assumes a degree of maturity and integrity and a feeling of responsibility on the part of the recipient. All too often, however, that has been absent. In the late 1970s the then British Foreign Secretary, David Owen, wrote a book called simply *Human Rights* in which he attempted to make exactly this point, and his words deserve repeating in full.

When I began to speak out for human rights and argued that a concern for human rights should permeate our foreign policy, I warned that there was a price to pay, and that the price was a little inconsistency from time to time. If I had to make that comment again I would no longer say 'a little inconsistency' I would say 'a very great deal of inconsistency'. Yet because these inconsistencies are probed and exposed publicly and often turned against the person who wishes to try and promote a sense of values, there is a danger that people will cease to proclaim principles and values; because they cannot be consistent and they cannot always justify every stance against previously stated or previously believed principles, they will cease to inject this particular issue into public life at all. And because the politician's compromises are very obvious, can be seen by everyone, can be dissected, editorialised upon and scathingly attacked, there has been a tendency to elevate possibly to an unrealistic height, the attraction of the man in public life who is the man of principle, the man of consistency, the man of unbending views. (p. 2)

The world is not perfect and democratic politics frequently reflects this. Politicians will sometime have to renege on their commitments, accept that certain ambitions are beyond their reach, dilute their plans due to the need for compromise, or possibly even sanction certain practices which in a perfect world they would never approve of. As Max Weber emphasized in *Politics as a Vocation* (1918), to adopt any other viewpoint is to adopt an unreal and 'infantile' view of politics that will always fail to reflect reality: 'no ethics in the world can dodge the fact that in numerous instances the attainment of "good" ends is bound to the fact that one must be willing to pay the price of morally dubious means'.

This may appear as a rather vicious or fatalist form of realism that risks strengthening the hand of those who seek to denigrate democratic politics but we cannot pretend that politicians are not from time to time compelled to make decisions of a magnitude that few of us are ever expected to face. Those decisions will frequently be made under immense pressure, on the basis of imperfect information, may lead to the loss of lives, will probably result in a situation that is less than perfect, and the individual politician with whom the buck stopped will have to live with the consequences of that decision for the rest of his life. So let us pause for thought and accept that without a good degree of maturity, integrity, and self-control we risk perpetuating a system that actually makes it very hard for politicians to be honest with us because modern societies have almost lost the capacity to hold a sensible and balanced debate about any issue. The intense and aggressive nature of the 'attack politics' that dominates Western democracies, and the fact that even the slightest inconsistency or glimpse of human frailty is likely to be vociferously exploited by opponents, sectional interests, and media channels, creates a powerful incentive for politicians to attempt to stage-manage events, never stray from their scripts, and seek safety in the constant repetition of bland sound-bites.

The fact that politicians rely on popular support to maintain their position and are constantly bombarded by an increasingly diverse range of competing demands makes demanding restraint or rejecting specific demands difficult. Democratic politics rejoices in the existence of difference and the smooth assimilation of different social groups and competing demands without resorting to authoritarian modes of control. The volcano, to return to an earlier metaphor, very rarely erupts but can also be used to encourage and facilitate positive change in non-democratic regimes. Recent developments in South Africa, Northern Ireland, and Burma illustrate the manner in which democratic pressures can forge peaceful transitions or the release of prisoners that many expected would never occur. As each of these three examples demonstrate, democratic pressures are generally 'slow-burn' in nature and frequently involve setbacks along the way—but that is the price we pay for seeking to govern through mutual accommodation and compromise.

What gives democratic politics its beauty, then, as a form of social organization is that it is *not* solely concerned with the fulfilment of societal demands but is equally tasked with the *rejection* of specific demands, possibly on the basis of resource limits, impracticability, fairness, a desire to protect the interests of less literate social groups, or even to protect the life chance of future generations from the detrimental behaviour of the current cohort. Politics is often about settling for less than what we want simply because we want to live without violence or the perpetual fear of violence from other people who want other things. In his original *Defence* Crick argued that the real danger of democracy's populist underpinning was that it may 'lead to false expectations...it may lead people to expect too much...the disillusionment of unreal ideals is an occupational hazard of free politics'. The question of 'unreal ideals' leads naturally on from this section's broader focus on the relationship between democracy and populism to the next section's focus: how *the politics of public expectations* provides a valuable way of both understanding contemporary political disaffection and also constructing a more optimistic view of why politics matters.

Great Expectations

There are some who would argue that democracy is *the* true form of politics, a form of societal organization and behaviour that is innately superior to other forms of political regime. My own ambitions are less evangelical but I do want to enthuse a new generation with the optimistic belief that democracy is a force for progress and that it generally delivers far more than most people realize. In order to close the gap that has apparently emerged between the governors and the governed, however, we need to develop a fairly candid and blunt account of what democratic engagement can and cannot provide and we need to be honest about the way in which democratic processes encourage politicians to promise more than they can deliver. We also need fresh tools and bold new ways of understanding the political world as it is currently unfolding. This must include new concepts and new perspectives that challenge dominant assumptions and through this

(1) *Offer* more discriminating methods of challenging anti-political arguments,

(2) *See* opportunities where others see dangers and

(3) *Create* the incentives on which a new public service bargain can be built.

Our thinking about the nature and limits of democracy must change and the central argument of this section is that a more honest grasp of the politics of public expectations provides a way to break out of the spiral of cynicism that appears to have emerged in so many established democracies.

Imagine for a moment two horizontal bars placed one above the other with a significant gap between them. The upper bar relates to *demand* and specifically to the promises that politicians may have made in order to be elected (in addition to the public's expectations of what politics and the state could and should deliver). The bottom bar relates to *supply* in terms of what the political system can realistically deliver given the complexity of the challenges, the contradictory nature of many requests and the resources with which it can seek to satisfy demand. The distance between the two bars is therefore the 'expectations gap', and recent survey evidence seems to suggest that in recent years the expectations gap has widened. With this simple framework in mind my argument is straightforward: the increasing evidence of political disaffection stems from the existence of an ever-increasing 'expectations gap' between what is promised/expected and what can realistically be delivered by politicians and democratic states. This argument can be placed within the contours of well-known debates concerning political behaviour.

Anthony Downs's *An Economic Theory of Democracy* (1957) provides the foundation for exploring these debates. In this book he sought to understand politics with reference to economic exchanges within society. Downs argued that political parties and politicians (as suppliers) and voters (as consumers) can be assumed to be rational and self-interested 'utility-maximisers' who engage in market-like transactions and relationships. Consequently political actors seek to maximize their chances of (re-)election by promising to deliver better services, but at a lower cost than the competitors (other political parties). This creates a bidding war in which the process of political competition artificially increases public expectations, only for these expectations to be dashed as the elected party either seeks to renege upon certain pre-election commitments or fails to achieve them. An economic theory of politics therefore seeks to provide an explanation for the frequent discrepancy between pre-election political rhetoric and subsequent post-election performance. It also allows us to understand the oft-quoted observation of Mario Cuomo on political campaigning:

You campaign in poetry. But when we're elected, we're forced to govern in prose. And when we govern—as distinguished from when we campaign—we come to understand the difference between a speech and a statute. It's here that the noble aspirations, neat promises and slogans of a campaign get bent out of recognition or even break as you try to nail them down to the Procrustean bed of reality.

With Cuomo's frank admission in mind, we can see that closing or reducing the size of the 'expectations gap' that has apparently emerged between the governors and the governed can be achieved in three main ways.

Option 1: increasing supply (moving the bottom-bar up);

Option 2: reducing demand (moving the top-bar down); or,

Option 3: a combination of Options 1 and 2 (close the gap from above and below).

This schema has empirical origins. As Director of the British Prime Minister's Policy Unit from 1997 until 2001, David Miliband sought to emphasize that the government's modernization agenda for public services was not going to dramatically increase supply. A marginal increase in performance might be delivered through efficiency gains but it was never going to close the 'expectations gap'. As Andrew Rawnsley's book *Servants of the People* (2002) explains, Miliband argued that the most important role for ministers was actually suppressing, shaping, and managing public expectations about what the government could achieve, or at the very least not inflating them further. This focus on both ensuring supply and managing demand in the context of public services provides us with a method of understanding not only the dysfunctions of democracy but also the challenges that constructing a more optimistic account of politics will inevitably face. The notion of an 'expectations gap' also allows us to tease apart the nature of governing in the twenty-first century in a little more detail, and in a way that accords with the previous section's emphasis on honest politics. It raises a number of questions about how we might as a society collectively break out of the cycle of broken promises that so often frustrates the public and instead cultivate a more optimistic, or at the very least balanced, account of what democratic politics delivers—and why it matters.

The essential point, however, is that although Option 1 (i.e. increasing supply) may have provided the default position for politicians throughout the twentieth century, it is no longer feasible. If the fifty years since the first publication of Crick's *Defence* can be characterized as the 'Age of Abundance', the five decades after the publication of this book are likely to become known as the 'Age of Austerity', as a combination of the global financial crisis, population growth, the emergence of a new world order, and the demands of addressing climate change conspire to ensure that democratic politics must in future focus on *reducing demand* as much (if not more) than *increasing the supply* of public goods. One hundred and seventy years ago in his *Democracy in America* (1835) Alexis de Tocqueville remarked, 'A new science of politics is necessary for a new world' and during the twenty-first century that 'science' of politics is undoubtedly still needed but it will inevitably focus on Option 2 (i.e. reducing demand), or more realistically Option 3 (i.e. closing the gap from above and below). Option 1 is simply not viable because the public's demands are insatiable, the problems facing society are too complex, the available resources are insufficient, and although managerial reforms within the public sector may deliver marginal efficiency savings, they will never close the gap. Saving politics from *itself* and embracing a more honest account of politics therefore demands accepting that focusing on *supply* is less important now than focusing on *demand*.

Let me put a little more flesh on the bones of this rather meagre framework by suggesting that the issue of public expectations can be seen as the basis of the relationship between the governors and the governed and therefore it is possible to identify at least two dimensions of public expectations. There are public expectations about political behaviour (i.e. the public to politicians), and political expectations about public behaviour (i.e. politicians to the public).

The first of these dimensions focuses attention on public pressure and the impact of public opinion on politicians. There is no reason to suggest that our present democratic institutions are by any measure perfect (indeed there are many reasons to suggest that they are not) but it is possible to argue that the democratic promise provides a fairly direct and responsive chain of delegation. Democracy provides a way of tying the self-interest of politicians to the public's interest by ensuring that they remain responsive to public opinion. We tend to take it for granted that we live in a democracy where it is possible to elect our rulers, to hold them to account (albeit imperfectly), and ultimately (should we chose) to 'kick the rascals out'. That is, a political system where one party or one candidate wins but at least the loser lives to fight another day. The chain of command is, however, arguably far weaker working the other way (i.e. in relation to the capacity of politicians to influence the public), as the need to secure and maintain public support makes it difficult for politicians to impose their views on the responsibilities of the public vis-à-vis politics and public services. Unless, of course, the politicians move towards more authoritarian forms of governing, a transition that would inevitably involve a transition from a *free* society to a *fear* society.

As has already been mentioned, those politicians and public servants who have spoken in favour of placing greater emphasis on the duties and responsibilities of members of the public to society as a whole in order to be able to deliver improved levels of service provision have frequently felt the force of a public backlash. Accusations of authoritarianism, bullying, discrimination, or harassment generally accompany any attempt by politicians or the state to introduce plans that would oblige the public to, for example, work longer in light of rising life expectancy, adopt a healthier lifestyle prior to medical treatment, seek to encourage parents to make sure their children have a good night's sleep and an appropriate breakfast before school, or the introduction of penalties for those who fail to recycle. Policies may well be 'good' in the sense of being sensible and being based upon clear evidence or obviously necessary due to changing demographics but they may at the same time be 'bad' in the sense of not being well received by those members of the public they affect directly. What makes 'good policy' and what makes 'good politics' are therefore frequently two quite different things. As a result, the rationalities of electoral competition generally make it very difficult for any political party to emphasize the need to change the nature of citizenship from being based around the individual as a *passive recipient* of public goods to being an *active citizen* in a more balanced political relationship. The public are unlikely to vote for a party that seeks to emphasize more responsible public behaviour, especially when other parties are promising to deliver 'more with less'. Reducing (or at the very least recalibrating) the public's expectations about what politics should and can provide in a way that seeks to re-emphasize the obligations and responsibilities of the public is therefore harder than most people understand. The public, and I make no apology for repeating this point, can be a selfish master to serve.

There are, however, green shoots that allow us to challenge dominant stereotypes and begin to sketch out the contours of a far more optimistic view of politics; one that does recognize the fact that not all politicians are corrupt and that democratic politics generally delivers high-quality public services. These green shoots exist in yet another 'gap' in relation to public opinions about everyday politics in general, compared to their specific personal experience of politics. Social surveys repeatedly show that if you ask members of the public how they view healthcare services, for example, *in general* they will use terms such as 'crisis' and 'a disgrace' but if you ask them about the last time they *actually accessed* medical services their evaluation is generally far more positive. The existence of this common 'perception gap' between how the public perceives services (generally negatively) as opposed to their actual experience (generally positive) across Western Europe and North America suggests that although democracy may be less than perfect, it is at least doing something right.

In pugilistic circles, to adopt a new metaphor, it is often said that when a boxer fights in their opponent's country, dominating every round of the contest is not enough to secure a win—only a knockout will do. The paradox of the 'perception gap' can be viewed as the same dilemma in a different context. Not only must politics (and therefore politicians) *deliver* high-quality public services; it must also *convince the public* that this is the case. Framed in these terms the 'perception gap' can be understood as a mirror-image of the 'expectations gap'. In the latter the public expect too much, because the political system incentivizes false or unrealistic promises, and the public are ultimately disappointed; but in the former the political system actually delivers public services but the public fail to believe or perceive that this is the case. The 'perception gap' therefore poses acute questions about *why* the public hold such negative general attitudes and *how* a more balanced and indeed honest relationship between governors and the governed might be developed. These are exactly the questions I want to explore in the next five chapters. But before moving onto the focus of my next defence, I want to reiterate the essence of democratic politics.

The Worldly Art of Politics

Politics is a worldly art due to the simple fact that it is sometimes based on processes that are ruthless, manipulative, and unappealing—and yet they deliver desirable and positive outputs. It is also worldly in the sense that it requires the capacity to connect with the public and inspire great hope and belief in the future. In the conclusion to the previous chapter I focused on the election of Barack Obama in 2008 to illustrate the dangers of creating a rhetoric–reality gap. In this conclusion I want to change both the country and the individual by focusing on the experience of Tony Blair when he was swept to power in 1997 in order to trace out the thin line between great expectations and dashed hopes. Making the connection between Blair and Obama is not difficult. In his memoirs, *A Journey* (2010), Blair states that 'When Barack Obama fought and won his extraordinary campaign for the presidency I could tell exactly what he would have been thinking. At one level, the excitement and energy created by such hope vested in the candidate has the effect of buoying you up, driving you on, giving all that you touch something akin to magic. The country is on a high and you are up there with them.' He goes on to note,

At another deeper level, however, you quickly realise that though you are the repository of that hope and have in part been the author of it, it now has a life of its own, a spirit of its own and that spirit is soaring far beyond your control. You want to capture it, to tame it and harness it, because its very independence is, you know, leading the public to an impossible sense of expectation. Expectations of this nature cannot be met. That's what you want to tell people. Often you do tell them. But the spirit can't be too constrained. And when it finally departs, leaving your followers with reality—a reality you have never denied and which you have even sought to bring to their attention—the danger is disillusion, more painful because of what preceded it. (p. 15)

Democratic politics therefore brings with it a danger of somehow creating a relationship based on deception, not a form of deception that is intentionally designed to mislead or trick but one based on the hope that hard work and hard choices can somehow be avoided; that there are, after all, simple and pain-free solutions to complex problems. This brings us back full circle to Crick's argument in his original *Defence* that democratic politics tends to 'lead people to expect too much and the disillusionment of unreal ideals is an occupational hazard of free politics'. Public disillusionment is running high and I want to calm the storm. Democracy has limits. It is not a panacea for the challenges of living in ever larger and ever more complex societies but beware of anyone who claims to have a perfect formula for the world's problems. There isn't one. There are no simple solutions to the world's problems but on any scale of assessment, democratic politics has delivered. The real paradox is why public confidence in democratic politics appears to have fallen so low at exactly the point when it is delivering so much, which is why this chapter has focused on the issue of public expectations in general and the existence of an 'expectations gap' in particular.

The notion of an 'expectations gap' not only weaves together the sections in this chapter but it also forms the common theme of every chapter. I want to explore the ways in which public expectations are created, shaped, and managed by various actors in society. I want to tease apart the manner in which the dominant paradigm of 'good governance', with its emphasis on the importation of private-sector-style relationships into the public sector, risks further inflating public expectations. I want to examine how politicians respond to the existence of competing pressures and demands and particularly how they adopt increasingly complex blame-shifting strategies or forms of distraction. I want to argue that the 'expectations gap' provides a way of understanding the difference between ideals and reality and I want to use this argument to make some provocative statements, to fly some kites and shake some trees. Not everyone will agree with me but I can no longer stand on the sidelines and watch a noble profession—public service interwoven with a belief in the capacity of collective endeavour—be the constant focus of ridicule and derision. Therefore having provided a defence of politics against *itself* by highlighting the internal contradictions of democracy and particularly the tension between democracy and populism, let me shift the focus to my second target— a defence of politics against *the market*.

3

A DEFENCE OF POLITICS AGAINST THE MARKET

Each person, withdrawn into himself, behaves as though he is a stranger to the destiny of all the others. His children and his good friends constitute for him the whole of the human species. As for his transactions with his fellow citizens, he may mix among them, but he sees them not; he touches them, but he does not feel them; he exists only in himself and for himself alone. And if on these terms there remains in his mind a sense of family, there no longer remains a sense of society.

Alexis de Tocqueville, *Democracy in America* (1835)

Too much and too long, we seem to have surrendered community excellence and community values in the mere accumulation of material things. Gross National Product ... measures everything except that which makes life worthwhile.

Robert Kennedy, University of Kansas (1968)

Goods assembled together in ownership make physical, visible statements about the hierarchy of values to which their chooser subscribes. Goods can be cherished or judged inappropriate, discarded and replaced. Unless we appreciate how they are used to constitute an intelligible universe, we will never know how to resolve the contradictions of our economic life.

Douglas and Isherwood, *The World of Goods* (1978)

The consumer has become a god-like figure, before whom markets and politicians alike bow. Everywhere it seems, the consumer is triumphant.

Gabriel and Lang, *The Unmanageable Consumer* (1995)

Distraction and diversion; markets and morality; self-harm and self-protection: these are the issues I want to explore in this chapter as part of a wider and more optimistic defence of politics. The previous chapter focused on the internal contradictions of democracy and particularly the manner in which the pressure to maintain a high degree of popularity creates incentives for politicians to over-inflate public expectations to the point where a rhetoric–reality gap is to some extent inevitable. Politics is therefore frequently characterized by soaring expectations and dashed hopes. My argument is that democratic politics would not be interpreted as failing so frequently and people would not 'hate' it as much as they do if it was judged against a more realistic set of expectations; if we could just cultivate a more balanced and proportionate understanding of why politics matters. That is essentially the argument this book is making and in this chapter I want to argue that the incursion of market-based values, relationships, and institutions within the public sphere has played a role in damaging public confidence in politics in at least five interrelated ways:

1. By failing to recognize the basic collective essence of democratic politics;

2. By imposing a rather crude view of what motivates human behaviour;

3. By promoting a thin model of democracy based around material consumption and individualism;

4. By hollowing out our capacity to make moral arguments and judgements; and

5. By promoting unrealistic public expectations about what the state can and should provide.

I am not encouraging voters to follow the advice of Bernard Baruch, an adviser to Presidents Woodrow Wilson and Franklin D. Roosevelt in the US, to 'vote for the man who promises least because he'll be the least disappointing', because to do so would be to let the pessimists, detractors, and politically depressive rob us of the sense of optimism and hope that democratic politics offers. But I am suggesting that if the public genuinely believe that politics (and therefore politicians) are failing them, this may well tell us more about the public's expectations than about the failure of our politicians. I am also making a very broad argument about the manner in which the dominant model of liberal democracy is tied to a pattern of mass consumption that relies upon constant economic growth. Debates and concerns about the sustainability of this model are moving up the political agenda not just because of environmental concerns but due to mounting evidence that more and more people are not only dissatisfied with politics but appear disillusioned and unhappy with life itself. Above a fairly low level of material well-being the link between individual prosperity and happiness is far weaker than is commonly assumed. Furthermore, the World Health Organization predicts that clinical depression will become the second most chronic global health challenge within a decade (around 150 million people are currently afflicted by the condition and around a million people commit suicide each year).

The first decade of the twenty-first century has therefore been marked (or even scarred) by a global bout of self-reflection on the relationship between politics, the market, and how modern societies interpret 'success' and 'value'. This is reflected in a flurry of interest in the 'new science of happiness', in books like Tim Kasser's *The High Price of Materialism* (2003), Barry Schwartz's *The Paradox of Choice* (2005), Alain de Botton's *Status Anxiety* (2005) and *The Architecture of Happiness* (2007), Richard Layard's *Happiness* (2006), Oliver James's *Affluenza* (2007), Dany-Robert Dufour's *The Art of Shrinking Heads* (2008), and Michael Foley's *The Age of Absurdity* (2010). These books, all in quite different ways, raise questions about the changing nature of the public sphere, the politics of abundance, and whether in embracing the market to the extent that we have, we may have lost our collective sense of worth and well-being. More specifically, this eclectic body of work arguably helps explain why individuals might feel increasingly dissatisfied in societies that seemingly offer an abundance of freedom and choice, due to the manner in which consumerist ideology thrives on the existence of dissatisfactions and the generation of high expectations. Once again, many of these issues are by no means new. For instance, Émile Durkheim's ground-breaking *Le Suicide* (1897), notably his focus on social anomie and displacement, provides a haunting prediction of the problems we face today. Yet at the same time all of these books on the topic of happiness and well-being either implicitly or explicitly make the case for democracy by emphasizing the value of deeper social relationships that are not driven by money or materialism and that reconnect individuals to a broader collective fate. The science of happiness therefore helps reveal exactly why democratic politics matters.

My argument is not against the use of market mechanisms or market-like relationships per se but is simply a plea for a more honest and open debate about the manner in which treating the public as consumers rather than citizens risks *increasing* the expectations gap that was discussed in the previous chapter while at the same time eroding the solidarity and sense of community on which democratic citizenship depends. The recent global financial crisis has brought these issues very much to the fore and although it does not foreshadow the end of capitalism it does remind us of the innate qualities of both the public sphere and the public sector and demands that we question the ideology of a free market and explore its limits.

In order to defend politics from the market and explore exactly how economic thinking has transformed the nature of politics in recent decades, this chapter is divided into four main sections. The first section focuses on the cultural contradictions: how an emphasis on individual consumption and material wealth risks fuelling social fragmentation. It therefore raises questions about consumerism, happiness, and the creation of 'false wants', which in turn allows us to further refine and develop this book's focus on the politics of public expectations. The second section seeks to tease apart the nature of markets and market logic in order to reveal its deeper moral core. This allows us to understand how marketization affects our relationships by stimulating individualized notions of material exchange, desire, rights, and reward to the detriment of non-market altruistic impulses and social responsibilities. Put simply, 'consumer capitalism' contains an internal dynamic that chips away at and erodes the collective foundations of democratic life.

The notion of collective foundations provides a link to the third section's focus: the impact of marketization on the public sector. The baseline argument of this section is not just that we have witnessed the commodification of public goods in a manner that knows the price of everything but the value of nothing but that to some extent marketization and the dominance of neo-liberal ideas has narrowed the sphere of politics and undermined our collective capacity, indeed our confidence, to engage in moral arguments about how to balance rights and responsibilities within a democratic framework. This is because the implementation of marketization within the public sector grates against the assumptions and impulses of democratic governance. The final section looks at the impact of marketization and particularly the notion of 'citizen consumers'. It suggests that to view the public as little more than consumers in a political marketplace, who should be encouraged to expect standards of service that they would commonly expect from the private sector, is the political equivalent of suicide, or at the very least self-harming.

One-Dimensional Man

Let me start by returning to a familiar theme: the tension that stems from the need to achieve a balance between popular participation in public life and the need for politicians to enjoy a fairly significant degree of governing capacity. I want to argue that the use of markets and the general thrust towards consumer capitalism has provided generations of politicians with a convenient method with which to divert the public's energy. I also want to argue that this strategy, while arguably being an understandable response to the pressures of governing, is pathological because it actually hollows out the spirit of collective democratic engagement by overemphasizing individualism.

Such diversionary tactics are by no means new. During the sixth century BC Peisistratos ruled Athens and became known as the 'friendly tyrant' due to the manner in which he was able to channel the democratic vitality of most citizens into their own private affairs. A focus on the accumulation of private wealth and material prosperity provided a useful strategy that generally ensured his potential opponents were not only scattered all over the country but were also so tied up in managing their own affairs that they lacked the time or inclination to attend to public affairs or hatch plots to overthrow him. The market was therefore a method of distraction or a surrogate for the feverish activity that might otherwise have been focused on the public stage. In terms of Jacques Rancière's work on the relationship between populism and democracy, the market provided a diversionary tactic that absorbed the intensity of democratic life and sated the 'the disorder of passions eager for satisfaction'. However, although it is possible to identify the creation of citizen-consumers and the expansion of markets and market-orientated reasoning into areas of social life traditionally governed by non-market norms, there is actually very little evidence that our passions have in fact been satiated: public expectations and demands continue to grow.

Let us begin by being honest about the impact of rampant and apparently unlimited consumer capitalism on democratic politics. Democracy does not mean the reign of the limitless desire of individuals, and a focus on material possessions and individual affluence arguably grates against the logic of democratic governance. Over time the unintended consequences of this strategy have become all the more obvious because promoting the quest for *individual* happiness meant advocating a form of private life and forms of social relationships that led to heightened expectations and escalating demands. These, of course, exerted a twofold effect: they rendered citizens unconcerned and relatively nonchalant about the impact of private decisions on the public interest while also undermining the authority of governments summoned to respond to the spiralling demands of society. Daniel Bell's influential *The Cultural Contradictions of Capitalism* (1976) focused on this specific point and argued that the social predilection for mass consumption was in direct conflict with the sacrifices needed to defend the common interest or 'public good' in democratic systems. The Trilateral Commission's investigation at around the same time into the erosion of public support for democratic politics in Europe, North America, and Japan, published as *The Crisis of Democracy*, echoed this point with a focus on how the development of consumption patterns in relation to culture, the economy, and politics had conspired to create insatiable public demands. This emphasis on insatiable public demands in the context of increasing material well-being throughout the second half of the twentieth century forces us to return to our focus on the politics of public expectations. More specifically, it poses rather awkward questions about the limits to growth and the nature of happiness.

John Maynard Keynes's essay 'Economic Possibilities for Our Grandchildren' (1930) provides a fitting starting point for a discussion about markets, politics, and happiness. It also facilitates a more sophisticated grasp of the politics of public expectations. Written at the height of the Great Depression, it predicted a distant and happy future in which living standards would have risen many times, the political economy would be stable, and work would become more of a pastime than a chore. Such beliefs were strangely common amongst classical economists. In *Principles of Political Economy* (1848) John Stuart Mill, for example, lamented the 'trampling, crushing, elbowing and treading on each other's heels, which form the existing type of social life', which he saw as but one of the disagreeable symptoms of one of 'the phases of industrial progress', and looked forward to a world in which 'while no one is poor, no one desires to be richer'. Karl Marx, in his *German Ideology* of 1845, pictured the citizens in his utopia hunting in the morning, fishing in the afternoon, and discussing poetry after dinner. Arguably the most recent and influential statement in this vein came with Herbert Marcuse's *One Dimensional Man* (1964), which dealt with the social construction of wants and desires, the pathologies of consumerism, and the prevalence of a thin or rather shallow model of democracy in which social connections were bought and 'socially constructed' through material items. With all our material wants now satisfied, argued Marcuse, our surplus energies should be channelled into play, not work.

The apparent optimism of the classical economists like Keynes, Marx, and Mill stemmed from their view of economic growth as being teleological, by which I mean a view of progress that would, like a journey from A to B, have a definite end point. That end point would be the production of sufficient material goods to allow a focus on leisure time over work. It was in exactly this vein that Marcuse's *One Dimensional Man* sought to understand how and why advanced capitalist production processes and consumerism appeared to be generating sources of 'unfreedom' (e.g. longer working hours, family breakdown, greater mobility, ever more stressful jobs, etc.) and why members of the public seemed so willing to work more even though their basic material needs had been fulfilled. The consumer lifestyle had therefore become a trap with individuals running ever faster, like a hamster in its wheel, to stand still. This situation was famously captured by the philosopher David Wiggins in his essay 'Truth, Invention and the Meaning of Life' (1976) using the story of a pig farmer who raised pigs to make money to buy more land to raise more pigs to make more money to buy more land to... *ad infinitum.*

The classical economists therefore set great store in the 'law of diminishing utility' by which, although buying one teddy, car, or new suit might generate great happiness, buying a second is less satisfying, and by the time you have ten teddies, cars or suits, buying another would provide no pleasure at all. It was for exactly this reason that Keynes predicted there would come a point 'when needs are satisfied in the sense that we prefer to devote our further energies to non-economic purposes'. The important contribution of Marcuse's analysis of the modern condition was the manner in which it revealed how 'false needs' are constantly created through advertising and the production of new and different goods (the latest football strip, the hottest fashion, the most up-to-the-minute gadget, etc.), even if this is detrimental in personal, social, or environmental ways (e.g. the disposal of old but perfectly good or repairable products, a lack of family time, etc.). In short, any defence of politics against the market must acknowledge the manner in which consumerism has created its own 'law of *un*-diminishing demands'. There is no final state of satiation.

This observation forces us to develop our focus on public expectations and public demands vis-à-vis politics along two distinct lines. There are those public demands that are *absolute* in the sense that we would feel and express them whatever our situation might be. As Abraham Maslow's *Motivation and Personality* (1954) emphasized from a psychological perspective and Ronald Inglehart explored from a sociological standpoint in *The Silent Revolution* (1977), absolute demands would be linked with survival and the scarcity of basic resources such as water, food, and shelter. There is, however, a possibly darker side to public expectations: those needs that are *relative* in the sense that we feel them only if their satisfaction raises us above and makes us feel in some way superior to our fellow citizen. The important element of this distinction is that although *absolute* needs may well be satiable, *relative* needs are clearly not, due to the fact that they increase with the general level. To return to the analogy of the expectations gap outlined in the previous chapter, the upper bar moves ever higher as the lower bar creeps up, all the incentives pushing upwards, never downwards.

Aristotle warned of this situation in his *Politics* by writing that 'all getters of wealth increase their hoard of coin without limit...[but] in this art of wealth-getting there is no limit of the end, which is riches of the spurious kind'. We should strive, Aristotle therefore argued, to acquire such items as are strictly necessary for a 'good life'. But what is the 'good life' and what do we mean by the 'common good'? How do we measure 'value'? On what basis do we distribute 'reward' within our society or define success? Where is the evidence that the constant accumulation of material possessions actually makes us happy? Defending politics from the market therefore takes us back to very basic questions about values, morality, and the nature of citizenship. I want to explore these questions in the remainder of this chapter but the main argument of this section is that achieving this steady-state equilibrium, by which I mean a balance between popular participation and governing capacity, cannot be achieved *solely* by channelling social life towards individual satisfactions because this risks hollowing out the very essence of politics (i.e. an emphasis on collective goods over individual demands). A mature and workable democracy must be that form of government and social life, as Rancière argues, that is capable of controlling the double excess of collective activity and individual withdrawal inherent to democratic life. The worldly art of politics and the art of living must therefore arguably coexist more closely than they have in recent decades. This is a point that demands we adopt a more fine-grained approach that focuses on the relationships between markets, morality, and citizenship.

Market Citizenship

This chapter is exploring the political consequences of one of the most striking features of the modern age: the expansion of markets and market-orientated reasoning into spheres of life and relationships that were traditionally governed by non-market norms. Defending politics against the market is therefore based on an understanding of the manner in which viewing the public as individual consumers of public services, rather than citizens of a broader community, risks not only over-inflating public expectations but also eviscerating the social fabric on which any democratic system depends. The design and promotion of a more positive account of politics, an account with the capacity to inspire, must therefore be one that nourishes the public sphere and is honest about the respective strengths and weaknesses of both the public *and* private sector. At the very least the global financial crisis suggests that, unless we want to let the market rewrite the norms that govern social institutions, we need a public debate about the moral limits of markets, because the hollowing-out of the public realm makes it difficult to cultivate the solidarity and sense of community on which democratic citizenship depends. The aim of this section is to explore the relationship between markets, morality, and citizenship and highlight the manner in which a reliance on economic theory has led to a certain narrowing or 'infolding' of democratic politics—and therefore how the renewal or revitalization of politics depends upon our ability to forge a new and richer sense of citizenship.

In addressing the relationship between markets and morality there is no better starting point than the 2009 Reith Lectures. In these, the American political philosopher Michael Sandel challenged the 'self-evident truth' that the institutions of the public sector should be structured and managed to emulate a well-functioning competitive market. His simple argument was that markets are by definition orientated by a specific morality: a morality based around individual self-interest.

The tension comes, to echo what has already been said, in balancing this individualizing force with the more collective pursuit of the common good. The final decades of the twentieth century were dominated by market triumphalism, privatization, and deregulation and although the 'progressive governance' approach of Bill Clinton, Tony Blair, and other world leaders in the 1990s softened the intense free-market approach of the 1980s, it still represented a general acceptance of the market as the most efficient allocator of resources. For Sandel, however, markets represent little more than institutional arrangements for the channelling of self-interest and greed and a way of seeking to harness that facet of nature towards the common good.

Until the global financial crisis the expansion of markets, and particularly the basic assumptions that the logic of the market brought with it, had rarely been challenged. To some extent the primacy of market-based norms and expectations had become almost depoliticized to the extent that anyone arguing in favour of non-market values, greater state intervention, or a direct role for politicians was immediately labelled as irrational and outdated. The 1980s and 1990s were, as we will see in the next section, characterized by a shift in the nature of public governance and a blurring of the boundary between the public and private sectors. This is reflected in the proliferation of for-profit companies in areas of the public sector, like schools, prisons, social care, public health, higher education, and policing, that were until recently governed by non-market values. Added to this is an almost unquestioned emphasis on 'customer choice', 'contestability', and 'empowerment' that attempts to solve social problems or motivate individual behaviour through material incentives. Cash payments and shopping vouchers have therefore become an increasingly common way of encouraging children to study, persuading teenagers to progress from secondary to further education, motivating clinically obese people to lose weight, and stimulating people to stop smoking. Why is it, we must ask, that the introduction of markets and cash rewards into the public sphere appears slightly distasteful to so many people? What is it that makes 'punishment for profit', for example, so objectionable? Why does paying someone public money to lose weight seem wrong? As we shall see, the simple answer to such questions forces us to understand the relationship between morals and motivations and how they combine to inform different models of citizenship, which has, in turn, major implications for democracy.

Markets and market incentives, as we have already noted, embody certain values and morals. They play to certain aspects of human nature and as such they provide a valuable tool of governance. More specifically market relationships promote certain ways of valuing not only the goods that are being exchanged but also defining the innate value of the individual or group with specific resources (labour, skills, knowledge, time, etc.). Market relationships are therefore imbued with an individualized logic that asks 'what's in it for me or us?' rather than 'what can I or we do to make a positive difference'. The exposure of previously public goods or private relationships to market forces generally involves a shift from *endogenous* motivations (internalized non-materialistic personal commitment) to *exogenous* motivations (individualized and material exchange relationships). This shift in the nature of relationships will be well known to parents who have fallen into the trap of seeking to motivate reluctant children to do their chores by introducing financial incentives. Once a monetary reward has been introduced for washing the dishes, doing homework, tidying a bedroom, or going for a bike ride, it is very hard to remove from future negotiations! Market incentives can therefore erode or replace non-market incentives that are thereafter extremely difficult to re-establish.

As Michael Sandel sought to emphasize in his Reith lectures, economics teaches us that people respond to incentives and although some kids might read books for the love of reading or ride their bike for the sense of independence and adventure it gives them, others may lack these real and very genuine (intrinsic) impulses. In this situation money can provide a useful form of leverage. The simple risk, however, is that monetary incentives may undermine intrinsic ones, leading to less reading or to more reading but for the wrong reason. Financial negotiations therefore become the basis of all relationships and a precursor to any form of domestic activity. The market is not therefore a neutral or innocent instrument, as many economists would argue, but it is a value-laden mode of governing with a tendency to skew relationships on a permanent basis. Payment alters how people perceive an activity, be it giving or receiving, and so may erode the intrinsic good of many activities. Market incentives define social relationships like parenting, teaching, loving, and caring as little more than commodities to be bought and sold (and too often corrupted and degraded). Put simply, market incentives change the basis of relationships.

Focusing on the incentives that underpin social relationships encourages us to move onto a bigger stage and examine the changing nature of citizenship. In a whole host of ways the concept of citizenship provides the bridge or the linkage between ideas of individual entitlement, on the one hand, and social responsibilities, on the other. More broadly, understanding the manner in which neo-liberal ideas have been translated into changes in not only the nature of citizenship (this section) but also the structure of the state (the focus of the next section) provides a way of exploring and therefore understanding the existence of public disenchantment with politics.

To grasp the relationship between marketization and citizenship it is useful to explore T. H. Marshall's classic work *Citizenship and Social Class* (1949). According to Marshall, citizenship is essentially a matter of ensuring that everyone is treated as a valued and equal member of society, and the way to ensure this is through the provision of universal citizenship rights. This is a model of citizenship that focuses on common concerns, collective deliberation, social connections, and loyalty to the democratic community itself. The concept of citizenship had at its core a *social bond* in the sense of a direct sense of community and loyalty. These citizenship rights, Marshall argued, had emerged in waves during recent centuries, from civil rights in the eighteenth century, political rights in the nineteenth century, through to social rights (education, healthcare, etc.) with the emergence of the large modern state during the twentieth century. This is clearly a rather sweeping approach to the notion of rights and citizenship and Marshall's analysis is sensitive to the manner in which specific forms of citizenship rights were acquired by different social groups at different times, in different countries, and for different reasons. But for Marshall the fullest expression of citizenship required a fully operational liberal democratic welfare state as the most effective way of delivering civil, political, and social rights to every member of society. This is often called a 'passive' or 'private' approach to citizenship because of its emphasis on universal entitlements and individual privileges rather than social obligations or public responsibilities.

From the mid-1970s onwards a powerful critique of citizenship rights emerged. Whereas Marshall argued that social rights allowed the disadvantaged to play a role in society and protected them from untrammelled market forces, an alternative way of thinking emerged in the form of the New Right that suggested social rights might in fact be creating a culture of dependency. Too many individually focused rights combined with a large welfare state that effectively created passive dependents had, so the argument went, become a barrier to a vibrant social sphere. The notion of citizenship has therefore been recast since the 1980s from a passive 'legal-status-and-rights' model to a more active 'citizenship-as-desirable-social-activity' model, which sought to emphasize the collective value of being a 'good citizen'. Lawrence Mead's *Beyond Entitlement: The Social Obligations of Citizenship* (1986) provides an influential account of this transition but it is sufficient for the purposes of this section simply to note that this transition hinged on the introduction of markets and market-based incentives. This was reflected in reforms that sought to extend the scope of markets in people's lives in order to emphasize the values of initiative, self-reliance, entrepreneurship, risk-taking, and self-reliance.

In his book *The Decline of the Public* (2004) David Marquand charts this transition through the final decades of the twentieth century from a focus on 'democratic citizenship' towards a model of 'consumer citizenship' that fed populist pressure but had little conception of non-economic values. To claim that citizens are being treated as consumers is to highlight the manner in which the government–citizen relationship is increasingly imitating patterns of choice and power found in the private sector. The user of public services is regarded primarily in 'self-regarding' terms that means they are expected to make decisions without reference to others and to behave as if they are simply engaging in a sequence of temporary bilateral relationships that bring with them little obligation to consider the wider political community, or act on its behalf.

The role of the state is therefore to react, like market actors, to the demands of their 'customers' and reflect a consumer culture based on mass consumption in which a proliferation of choice and personalized services theoretically enables a wide variety of wants and desires to be satisfied. Yet the notion of a consumer-citizen brings with it a host of problems. In some areas of the public sector identifying the consumer of public services is actually quite difficult. In relation to policing, for example, is the 'customer' the victim or the criminal? How does economic logic deal with the fact that many 'customers' of public services, like the mentally ill, are the focus of enforced consumption? The emergence of a marketplace democracy is also tainted by a naive belief in the existence of a level playing field, on which all individuals and

groups can make their claims effectively. In reality, however, the existence of 'voice' and 'choice' tends to reflect pre-existing social inequal-
ities and may therefore simply result in what might be termed the
'dictatorship of the articulate'. Most importantly for the argument of
this book, however, is that the rise of the consumer-citizen brings with
it the risk of inflating the expectations gap. The public sector has limited resources but extensive demands and the only way of managing
this gap is through some form of rationing or priority setting. The
danger of emphasizing consumer choice, therefore, is that it risks
encouraging the public to make demands that simply cannot be delivered. Reducing everything down still further, any defence of politics
against the market has to focus on the basic incompatibility between
individualism and collectivism. The creation of a marketplace democracy based upon individuals as rational consumers of public services
rather than citizens of a richer democratic community is likely to be
constrained by its foundation on a splintered logic. In order to appreciate the impact and implications of this splintered logic the next section
focuses on the marketization of the state.

Government by the Market

This chapter is trying to stimulate a more open and balanced debate
about how the gradual but constant expansion of markets and market-
like relationships into the public sphere has altered the relationship
between individuals and politics. My argument is that treating individuals as consumers in a marketplace, rather than citizens in a democracy,
without any public debate or countervailing measures, risks inculcating
a set of values which are anathema to democratic politics. The logic of
the private sector and that of the public sector are at root antagonistic—
they splinter rather than unite—and I hope to have shown this in the
first section's discussion on morality and markets and in the second section's focus on citizenship. My aim in this section is to reveal the practical impact of this splintered logic on the public sector itself with the
intention of revealing the manner in which the increasing encroachment of the market has undermined certain collective values and institutional capacities without there even being much of a public debate.
I want to suggest that a rather ironic relationship exists between the
dominant neo-liberal-inspired paradigm of 'good governance' and the
all-pervasive sense that democratic politics is somehow failing. Could it

simply be that the introduction of market norms, values, and expectations risks creating a rhetoric–reality gap that can only increase the gap that has apparently emerged between the governors and the governed? Does the solution to closing the gap lie in attending more closely to what we have, both materially and socially, rather than continually demanding more? How might the hierarchy of values that shapes modern liberal democracies be recast in order to give greater emphasis to moral arguments concerning civic virtue and trust? To respond to these questions, I want to make a very bold distinction between what I call the 'Logic of the State' and the 'Logic of the Market'.

Albert Hirschman's influential *Exit, Voice and Loyalty* (1970) provides the intellectual roots of this distinction and takes us back to a debate we have already touched upon as part of a discussion about the manner in which the state and the market adopt very different approaches when faced with limited resources. To recap, market-based allocation mechanisms operate on the basis of *internalized* rationing systems (i.e. individuals make personal choices about where and when to spend their money) because free exchange, in theory, is intended to match supply and demand in an efficient manner. State-based allocation mechanisms operate on a fundamentally different basis. Democratic collective decision-making frameworks involve an *externalized* rationing system in which decisions concerning policies and services (and paying for them) are imposed and enforced by the state. This externalized rationing system may sometimes appear overly centralized, controlling, and even unfair but it has been established and sustained on the basis of a coherent logic based upon at least three tenets.

1. That externalized/imposed rationing is necessary to avoid the dilemma in which multiple individuals acting independently in their own self-interest can ultimately destroy a shared limited resource (known in the academic literature as 'collective action problems').

2. Externalized rationing is also viewed as necessary in order to avoid inferior social outcomes and protect individual freedoms. Driving laws, for example, limit individual freedoms in some ways in order to produce the situation in which everyone can drive relatively safely.

3. Centralized decision-making and external rationing is viewed as vital because many individuals share certain values concerning the

need to protect sections of society from the vagaries of a pure market. This generally involves the provision of a social safety net in terms of state benefits, an educational and healthcare system that does not discriminate on the basis of money, and a variety of social services concerned with supporting, protecting, and retraining disadvantaged social groups.

In short, the Logic of the State was intended to inculcate certain values that stand in direct opposition to the Logic of the Market and it was for exactly this reason that Crick viewed the democratic state as a counterweight to the pure market. As such, the 'Logic of the State' accepted that in a system based upon an externally imposed rationing system some people would take out more than they put in and not everyone would receive the level of service provision they might wish for.

As a host of books, studies, and reports make clear, the final decades of the twentieth century were dominated by a shift in the dominant paradigm of 'good governance' whereby the Logic of the State became displaced by the Logic of the Market. This was reflected in the global trend towards 'New Public Management' and sweeping processes of privatization, deregulation, contracting-out, hiving-off, and the injection of market-like relationships wherever possible. *Reinventing Government*, to use the title of David Osborne and Ted Gaebler's influential 1992 book on public sector reform, was therefore infused with neoliberal beliefs about the innate superiority of the market in terms of organizational efficiency and the efficient allocation of scarce resources. The entrepreneurial spirit may well have transformed the public sector but the jury is still out on whether this should be judged as a positive development. However, before I explain why this is the case I want to step back, very briefly, and consider the bigger picture when market-based reform strategies were emerging as a rather simple solution to the problems of governing during the late 1970s. This was a period, as has already been discussed, when concerns regarding political overload, de-legitimation, and democratic bankruptcy were very much to the fore in the light of social and economic unrest across North America and Western Europe. There was a widespread sense that politics was promising too much but delivering too little. What we might now define, using the simple framework discussed above, as an 'expectations gap' had developed and therefore a relatively simple set of options presented themselves:

Option 1: increasing supply (moving the bottom bar up);

Option 2: reducing demand (moving the top bar down); or,

Option 3: a combination of Options 1 and 2 (close the gap from above and below).

In this context the Logic of the Market appeared to offer a win–win solution because it promised to increase supply (Option 1) without requiring significant additional financial investments. Efficiency savings and the generation of 'more bang for each buck' through the injection of the market or market-type relationships would solve the 'crisis of democracy' that the Trilateral Commission had examined in such detail. What the subsequent spread of New Public Management throughout the 1980s and 1990s masked, however, was any deeper discussion concerning the limits of politics, the responsibilities of individuals to society, how markets altered social relationships, or the pathologies of Marcuse's 'one dimensional man'. Reducing demand (Option 2) was simply never acknowledged as a viable political option despite growing concerns about both the long-term impact of mass consumption on the environment, and the inflationary pressures created by the internal contradictions of democracy. Taking these themes of restraint and demand a little further provides a way of adding practical detail to these arguments, so let me spend just a little time daring to challenge the Logic of the Market and standing up for the Logic of the State by focusing on two simple issues: the public service ethos and individualized demands.

The Public Service Ethos

In terms of exploring the manner in which New Public Management and marketization have led to the 'hollowing-out' of the state, there is a wealth of material on institutional reform and the 'unbundling' or 'unravelling' of the public sector—from Australia to Canada and all points in between—as a result of attempts to try and create markets, deliver choice, and enforce contestability. Institutional structures, like children's building blocks, are relatively easy to demolish and rebuild. What is far harder to recreate is the cultural glue that binds public sector organizations together in the form of a shared set of values, ethics, and motivations that puts the greater good before individual benefit. The public service ethos is generally accepted to involve a combination of high ethical standards (trust, propriety, etc.) and a degree of altruism in which individuals commit to working within the public sector due to a sense of personal commitment and loyalty to collective action, and for which they will be rewarded with a secure job, a moderate income, and even the possibility of a public honour or distinction for senior or outstanding public service. Phrased in this way, the public service ethos can be interpreted as a form of cultural resource that promotes a high-trust, high-commitment workforce.

The rise of what John Clarke and Janet Newman labelled *The Managerial State* (1997) was, however, based on a critique of modern social democracy that interpreted the public service ethos as little more than a myth. What is more, it labelled the public service ethos as little more than a veil for the maintenance of a system in which public sector employees were able to persist in self-serving forms of behaviour. Altering the incentives and sanctions framework for public service employees by opening up their services to the discipline of the market and introducing new forms of performance-related pay was viewed as a thoroughly 'modern' and appropriate response. Three decades later the problems and unintended consequences arising from this market-based reform logic have been documented extensively. These include the commodification of tasks into 'price per unit' variables with little acknowledgement of the true role or work of a doctor, nurse, teacher, or police officer; the introduction of crude targets and an explosion of audit mechanisms and expensive compliance mechanisms; the creation of delivery chains of increasing length and complexity in which each organization is focused on achieving 'their' objectives; the gradual de-skilling of the state as more and more areas of expertise transfer into the private sector; the sapping of morale amongst public service professionals as their capacity for innovation and discretion is increasingly eroded; the simple fact that private sector providers do not share information about the procedures and practices that may allow them to claim 'best practice' status due to a need to protect their market position; and the rather perplexing fact that there is very little hard evidence that New Public Management has actually delivered the efficiency savings it promised.

But there is a deeper and more basic failing: the baseline definition of those working within the public sector as *homo economicus* (as rational and narrowly self-interested actors whose sole desire is to possess wealth). Have those perpetuating this view ever spent time in an inner-city school on a Monday morning, a benefits office on a Friday afternoon, or an accident and emergency department on a Saturday night? Do they really think that those street-level bureaucrats whose motivations they define and dismiss with such apparent ease are only in it for the money? My argument is not that money does not matter or that performance should not be rewarded but that for the majority of public service employees, from social workers and police officers to local government officers and classroom teaching assistants, it is the job (i.e. the opportunity to play a positive role in society) that motivates them. The Logic of the Market therefore introduces a rather unfortunate assumption that public employees are knaves (interested in personal gain) rather than knights (honourably committed to the public good) and appears unable or unwilling to entertain the notion of *homo reciprocans*, which states that individuals are primarily motivated by the desire to improve their environment, nurture others, and feel part of a collective whole.

The irony of the current situation is that the Logic of the Market is totally one-sided. It is irrational and out of balance because it places all the pressure on the public sector, through the introduction of ever more divisive and risky market-based reforms, but shies away from addressing the more important demand side of the relationship on the part of the wider public. More specifically, and here lies the rub in terms of democratic disengagement and declining levels of public trust, the implicit logic of marketization as the dominant paradigm of 'good governance' brings with it a clear tendency for politicians and their officials to compare public services with those provided by the private sector. Furthermore, the public are increasingly encouraged *to expect and demand* the same standards of personalization, choice, and control in their interactions with the state that they enjoy with organizations within the private sector. The conception of citizens as consumers risks inflaming rather than reshaping the public's expectations, which is a theme that leads us to investigate the impact of the market's emphasis on responding to individualized demands.

Individualised Demands

Advocates of New Public Management shared the assumption that the 'old' model of public services was outdated and unresponsive. Their reform prescriptions were informed by models, drawn from books like

Hirschman's *Exit, Voice and Loyalty* that suggested individuals have two options when faced with an organization that is providing a declining or unsatisfactory level of service. They can *exit* (withdraw from the relationship and move their custom to an alternative provider) or they can use their *voice* by complaining and through this possibly alter the behaviour of the organization. The Logic of the State was based around the *voice*-type mechanisms, through which individuals could seek to have their views taken into account. The Logic of the Market, on the other hand, dictated that 'exit' mechanisms were crucial, as those who felt their voice was not listened to could take their custom elsewhere. How an individual deployed their *voice* and *exit* capacities depended on a host of factors including their long-term personal commitment to an organization (i.e. their loyalty), the availability of complaints mechanisms, and the existence of alternative providers that made exiting a viable option.

The intrusion of the market into the public sector therefore brought with it an attempt to not only strengthen voice-based mechanisms (complaints procedures, user-panels, charters, etc.) but more importantly by attempting to create a rights-based system in which a range of competing providers, be they schools, day-care centres, housing associations, probation services, or hospitals, would compete for custom and through this make 'exiting' a central element of an individual's relationship with the public sector. This is reflected in the use of legally enforceable social entitlements, public service guarantees, personalized budgets, individualized care packages, and an increasing use of voucher schemes. And yet for politicians to encourage members of the public to expect those levels of service from the public sector that they are used to receiving from the private sector is akin to cultivating expectations that cannot be realized. As Catherine Needham concludes in her book *Citizen Consumers* (2003): 'The fundamental danger is that consumerism may foster privatised and resentful citizens whose expectations of government can never be met, and cannot develop the concern for the public good that must be the foundation of democratic engagement and support for public services.'

By indulging in this behaviour without massive increases in resources politicians are arguably deluding the public about the capacity of the state and unwittingly increasing the 'expectations gap'. The state was never designed, resourced, or expected to compete with the market. The state possessed (and still retains) certain qualities and characteristics that can never be replicated in a profit-driven organization, but by inflaming individualized public expectations we do little to foster or safeguard those facets of collective endeavour (the public sector ethos, compromise, civic friendship, public service, trust, respect, mutual obligation, compassion, altruism, democratic citizenship, etc.) that had taken more than half a century to build.

This is not an argument against the market but in favour of a more balanced account of citizenship that is based upon a deeper set of governing relationships and which goes beyond facile assumptions that conjoin human nature and self-interest. Our current model of liberal democracy risks eviscerating the very essence of democratic life by squeezing out and failing to respect those deeper relationships and motivations than cannot be reduced to material reward and mass consumption. The dominant model of public sector reform and public governance also grates against the logic of collective democratic engagement (the former emphasizing the rights-based fulfilment of individual demands, the latter emphasizing restraint, shared understanding, and individual obligations to society). It is in exactly this vein that Gerry Stoker concludes his book *Why Politics Matters* (2006) by writing, 'The discourse and practice of collective decision-making sits very uncomfortably alongside the discourse and practice of individual choice, self-expression and market-based fulfilment of needs and wants...so it turns out that a propensity to disappoint is an inherent feature of governance even in democratic societies.' With this thought in mind it is possible to step back and reflect upon the broader relevance of this defence of politics against the market.

Politics against Markets

Humans are complex animals. They are both selfish and social and this is reflected in the physiological evolution of the brain and the manner in which the two sides of the human brain interpret the world quite differently in terms of the application of values, assumptions, and priorities. The left hemisphere is detail-orientated, prefers mechanisms to living things, and is inclined to self-interest; the right hemisphere, by contrast, has greater breadth, flexibility, and generosity. The two sides of the brain therefore possess coherent but quite incompatible ways of experiencing the world. Recent neuro-scientific studies suggest that a shift in the relationship between the two sides of the brain is occurring as the independent self-attending left hemisphere is increasingly taking precedence over its more altruistic society-centred right side. In *The Master and his Emissary* (2009) Iain McGilchrist suggests that we may be about to witness the final triumph of the left hemisphere at the expense of us all and with potentially disastrous consequences. McGilchrist's book is not only a masterpiece in its own right but it also provides a very broad stage on which to position this chapter's focus on the gradual but constant incursion of the market and market-based principles into the public sector.

In a sense the shift from *democratic citizenship* towards a more individualized model of *consumer citizenship* risks speaking exclusively to the left hemisphere of the brain while failing to nourish, stimulate, and sustain that element of the human nature or neurological programming that longs for a sense of collective place, responsibility and value. The social commentator Will Hutton once wrote that 'to construct a civilisation around the nostrum that the public realm is morally, economically and socially inferior to the private realm is to submit to an alien barbarism in which what we hold in common is permanently placed as second best', and for some reason this statement haunts me when I seek to understand the challenges we collectively face. Like the two sides of the human brain, the Logic of the State and the Logic of the Market coexist. They apply a quite different set of values and assumptions to the world but neither should be assumed innately superior.

Pericles, the great champion of democracy in ancient Athens, praised individual initiative, but also warned against the citizen who lives only for himself. He said that such individuals have no right to be part of the city-state upon which their flourishing depends. He had a noun for such folk—*idiotes* (from which we get a well-known English word) and my concern is that we have all become slightly too concerned with what we can get for ourselves rather than what we can do for each other. The ethics of the free market encourage us to live self-interested lives and yet a democracy cannot exist as a company of strangers, as it rests on the existence of deeper bonds (bonds that we risk undermining by defining citizenship in purely consumerist terms) and a recognition that an individual's position in the world relies to a great extent on the lives of others. Rights and entitlements clearly play a role in the modern world and should not be dismissed lightly but their legalistic and individualizing thrust is exclusive and must be balanced against a richer account of democratic duty. This balance is too often missing and to a great extent individual rights have themselves become little more than commodities to be exploited. This is demonstrated by those who assert their rights in a selfish way without regard to the rights of others. There is, as Michael Sandel argued in his Reith Lectures, an urgent need to question the assumptions of the 'good life', the legitimate boundaries of the market and the form of citizenship promoted by consumer capitalism. Continuous material acquisition and wealth may dazzle and entertain, it may well flatter our vanity but it will ultimately disappoint. The pig farmer who constantly accumulates more land and more pigs in order to acquire even more land and more pigs is unlikely to be happy but simply lost in a strained and contradictory landscape of values.

The simple argument of this chapter is that democratic politics needs to be defended from a moral hierarchy that perpetuates crude assumptions about the innate superiority of the market and equates happiness with material consumption. We may have become richer in material terms but the evidence suggests that we have also become self-centred, self-interested, and self-regarding. The global financial crisis may have provided a rather extreme example of what Sue Gerhardt describes as *The Selfish Society* (2010) but it also pushed the issue of markets and morality back within the contours of public debate. The state has now made something of a comeback and the ideology of the free market is no longer uncontested. The global financial crisis demonstrated exactly why politics does matter. The moral limits of markets and the role of the public sector in protecting non-market norms were rediscovered as a reaction against purely privatized notions of the good life. A defence of politics against the market therefore stands upon an awareness of the pitfalls of individualism and rampant consumerism. Democratic politics matters because it is at root a civilizing activity and as a consequence demands some sense of civic virtue or understanding—a sense of how to live as if we were human.

If the 'art of living', to adopt Keynes's phrase, can no longer be solely equated with material possessions, economic prosperity, and personal choice because too many of us are simply unhappy, then we must be brave enough to articulate a shared vision of acceptable behaviour, be very clear about collective responsibilities, and not afraid to suggest that individuals sometimes need a very clear nudge from the state to encourage them to act in ways that deep down they know are just. Yet as has already been mentioned, for many of us our traditional moral anchorages, like the church, the trade unions, and our families, have been undermined and we lack the confidence to make moral judgements or defend certain viewpoints, due to an awareness of the unavoidable plurality of convictions that exists in a modern society. As a society we need to define certain baseline civic virtues if we are to cultivate a more optimistic, revitalized, and forward-looking approach to politics. We can no longer avoid complex questions by defining them as economic issues to be decided by the market; we need to be braver and define the type of human character we want to nurture: explore how members of a political community should engage with one another and the kind of world we want our grandchildren to live in. We then need to consider the role that an active state might play in supporting this vision. In the aftermath of the global financial crisis I certainly detect an appetite for change and a public life with a purpose. The election of President Obama was fuelled by this demand as he dared to articulate a politics of moral and spiritual aspiration and was not scared to define wrong and right.

The suggestion that, as a society, we sometimes avoid tough questions by defining them as economic issues to be decided by the market, rather than political issues to be decided by politicians, not only reflects the impact of the 'bad faith model of politics' but at a much broader level it reveals a need to rediscover our collective self-belief. Our naive faith in the market has left us dependent on a weak form of 'life politics' that focuses on individual responses to social problems. The twenty-first century will be shaped by challenges that cannot be ignored and cannot be addressed on a purely individual basis. To suggest that they could would be to sustain a process of mutual deception that benefits no one. Our confidence may be shaken, the 'Age of Abundance' may well be slipping into an 'Age of Austerity' that might to some people look bleak and threatening, but the twenty-first century also provides great opportunities and new prospects for those who take the lead and trumpets the great benefits and potential of democratic politics.

In order to do this we need to adopt, as this chapter has argued, a more cautious approach to the use and value of markets. Democratic politics provides a valuable counterweight to the pure market and the need for this mechanism in the twenty-first century should not be underestimated. A defence of politics against the market forms just one part of a much wider defence of politics against a collection of strategies, tools, and tactics that each in their own way have attempted to narrow the sphere of conventional democratic politics by defining many issues as beyond the legitimate control of politicians. This is an issue that takes us into the terrain of Noam Chomsky's *Hopes and Prospects* (2010) and his belief that financial liberalization combined with the privatization of public services has weakened the viability of democracy: 'with services privatised, democratic institutions may exist but they will mostly be formalities because the most important decisions will have been removed from the public arena.' By focusing on the shifting arenas in which decisions that concern the public now take place Chomsky reminds us that 'Keep the politicians out!' was to some extent the rallying cry of the decades that spanned the millennium.

The belief that politicians were not to be trusted and that it was somehow possible to take politics 'out of politics' has led to a change in the nature of modern governance. This is a change based upon the transfer of power from those whom we elect to those we do not elect (like, for example, judges, economists, scientists, bankers, accountants, technocrats, ethicists, etc.) but who are for some strange reasons considered as more legitimate and trustworthy than elected politicians. My warning in this context is simple. We cannot elect politicians but then deny that they have a legitimate role. We cannot allow politicians to avoid tough choices by simply giving up certain powers. We cannot depoliticize the sphere of democratic politics by creating numerous centres of fugitive power that simply create complex blame games. We cannot assume that scientists, judges, or anyone else has the capacity to arrive at 'better' decisions than mere politicians. In short, if we are to restore our confidence in politics and replace the 'politics of pessimism' with a renewed 'politics of optimism' then we urgently need to defend politics against *denial*.

4

A DEFENCE OF POLITICS
AGAINST DENIAL

We are in the presence of a regime that, I believe can be called tele–post–democratic oligarchy…a post–democracy in which the vast majority of citizens do not 'choose' and not 'elects' but ignores, silent and obedient.
                    Danilo Zolo, *Democracy and Complexity* (1992)

A nasty little thought…Would the country be better off if more policy decisions were removed from the political thicket and placed in the hands of unelected technocrats?
                    Alan Blinder, *Is Government Too Political?* (1997)

The transfer of power to technocrat-guardians might undermine the legitimacy of government. People might become alienated from, and eventually rebel against, a system in which power is closely held, even if technocratic-guardians tend to make decisions that are manifestly better for the public in the long-run.
                    Alisdair Roberts, *The Logic of Discipline* (2010)

That strategy involved the depoliticization of key domains, in the sense of removing them from the spheres of partisan, electorally influenced politics, and replacing these potentially democratic forces with the routines of low politics. In this way, governing issues were converted into grist for the mill of specialized elites. The exhaustion of that strategy has produced hyper-politicization.
                    Mick Moran, *The British Regulatory State* (2003)

Boundaries and borders; discipline and restraint; expansion and control; confidence and opportunity: these are the issues that concern this chapter as part of a defence of politics against the global trend towards the depoliticization of democracy that has emerged in recent years. This trend is reflected in reforms that have transferred an increasing range of powers from elected politicians to unelected experts or have implemented new rules and procedures that significantly reduce the flexibility and discretion enjoyed by politicians. Narrowing the range of issues on which politicians can exert direct control has been promoted by a vast range of think tanks and pressure groups as a solution to both public policy and constitutional challenges and was described by the European Policy Forum as 'one of the most promising developments since the last war: the depoliticisation of many government decisions'. At the global level the World Bank advocates large-scale depoliticization as a central aspect of building state capacity and market confidence while the United Nations organizes conferences and seminars with such themes as 'depoliticizing governance'.

The last chapter concluded with an emphasis on political confidence and self-belief. This chapter continues this theme by exploring why politicians, having spent years campaigning to win power, now seem strangely willing to hand power over major policy areas to an assortment of technocrats, accountants, scientists, ethicists, and judges. This statecraft was summed up in the announcement in 2002 by Labour peer Lord Falconer when he was a leading member of the British government: 'What governs our approach is a clear desire to place power where it should be: increasingly not with politicians, but with those best fitted in different ways to deploy it.' He went on to note that 'This depoliticising of key decision-making is a vital element in bringing power closer to the people'.

However, depoliticization rarely brings power closer to the general public and is more accurately viewed as the transfer of power *between* competing elites. Put slightly differently, depoliticization represents the denial of democratic capacity and the narrowing or infolding of the public sphere. It is for exactly this reason that I want to defend politics from those forms of modern governance that involve an attempt to remove issues and functions from the thicket of day-to-day party politics.

Looking more broadly, it is fascinating to observe the parallel development of two quite different historical trends towards the end of the twentieth century. Francis Fukayama's *The End of History and the Last Man* (1992) famously argued that the collapse of the Communist states in Eastern Europe marked the triumph of liberal democracy. History was, for Fukayama, directional, and its end point was capitalist liberal democracy. There is, in fact, no end point to history and what is particularly interesting about the last two decades is the manner in which mature liberal democracies embarked upon a strategy of political denial that hinged on a commitment to depoliticization. It is for exactly this reason that many scholars and social commentators suggested that liberal democracy had been eclipsed by a new technocratic model of politics in which the role of elected politicians is minimal. Carl Boggs's *The End of Politics* (1999), Colin Crouch's *Post-Democracy* (2004), and Colin Hay's *Why We Hate Politics* (2007), to highlight just a few key texts, all pinpointed depoliticization and the politics of denial as the root cause of a decline in public confidence in political processes, political institutions, and politicians.

Recent history therefore reveals not a single path to a relatively distinct model of liberal democracy but a dual process of *democratization* (for those countries that were until recently communist or authoritarian regimes) and *depoliticization*, or what others prefer to label *de-democratization*, in mature democracies. This twin-track approach to politics can itself be viewed as the outcome of a deeper collision of ideas about the virtues and limitations of democratic systems. What this deeper collision really signified, however, was the very basic system-wide tension between popular involvement in politics, on the one hand, and stable governing capacity, on the other.

If we are to defend politics and make the case for democracy we need to be able to argue that elections matter in the sense that the people the public select to govern will actually have the power and confidence to make tough choices. It is very hard to persuade the public to re-engage with politics and to have some confidence in politicians when they are constantly faced with politicians who deny their own capacity to act. In terms of understanding why the politics of denial has emerged as a dominant form of statecraft, it is necessary to appreciate both the external contextual drivers and the more specific internal drivers of this denial. The external driver is largely *ideological* and rests on the broad acceptance of the 'bad faith model of politics'. Politicians, so the argument goes, are not to be trusted, they are likely to promote their own short-term political interests above sensible long-term policy-making, and, as a result, lack discipline and credibility. The 'Logic of Discipline', as we shall see, promotes the wholesale transfer of decision-making capacities from politicians to a range of non-elected 'independent' experts who are viewed as being better placed to make decisions about the allocation of scarce resources.

This external driver is, however, supplemented by an internal driver that has generally been overlooked in the wider literature: depoliticization. Through the transfer of functions to agencies, boards, or commissions, depoliticization provides politicians with a means of managing the issue of overload and of regulating the range of issues for which the state is now expected to exercise some element of control. It also provides a way of utilizing the skills and knowledge of experts in relation to technical or scientific areas of policy where politicians lack specialist skills. Hiving off certain functions can also deliver great benefits in terms of taking an issue out of the aggressive sphere of partisan politics and creating some political space, or distance, within which a more considered discussion of the best way forward might take place. What we might label 'the politics of ABC' (i.e. agencies, boards, and commissions) also intensifies the challenges of governance, due to the manner in which the nature and structure of the state is increasingly fluid and fragmented. The darker side of the politics of denial, however, rests not just with the complex institutional architecture that it spawns but in the deeper lack of political confidence that it reflects. Drawing upon the advice of experts seems to me a wholly sensible approach to governing but in many areas the situation has progressed to the point that experts now *make* the final decisions. Politicians seem to have lost confidence in their own capacity to make decisions.

The topic of depoliticization therefore forms a novel angle from which to understand why politicians seem increasingly willing to hollow out their own governing capacity and also why the public appear increasingly uninterested in conventional politics. Focusing on depoliticization also poses new questions about the management of public expectations and whether any polity that rests on popular support can ever take unpopular decisions. There is often, as we have seen, a big gap between what makes 'good politics' and what makes 'good policy'. The politics of denial sheds new light on why politicians tend to act in the way they do; and whether you, the reader, might act in exactly the same way if you were unfortunate enough to be placed in their shoes. If you had to face the difficult choices of governing; if you were the focus of an orgy of expectation; if *you* operated in an environment in which every utterance and potential gaffe, irrespective of where it was spoken, was likely to become the focus of a media feeding frenzy and in which every omission was immediately defined as a snub against your colleagues; if you knew your errors would be amplified and your successes dismissed; and if you were personally responsible for a vast range of issues about which you actually knew very little; if you were subject to a great number of incompatible demands . . . would the politics of denial not suddenly become an attractive option? Is it possible that politicians are not so unlike the rest of us after all and that we would behave exactly like they do if put in their position? Let me develop this question by setting out the main claims of this chapter:

1. The adoption of an avowedly anti-political agenda reflects a systematic crisis of confidence.

2. Depoliticization, in all its forms, represents a dangerous illusion. It is the denial of politics while continuing politics by other means.

3. Transferring responsibility to unaccountable and unelected actors is an odd response to concerns about the efficacy of the democratic process.

4. It is incredibly hard to revitalize the public's interest and belief in the relevance of democratic politics when politicians constantly disavow their responsibility for almost all matters.

5. The global financial crisis has undermined the 'Logic of Discipline' that suppressed the role of politicians and has created new opportunities.

Before examining each of these claims in a little more detail I want to use the fact that my defence of politics against *denial* sits at the midpoint of this book to take stock very briefly and reflect on some of the arguments that have already been made about the need to defend politics from *itself* (Chapter 2) and from the *market* (Chapter 3), but also to look forward to how the later defences, focusing on *crises* (Chapter 5) and the role of the *media* (Chapter 6) augment and develop my core argument about the need to make the case urgently for democratic politics (the focus of Chapter 7). Although blaming politicians for the ills of the world might provide a useful emotional anaesthetic, in reality, where failings do exist, they are undoubtedly systemic in nature and we are all to some degree complicit.

I know this is a highly unfashionable argument to make and please forgive me once more if I dare to suggest that too many critics of democracy have become too adept at demanding, condemning, and carping and too reluctant to step into the arena themselves in order to try to make a positive difference. Democracy is not perfect—I have been more than open about this fact—but its basis on tolerance, compromise, and mutual understanding make it by far the best way for increasingly complex societies to rub along together, 'rub along' being a carefully selected phrase because democracy will always create sparks, tension, and a degree of friction due to the simple fact that everyone will not get everything they want all of the time. But that is the beauty of politics, not its failing. It is a civilizing and human activity and, as the repeated bailout of the Greek economy in 2011 illustrated, politicians will sometimes be required to make unpopular decisions in order to accommodate certain interests, compromise with other countries, prevent the spread of problems, or even protect future generations.

My aim is not to provide 'answers' or convince you that I am 'right' (and you are 'wrong') but simply to suggest to you that the dominant anti-political sentiment that implies that politics no longer matters, that political processes fail more frequently than they succeed, and that politicians are all corrupt is wrong. Political processes will certainly fail from time to time because the challenges they face are complex and the resources they have are limited. Politicians will also make mistakes because they are human and we expect them to make decisions on the basis of partial information and under great pressure. We also place demands on them that are generally beyond the capacity of mere mortals. I do not deny that much of the public distrust of politics, in general, and politicians, in particular, has been self-inflicted. The Monica Lewinsky Affair in the United States and the MPs expenses scandal in the United Kingdom, for example, both tarnished the image of politics; but they also revealed a democratic process functioning precisely as it should do. President Clinton was impeached and the 2010 General Election in the United Kingdom delivered the largest turnover of MPs in modern political history. There was no bloodshed and politicians were forced to take notice of public opinion. Problems there undoubtedly are, but do not let us overlook our good fortune. We take it for granted that we live in a democracy where it is possible to elect our rulers, to hold them to account, and ultimately to remove them. Democracy, and therefore 'politics' and politicians, has delivered most of the things, both material and social, that we now take for granted as essential elements of a civilized life. Chris Mullin, himself a former politician who served in the House of Commons for over twenty years, captured this need to put things in perspectives when he wrote,

Yes, we have our problems but, my goodness, what would some young person born in Iraq, Afghanistan, Kosovo or anyone of a hundred other countries not give to change places with us? If life here is so miserable why do we imagine thousands of people are risking their lives, crossing deserts and mountains, waiting months, even years, in squalid camps to be smuggled into our country? Because, compared to them, we have lives of unimaginable good fortune.

Putting things in perspective also demands that we acknowledge the manner in which we live in an age, as the last chapter's defence of politics against the market emphasized, in which it is fashionable to demand instant results but where instant results are not available. Politics is not as simple as it once was, politicians are not as powerful, the public is more diverse, and the challenges we face more expansive and complex. But if the public's expectations and demands of politics have outstripped supply, the popular basis of democratic engagement also makes it very difficult for politicians to speak the truth. The public, as I have already emphasized, can be a selfish and capricious master to serve and political competition, as I have also sought to stress, generally incentivizes the promotion of false hopes and the inflation of expectations over a rather more restrained but honest account of the challenges faced. If Obama's rallying call of 'Yes, we can' had been replaced by 'We might be able to do this' his campaign would have undoubtedly lost the zest and energy that propelled him into office. What Barack Obama injected into American politics, and what so many established democratic societies seem to have lost, was confidence. My concern is therefore that the pervasive anti-political sentiment that is almost tangible in some countries reflects a deeper loss of confidence, not just of the wider public in the democratic framework, but also in the self-confidence of politicians in their own ability to govern and make decisions.

Politics and Fate

Understanding the changing nature of democratic governance and how this links with political apathy and disengagement, let alone deeper arguments concerning the tension between popular pressures and political restraint, is actually quite simple. The public increasingly demand more public spending but less taxation; politicians need to win office and so there is a systemic motivation to promise far more than you can actually deliver. Rhetoric–reality gaps are therefore common, as are soaring expectations followed by dashed hopes. Getting into office is consequently all about telling the public what they want to hear, rather than what they might need to hear. However, the high cost of that strategy will inevitably come home to roost once in office. In this section I want to examine the changing boundaries of politics and particularly how some issues are 'organized out' of politics. My argument is simply that it is possible to identify three broad spheres or areas of politics and then use this framework to highlight the manner in which functions and responsibilities have been increasingly located within a strangely opaque and theoretically depoliticized sphere. Having isolated this institutional pattern it is possible to explore and identify the beliefs and assumptions that drive this process and then discuss how it relates to a broader lack of confidence in politics.

If the thought of following this theoretical train of thought over the next few pages seems simply too painful, let me implore you to read on. Certainly take a break, go for a run, or do anything that refreshes both your body and mind; take a day or a month or a year but whatever you do don't give up on this book. Too many people are suffering from the fatigue and exhaustion that accompanies disillusionment because they think that politics no longer matters and is at an end. Do not be mistaken. Democratic politics retains a capacity for renewal and delivering fresh hope but I need you to undergo the fatigue of supporting it by engaging with the arguments contained within the pages of this book. My hope is that by the time you have read my defence of politics against its foes you might also be willing to put your head above the parapet and speak out in its defence.

This personal plea from the author to his reader may well be unconventional but Bernard Crick, from whose inspiration this book is born, was not the most conventional of people. He viewed democratic politics as a counterweight against a number of social risks. Politics provided a way of pooling resources, working together, and taking control of our lives in a way that would simply be impossible without some form of shared collective endeavour. 'Mere politics' is therefore the opposite of fate, fortuna, or 'mere luck'. It signifies a realm of choice and contingency through which human societies can shape who they are, how they live, and what they value. The distinction between 'politics' and 'fate', however, encourages us to lay down some simple boundaries in order to explain and understand the changing nature of both the state and political rule. In this regard, we can identify three broad, to some extent overlapping, but still relatively clear spheres:

1. The *governmental sphere,* encompassing those functions and issues for which elected politicians are directly responsible.

2. The *public but non-governmental sphere,* encompassing a vast range of functions and issues for which there is a general acceptance that the state should play a role but not under the direct control of politicians.

3. The *private sphere,* encompassing those issues and debates where individuals have some level of direct control, like in relation to sexual behaviour or parenting, but where it is generally thought politicians and the state should play little or no role.

Like the layers in a Russian doll, each of these three spheres is seen to be politicized to a lesser extent than the preceding one and beyond the private sphere exists what we might simply call 'fate', where nature rules in the absence of any capacity for human agency. The edges of these layers are frequently blurred but for the purposes of this section we can simply acknowledge how these three layers help us detect and trace different forms and gradations of denial. So, for example, the decision to delegate responsibility for the regulation of medicines from a department of state to an independent body of experts would involve a form of denial that politicians were best placed to take certain decisions and would therefore involve an attempt to depoliticize by transferring it from the *government* to the *public but non-governmental sphere.* The decision by a new Prime Minister or President to institute a national anti-obesity strategy for the first time or to outlaw the wearing in public of a specific religious garment would, by contrast, reflect an attempt to strengthen political control over an issue (i.e. politicization as the issue shifted from the *private* towards the *public* or *governmental* spheres). Similarly, the creation of the Mississippi River Commission on 28 June 1879 (to return to an organization we discussed in Chapter 2) would, according to this approach, represent a form of politicization whereby an issue, in this case the flow of the longest river in North America, was elevated from the realm of fate to the public sphere. Conversely, refusing to accept that global warming existed or that humankind can do anything about it would place that issue squarely within the realm of 'fate'.

The simple point that this framework allows me to illustrate is the manner in which democracy has increasingly been subject to a process of depoliticization that has shifted more and more functions, roles, responsibilities, and decision-making powers from the governmental to the *public non-governmental sphere* (or what we might more simply call the 'grey zone', to adopt a popular and helpful term first coined in Denmark). This development is reflected in the explosion of what are variously termed 'extra-governmental organizations', 'para-statals', 'hybrids', 'quangos', and 'fringe bodies' that now undertake administrative, regulatory, quasi-judicial, decision-making, fact-finding, and sleaze-busting activities at one remove from elected politicians and democratic oversight. It is the swelling of the grey zone that connects the OECD's (Organization for Economic Cooperation and Development) *Distributed Public Governance* (2002), Jonathan Koppell's *The Politics of Quasi-Government* (2003), Frank Vibert's *The Rise of the Unelected* (2007) with books that have a much broader focus on the nature and future of modern politics, like John Keane's *The Life and Death of Democracy* (2009) with its focus on the emergence of 'monitory democracy'. The grey zone becomes the battleground, or arguably the dumping ground, for deeper tensions within the democratic model.

Let me explain this analogy in a little more detail. My baseline argument in this book is that increasing numbers of people have become disaffected with democracy because they feel that it does not deliver on its promises and that politicians lie and never give a straight answer. Politicians over-promise and under-supply because they operate within a structure that makes it very difficult, if not impossible, for politicians to tell the truth because if they did so nobody would vote for them. As a result we all engage in a system of mutual deception and distrust and politicians resort to ever more extreme ways of managing unrealistic public expectations. The grey zone becomes the arena in which these tensions are inevitably played out and the terrain in which more and more responsibilities are placed. It is therefore possible to identify a twin process of both *depoliticization* and *politicization* that both serve to augment the grey zone.

Depoliticization. The public demand more and more but are unwilling to pay for more or accept any policies that may lead to a decline in their standard of living. Squeezed between the rationalities of *good politics* (give the public whatever they want) and *good policy* (the need to restrict supply, impose discipline, make unpopular decisions) politicians have increasingly delegated tasks to organizations that sit within the murky grey zone.

Politicization. New fears, the social amplification of risk, technological developments, changing expectations, etc. lift issues from the realm of fate and the private sphere to the level at which society demands a collective response. The existence of widespread concern about the effectiveness and trustworthiness of politicians and political processes creates a willingness to tap new forms of legitimacy (expertise, experience, independence, etc.) that again leads to a focus not on conventional politics but on the grey zone.

The twin processes of politicization *and* depoliticization have in recent decades led to a structure of democratic governance that is markedly and increasingly shaped like a ring-doughnut, as centripetal (i.e. outside-in) and centrifugal (inside-out) pressures have both operated to locate new and established functions and responsibilities within a burgeoning grey zone. Viewing the structure of the modern state as a ring-doughnut might not be the most conventional approach to understanding the structure of the modern state but that is why it is so useful. The hole in the centre of the doughnut represents the *governmental sphere* and reflects the manner in which the central and direct governing capacity of politicians has, due to a range of factors, been significantly reduced in recent decades. This is reflected in a large amount of research and writing on the 'hollowing out of the state' since the mid-1990s. The main ring of the doughnut represents the *public but non-governmental sphere* that has ballooned over the same period. Indeed, research by the OECD (*Distributed Public Governance*, 2002) discovered that in a vast range of countries the 'grey zone' now constitutes over 75 per cent of the public sector in terms of both expenditure and personnel. We can therefore identify a mirror-image development involving the shrinking or hollowing out of the governmental sphere, and the simultaneous growth of the non-governmental sphere. This shift in the nature of governance may help us understand public disengagement from politics. The institutions of modern politics tend often to be led by individuals who are neither elected nor directly accountable to the public. In this context it is not so much that the public 'hate' politics, but they do not understand why so many functions and powers appear to have drifted away from elected politicians. In order to shed light on this issue we need to explore the blame game.

The Blame Game

One of the central arguments of this book is that the public do not 'hate' politics but that they have simply lost touch with it in terms of understanding who makes decisions, through what processes, and why politicians increasingly seem to deny that they have any capacity to influence an increasing range of issues. The curious element of this theme is that politicians and academics also generally find it very hard to understand who does what, how, and why! The notions of 'unbundling' and 'unravelling' may form central tenets of the 'good governance' agenda but the practical implementation of these processes has too often led to a dense, complex, and generally unmapped institutional terrain. Elected politicians are therefore *directly responsible* for less and less at exactly the time when the state (in all its organizational forms) has assumed control for more and more. And yet the term 'depoliticization' also brings with it an attempt to cultivate a rather narrow view of 'the political' within the public's consciousness. My point here is simply that, as we shall see in later sections, an issue becomes no less political in terms of its social impact or importance just because the process through which decisions are made is altered. Politicians also make decisions about what functions to hive off, where to limit their discretion, and when to use emergency intervention powers. The politics of denial therefore masks the continuation of politics by other means, in arenas of power that are less amenable to public scrutiny and control. This, in turn, raises questions about blame-shifting and how to maintain reasonably clear lines of democratic scrutiny while at the same time governing through increasingly fluid networks that offer a fuzzy form of accountability.

'Fuzzy' in the sense that no one politician or public body can be held clearly responsible for a specific act of failure, sin, or omission therefore seems part and parcel of the transition from govern*ment* to gover*nance* (the latter term embracing the role and growth of the grey zone). Indeed, finger-pointing, buck-passing, denial, 'spin' activity, and blame avoidance appear to pervade the governmental sphere and the grey zone in equal measure. The central question, however, is not so much whether blame games exist but *why* and it is in answering this question that we are able to cut back into some of the deeper contradictions of democracy and further explore the issue of public understanding and public expectations. For the media and the public blame games exist because of the 'self-evident truth' that politicians always attempt to hide their corrupt behaviour or failed policies by seeking to shift the blame onto the shoulders of others (e.g. bureaucrats, the previous government, etc.). In some cases this interpretation may be absolutely correct but in the majority of cases the explanation is far less scandalous: modern government and governance is, as has already been emphasized, incredibly complex. If political responsibility appears extraordinarily elusive (and I'm not actually sure it is in this world of freedom of information and electronic communication), the main reasons for this surely take us back to systemic failings rather than individual error.

The systemic failing in this case lies in what Christopher Hood calls 'The Logic of Blameworld' (see *The Blame Game: Spin, Bureacracy and Self-Preservation in Government*, 2010). As Hood shows, governing and public sector management take place within a low-trust/high-blame political environment in which success will rarely be publicly acknowledged but failures will be publicized and amplified by a vast range of actors who have something to gain by adopting a cynical stance. At the same time, the social demands have become more complex, the tools of governing more specialist, and the nature of 'attack politics' ever more aggressive. As a result, politicians are primarily motivated by the desire to avoid blame for unpopular actions and decisions rather than by seeking to claim credit for popular ones. The risk of blame therefore outweighs the risk of success in modern politics and, as a result, depoliticization provides a quite rational self-preservation mechanism for a politician faced by expansive demands but shrinking resources. Delegating power or 'tying one's hands' therefore provides a way of offsetting the simple fact that politicians cannot satisfy the frequently contradictory demands they are faced with (they cannot make 'all sad hearts glad').

Avoiding blame rather than seeking reward appears a rather pessimistic approach to governing and yet what I am attempting to explain is that it is *the system of democratic politics* with its internal tensions and hidden contradictions which conspires to create a shallow 'blame world' with all the finger-pointing, buck-passing, denial, and blame games that frequently convince the public that the politics is failing and politicians are not to be trusted. Democratic politics is messy, invidious, frustrating, and cannot deliver simple solutions to complex problems. So if we want politicians to provide straight answers and make decisions, we need to spend more time rethinking democratic accountability. We need to challenge not simply the Logic of Blameworld, which is itself a symptom of a deeper condition rather than a cause, but a more basic logic that has undermined democratic politics for too long: the Logic of Discipline, which is the theme of the next section.

The Logic of Discipline

Jacques Rancière may well have been correct when he wrote in *On the Shores of Politics* (1995) that 'depoliticization is the oldest task of politics' but that does not mean that we have to accept that what has shaped the recent past must shape the future. In order to shape the future through a more optimistic and balanced account of politics, we need to understand and critique the Logic of Discipline, a term first coined by the political scientist Alastair Roberts in his book of the same name (2010). This is a political philosophy premised on a deep scepticism about the capacity of democratic processes to make sensible policy choices. The Logic of Discipline sought to impose constraints on politicians, public servants, and the public, often by shifting power to technocrat-guardians who were shielded from political influence. As such, it placed great faith in the power of legal changes (new laws, treaties, contracts, rules, etc.) and institutional innovations (delegation, privatization, etc.) to produce significant alterations in the performance of governmental systems. Opponents of discipline, however, emphasized the damage to democratic values that followed from the empowerment of new groups of technocrat-guardians.

The Logic of Discipline can be viewed as a reaction against the inflationary pressures that democratic politics promotes. If politicians cannot discipline public demand, due to their need to curry public support, so the argument goes, then the sphere of democratic politics must be restricted and functions placed in the hands of those with the capacity to make unpopular decisions. This logic is in a sense anti-political in nature as it revolves around the emptying of political debate and its replacement with technocratic administration. The use of independent 'fringe' or 'hybrid' bodies, in an attempt to defuse particularly salient issues or discipline certain interest groups, is not in itself a new development. However, in recent decades the pace and scale of this approach to governing has increased markedly and underpinned debates concerning the 'hollowing-out of the state' towards the end of the twentieth century. More importantly for the argument of this book, the Logic of Discipline can be understood as the economic equivalent of the 'bad faith model of politics' and in this regard its assumptions and prescriptions for change were relatively straightforward: the insertion of political competition into public governance and decision-making will only produce policies that are short-sighted, unstable, or designed to satisfy the selfish concerns of powerful voting blocs, well-organized special interests, or the bureaucracy itself. The only cure, therefore, for the malady of politicization and political interference in public affairs is reducing the capacity and role of politicians, or at the very least imposing tight constraints on discretion. Governmental processes must therefore, according to this view, promote the virtues of far-sightedness, consistency, and public-spiritedness by placing significant constraints and restrictions on the capacity of politicians so that they cannot make self-interested decisions. Depoliticization can therefore occur through a number or combination of measures that include,

Institutional depoliticization involving the wholesale transfer of responsibility for decision-making to an arm's-length organisation;

Procedural depoliticization that rests on the introduction of new rules, laws, or contracts that limit the discretion of politicians or prescribe certain policy options completely; or

Ideological depoliticization that entails the promotion of a 'there is no alternative' narrative concerning certain issues and therefore denies the existence of political options.

Let me provide just one example that brings each of these forms of depoliticization together in just one policy sector. The global trend towards the creation of independent central banks provides an important example of institutional depoliticization and the Logic of Discipline. Prior to independence many national central banks were under the direct control of finance ministers who were members of the government and accountable to the popularly elected legislature. Under these arrangements it was argued that central banks frequently faced political pressure to stimulate short-term economic activity at certain points in the electoral cycle despite the long-term inflationary effects.

Politicians were viewed as being unable to make credible commitments and, as a result, the virtues of far-sightedness and stability were ignored. The Logic of Discipline therefore suggested that strengthening governance could only be achieved by weakening politicians. The creation of 'independent' banks was therefore intended to allow bankers and economists to make sensible but politically inexpedient decisions about monetary policy and the dysfunctions of democracy were to some extent remedied through what could be described as the outsourcing of politics.

In his book *The Quiet Revolution* (2004) Alan Blinder, himself a former Vice Chairman of the US Federal Reserve System, highlights the little-known but profound revolution in the politics of central banking that has occurred. In *The Logic of Discipline* (2010) Alastair Roberts developed and expanded this analysis to include tax collection, regulatory bodies, the changing role of courts, and the governance of long-term infrastructure projects. My own argument is that it is possible to trace the gradual penetration of this politics of *denial* into an increasing range of policy areas including the accessibility of medicines, agricultural subsidies, science and technology, housing aid, regional development, overseas aid policy, and the availability of social benefits. The authority of expertise, rather than any other form of political reasoning or ethics, has become the dominant language of political justification and, as a result, debates are carefully framed, frequently with spurious references to the inevitability of globalization, to suggest 'there is no alternative', and policy choices are presented as little more than neutral technical exercises. Is it any wonder that the public tune in but then switch off when all they see is little choice, less democracy, and the promotion of an at*myth*sphere in which the capacity of politics to change is denied?

As we have seen in this section, the pervasive Logic of Discipline has fuelled a broad shift towards the depoliticization of democracy. This process has rested on a set of assumptions that were ingrained with a deep scepticism about the merits of conventional democratic governance, the behaviour of politicians, and the capacity of societies to discipline themselves. The result has been a narrowing or infolding of democratic politics that has offered the public little in terms of rebuilding public confidence or trust in politicians or political processes. Challenging the Logic of Discipline, particularly in the light of recent global events, therefore provides a way of reanimating democratic politics and posing fresh questions about perennial themes and issues. It is to this critique of the Logic of Discipline and towards a more vibrant account of the future of democratic politics that I now turn.

Democratic Challenges, Democratic Choices

This book is rooted in an optimistic account of politics. It rejects the 'bad faith model of politics' and instead highlights the capacity of democratic regimes to respond to internal tensions and external challenges. My faith in politics is not blind; it is not a perfect system of rule because there is no perfect system; but history reveals a rich history of democratic adaptation and success. A new 'politics of optimism' will only emerge, however, not only when we recognize that democratic choices exist and that those who suggested 'there is no alternative' were wrong but also when we all accept that *rights* bring with them social *responsibilities* that cannot be denied. So let me buck the trend by arguing in favour of politicization and the expansion of the democratic sphere. If there has been a 'quiet revolution' that has narrowed the parameters of conventional democratic politics, I want to provoke a very loud debate about the need to revitalize politics by recruiting politicians with the nerve and confidence to make tough decisions. And yet by putting the Logic of Blameworld and the Logic of Discipline at the core of this chapter I have attempted to illustrate how *blame fuels denial*. The Logic of Blameworld and the Logic of Discipline can therefore be viewed as mirror-image developments: the former seeks to blame politicians for more and more while the latter seeks to limit the sphere for which politicians can be held directly and personally responsible. In this section I want to push this argument a little further and consider its broader implications by locating it within the contours of the wider debate concerning the tension between democracy and populism.

When all is said and done depoliticization represents the relocation or reconfiguration of political power. Indeed there are clear correlations between the three forms of denial outlined above (*institutional, procedural,* and *ideological*) and Stephen Lukes's classic book *Power: A Radical View* (1974), in which he identifies three main forms of political power. Lukes's 'decision-making' power is clearly related to what I have termed 'institutional depoliticization' as decision-making capacities are transferred to 'independent' public bodies. His 'non-decision making' power is clearly related to procedural, rule-based depoliticization in that politicians agree to abide by set frameworks and therefore forgo or significantly diminish their discretion. Finally, Lukes's 'radical view', which involves power being retained and controlled through processes of thought control, has a clear resemblance to what I have described as ideological depoliticization. With the link between depoliticization and power in mind, let me now begin to challenge the Logic of Discipline in order to reveal the existence of alternatives.

First and foremost, the Logic of Discipline is undoubtedly based upon what Roberts correctly describes as 'naive institutionalism', naive in the sense that the trend towards depoliticized modes of governance simply assumed that, although politicians could not be trusted to act in the public interest, in some strange way, everyone else could be so trusted. The independent experts to whom decision-making powers were transferred were therefore simply assumed to be able not only to identify what the 'public interest' was but also to identify how it could be best protected. Market-based assumptions about the self-interested basis of human nature were applied to politicians but apparently not to a whole host of other professional groups, who for some reason could be trusted to govern in the public's interest. The global financial crisis suggests that a great deal of this trust was misplaced. More broadly, the Logic of Discipline contained a naive faith in the capacity of scientists, technicians, ethicists, and other experts to find simple and relatively uncontroversial answers to questions that are in fact both complex, moral, and inherently political in nature. Political and ultimately moral dilemmas cannot be reduced to technical questions for which an 'objective' rational answer can be found. In *Nature's Experts* (2004) Stephen Bocking recognizes this simple issue and shows that scholars of science, just like practitioners of politics, are likely to be strong on diagnosis, but less strong on prescription. He also reveals how scientists tend to locate their advice within pre-existing political discussions and as such inevitably become politicized. In this regard, Bocking quotes the American sociologist of science Dorothy Nelkin: 'As scientists debate the various sides of politicized issues, their involvement undermines assumptions that have given experts their power as the neutral arbiter of truth.' By participating in political debates as advocates of one position or another scientists automatically reduce their claims to authority and science becomes simply 'politics by other means'. Depoliticization or what we might call the denial of politics *is* 'politics by other means'.

This is a point that brings us back full circle to a focus on the boundaries of democratic politics, the relationship between *depoliticized* and *politicized* modes of governing and the fact that democracy is a 'double-barbed' concept. By this I mean it brings with it certain values that may not at first glance appear compatible. These are the promise of freedom (to own, to speak, to congregate, to travel, to vote, to choose) alongside the need for restraint (in terms of sometimes being willing to set aside individual demands for the greater collective good). The politics of *denial* is therefore framed by the wider tension between democracy and populism and questions concerning whether democracies can discipline themselves. The Logic of Discipline emerged as a direct result of an awareness of the economic contradictions of democracy that were discussed in Chapter 2. Democratic competition encouraged politicians to constantly promise 'more for less' and rewarded those who pandered to voters rather than those who sought to dampen public expectations. The overall effect was a bias in favour of expansion that was reflected in the upward trend of expenditure and debt, even greater demands, and the existence of an ever more obvious rhetoric–reality gap that was undermining public confidence in politics and trust in politicians. Depoliticization and the Logic of Discipline therefore provided a mechanism through which unpopular decisions could be taken: the deliberate suppression of political participation rights on the basis that society will be better off in the long run.

Looking back on the last three decades or so it is odd that the 'triumph' of liberal democracy was accompanied by such extreme scepticism about the trustworthiness and motivations of politicians. As a result, democratic governance has been increasingly marked by contradictions that take us right back to John Lukac's work on democracy, populism, fear, and hatred (discussed above). For Lukac the defining challenge for modern governance was how to manage the virulent forms of populism that had been unleashed but could not be easily accommodated within the established institutions of liberal democratic government. The rush of populism posed new and urgent questions about society's capacity to make much-needed but unpopular decisions about the protection or distribution of scarce resources. The Logic of Discipline provided an answer to these questions but the global financial crisis that erupted in late 2007, and continues to send after-shocks around the world, destroyed the notion that depoliticization is feasible; that is, that some issues or topics can be made non-political. It appeared that poorly regulated markets were prone to exactly the same vices (short-termism, self-interest, greed, etc.) as unconstrained democratic states.

The financial crisis exposed the shallowness of anti-political arguments as the state (and therefore politics and politicians) suddenly assumed centre stage. The market-led theories that had defined the reform agenda for at least three decades suddenly crumbled in the face of massive injections of public money to stabilize the market, and politicians from across the political spectrum suggested a need to *politicize* certain functions as part of a more interventionist and statist position. By August 2009 the *Financial Times* confidently stated that 'The era of economic theocracy, in which unelected experts ran the global economy, is over'. My aim in highlighting this fact is not to reopen the 'small state versus big state' debate but simply to emphasize that the financial crisis revealed why politics matters. It supported Crick's view of politics as a counterweight to the market and his faith in the value of collective action.

The politics of denial was not, however, mortally wounded by the global financial crisis. Depoliticization is a growing and global phenomenon. The European Union, for example, represents the crucible of technocratic depoliticized governance and its institutions sit at the centre of a sprawling web of 'independent' agencies whose accountability is both distant and diffuse. Moreover, a number of social challenges, not least the challenge posed by climate change, are combining to generate renewed interest in the politics of denial and the supposed benefits of depoliticizing democracy. This renewed faith in the Logic of Discipline, and the lack of faith in the idea of democracy that it reflects, brings this chapter back to where it started and to a focus on confidence and self-belief. I want to understand why, when democratic politics has delivered so much, so many people appear so scared, so apologetic, so feeble, and almost crippled by fear, so imbued with doubt and apparently lacking in mission. I want to argue that crises bring with them opportunities; that the future lies in our own hands and that if we face the challenges that lie ahead with our heads slung low and our self-belief in tatters then we will end up on the losing side while those who dare to step out of the shadows with an energy derived from a new politics of optimism will prosper. In order to do this, however, we need to calm the storm that currently surrounds politics and it is for exactly this reason that the next chapter presents a defence of politics against possibly the most overused word in the political lexicon—*crisis.*

5

A DEFENCE OF POLITICS AGAINST CRISES

The politics of fear appears to dominate public life in Western societies. We have become very good at scaring one another and appearing scared...being scared has become a culturally sanctioned affectation that pervades all aspects of life.

Frank Furedi, *Politics of Fear* (2005)

The most gruesome amongst the added fears is the fear of being incapable of averting or escaping the condition of being afraid.

Zygmunt Bauman, *Liquid Fear* (2006)

Democracy, like communism, is a nice idea, and it is a pity that neither works. If there was a way of saving democracy then we should save it, but it is unlikely that there is any such way because the ordinary person or 'mass man' is not made of the right heroic stuff necessary to meet the challenge of our age...it is too late to rely upon an evolution of true democracy through bottom-up reform. The performance of humanity to date suggests that we will move towards crisis, followed by disorder and authoritarian rule.

Shearman and Smith, *Climate Change Challenge and the Failure of Democracy* (2008)

Our civilization could self-destruct—no doubt about it—and with awesome consequences, given its global reach. Doomsday is no longer a religious concept, a day of spiritual reckoning, but a possibility imminent in our society and economy. If unchecked, climate change alone could produce enormous human suffering. So could the drying up of the energy resources upon which so many of our capacities are built. There remains the possibility of large-scale conflicts, perhaps involving weapons of mass destruction. [And yet] For most of us there is a gulf between the familiar preoccupations of everyday life and an abstract, even apocalyptic, future of climate chaos.

Anthony Giddens, *The Politics of Climate Change* (2009)

These are the times that try men's souls. By focusing this chapter on crises and catastrophes, meltdowns and metaphors, fears and fantasy, dread and disaster, risk and resilience, and (ultimately) hope and optimism, I want to make the case *for* democratic politics. We live in a world that seems to stumble from one day to another managing successive crises; in a world in which everything seems strangely transient, precarious and risky; in a world where we focus not on enjoying life or striving for something 'good' but rather on avoiding danger and preventing 'the worst'. It is as if we have become cowed and scared of living and this is reflected in regular moral panics and bouts of hysteria as risks become over-inflated, misconstrued, and most of all deliberately exaggerated by those who have something to gain from the politics of fear. In reality the world has never been a safer place. Most humans have never been so secure and it is democratic politics that has delivered these achievements. That is not to say that very real and far-reaching threats do not exist or that democracy is perfect but it is to highlight a modern social paradox that increasingly witnesses major social reactions to 'crises' that are in fact either non-existent, statistically insignificant, or simply part of the ebb and flow of day-to-day politics. What makes this paradox even more interesting is the manner in which at the very same time we largely ignore some of the most pressing threats to human life and social existence, threats that raise questions about the limits and nature of democratic politics that cannot be ignored indefinitely.

The starting point for this chapter is therefore that everything frequently appears upside down and inside out and this reflects the fact that *fear sells*. Our sense of dread, fear, and anxiety, which manifests itself most clearly in a belief that politics is failing, is driven not by logic or rationality but by phantom fears that are created by political actors (many of them largely invisible to the public) in order to make money, win votes, sell products, secure research funding, highlight issues, distract attention, or gain public support. Put slightly differently, there is a political economy of fear that allows ambient insecurities concerning the changing nature of society and the availability of more (but not necessarily accurate) information to be manipulated for self-serving means. Replacing the current 'politics of pessimism' with a more buoyant 'politics of optimism' will only occur when we challenge those who benefit from creating a climate of fear, instability, and crisis. This is a conclusion that takes us back to the very heart of Crick's original *Defence* and especially to his *cri de coeur* that 'Man cannot live by fear alone or he will fear to live'. To live, to enjoy, to engage, to be proud of our past achievements, and to have hope and confidence in our collective capacity to change the future are the only ways of resolving the pressing challenges that will undoubtedly shape the twenty-first century.

My argument is that, distilled down to its very simplest form, the *crisis of politics* (by which I mean the erosion of public support for politics and politicians) reflects the *politics of crisis* (the use of crisis-inflation strategies in order to scare the public into behaving in a specific way). As part of this argument I want to suggest that we have lost our capacity to discriminate between social pathology or breakdown, on the one side, and social normality and social order on the other. Furthermore, what has changed in the last fifty years is not so much the existence of various forms of risk but the specific *nature* of those risks and the fatalistic *spirit* in which those 'new' risks are approached. Moreover, although the climate change challenge adds a rather stark dimension to debates about the 'life and death' of politics, we must reject those who would argue in favour of the 'authoritarian alternative'. In order to develop these points this chapter is structured around four simple questions:

1. If we are safer than we have ever been, why do we still feel so fearful and precarious?

2. How can we understand and distinguish between certain types of risk?

3. If climate change represents the most pressing threat to humanity why has the political response been so weak?

4. How do the answers to these questions help us understand the 'crisis of politics' and through this develop a more buoyant and optimistic account of democratic politics?

In order to engage with these questions I will focus on four main themes: the notion of liquidity (explained in the next few pages); the changing nature of risk; climate change and the 'authoritarian alternative'; and the theme of collective confidence. These issues, as we shall see, conspire to produce a form of 'disaster capitalism'—a phrase borrowed from Naomi Klein's influential *The Shock Doctrine* (2007)—in which threats, disasters, catastrophes, and crises are at one and the same time everywhere and nowhere. We are kept in a constant sense of anxiety and panic by the actions of those who have something to benefit from the politics of fear. If we could only turn down the shrill rhetoric of crisis and disaster that dominates social discourse and for a moment reflect on everything we have and everything we have achieved, maybe we could see that the fabric of politics is not quite as threadbare as many think.

Let me give you a brief example to demonstrate this point. If the financial crisis that began in the sub-prime market of American housing represented the near meltdown of the banking system then the Fukushima disaster in March 2011 provides an example of a quite different near meltdown. A forty-year old nuclear reactor that was designed to withstand at most a 6-metre tsunami was hit by one of almost three times that height. The result was a disaster but not a crisis. The fact that the nuclear plant was not completely destroyed could be interpreted as a major success that reflects not only modern standards of technological resilience but also the value of close state-based regulation. There are around five hundred nuclear power stations in the world but only three recorded major disasters in history (Three Mile Island, Chernobyl, and now Fukushima). My intention in highlighting this fact is not to advocate nuclear energy but simply to put the issue in some kind of perspective, especially in light of the decision of several countries to close all their nuclear power plants.

Defending politics 'against crises' is like attempting to unravel an incredibly large and tight knot, a Gordian knot that is too tangled and twisted to be neatly untied due to many complex issues that have become interwoven and therefore difficult to extract with any clarity. These include scientific debates concerning the measurement of risk, sociological debates concerning the social amplification of risk, economic debates concerning financial flows and risk, debates concerning evolutionary psychology and 'fight, freeze or flight' responses, governance debates concerning risk-regulation regimes, and democratic debates concerning the capacity of politicians to take unpopular decisions. If the knot is too twisted and tangled it must be cut and my cutting tools are crude and simple. The first is the concept of *crisis inflation* which focuses attention on the manipulation of public fears and anxieties in order to open new markets, sell more papers, or pressure politicians into passing laws that may benefit a section of society only at the expense of the majority. The second tool is the concept of

crisis denial that draws attention to the manner in which public concern and therefore political responses tend to focus on what might be
termed secondary matters or false fears instead of focusing upon the
primary crises that threaten human survival. The concepts of *crisis
inflation* and *crisis denial* are clearly to some degree interrelated as the
politics of fear (and indeed the political economy of fear) may lead to
the amplification of public concerns about secondary issues, which
then diverts attention from more important and more difficult primary risks.

This simple distinction between *inflation* and *denial* provides us with
the means of beginning to unravel the various debates and schisms that
litter the existing research and literature on the politics of fear and the
changing nature of risk. Take, for example, the apparent conflict
between a body of largely sociological and psychological writing that
suggests the world is far less dangerous and threatening than most people believe and compare it with the significant body of more scientific
scholarship that appears to argue the complete opposite. The former
more buoyant body of work would include Christopher Booker and
Richard North's *Scared to Death* (2007), Simon Briscoe and Hugh
Aldersey-Williams's *Panicology* (2008), Dan Gardner's *Risk* (2008), and
Philip Alcabes's *Dread* (2009), which, in each their own ways, try to
understand why social anxieties and sporadic episodes of mass hysteria
appear more common when the world is generally far safer and more
stable than at any time in history. The latter more gloomy body of
work would include Franz Broswimmer's *Ecocide* (2002), Jared Diamond's *Collapse* (2004), Ronald Wright's *A Short History of Progress*
(2004), James Lovelock's *The Revenge of Gaia* (2006), James Hansen's
Storms of my Grandchildren (2009), Eugene Linden's *Winds of Change*
(2007), and most famously Al Gore's *An Inconvenient Truth* (2006).
Although these bodies of work may at first glance appear incompatible, they are actually focused on two ends of the same argument. The
former body of work focuses on *crisis inflation* and why a heightened
sense of vulnerability surrounds a host of issues that statistically offer
very low risks (avian flu, stranger danger, predatory paedophiles, feral
hoodies, asteroid hits, economy-flight syndrome, bio-terrorism, etc.),
whereas the latter body of work focuses attention on *crisis denial* and
the absence of any major public concern or political response concerning a host of issues that pose far more far-reaching threats (climate
change, over-population, resource depletion, etc.).

This focus on *crisis inflation* and *crisis denial* reintroduces the issue of public expectations, and particularly the existence of an 'expectations gap'. The 'gap', as Chapter 2 explained, arises from a disparity between what the public demands and what politics can supply. The dynamics of political competition, so the argument suggests, encourages politicians to over-promise but then under-supply, which gradually undermines public confidence and trust in politics. Taking this language of supply and demand into the sphere of public anxiety and risk management allows us to view *crisis inflation* as the process through which the upper bar increasingly rises, due to the definition of an increasing range of issues as 'crises' that signify systemic failure and collapse and therefore demand immediate and far-reaching action. The *politics of crisis* therefore injects its own brand of inflationary pressure on politics by increasing the range of issues for which politicians are expected to assume responsibility. In order to try to respond to the public's concerns and demands, politicians attempt to lift the bottom bar (i.e. supply) through the implementation of increasingly elaborate risk-regulation regimes.

Closing the gap from above (i.e. by reducing demand) is almost impossible as the nature of contemporary politics rarely provides political space for a considered or mature debate concerning the statistical likelihood of risks but instead places great pressure on politicians to respond rapidly to specific events, public concerns, or media scare stories. Developments in global communication and information technology further increase these pressures as the internet fails to distinguish between credible experts and scaremongers. Mobile phones allow grainy images of riots, shark attacks, or natural disasters to be transmitted around the globe in seconds and yet the aggressive, adversarial, and immediate nature of 'attack politics' provides little space for reflection before the incumbent politician is derided as dithering and incapable of taking decisive action. In many cases, however, the specific nature of the problem has been exaggerated by the process of crisis inflation to the point that the political response itself risks inflaming rather than quelling social concerns.

The language of *supply* and *demand* and a focus on the politics and management of public expectations brings us back to the simple issue of limits and responsibilities. Politics cannot make life risk-free; it cannot prevent natural disasters; it cannot 'make every sad heart glad', but the history of democracy is clearly tied to the eradication and control of certain risks. The risk of poverty, disease, slavery, mass rapes, torture, and infant mortality—risks that still remain very real in large parts of the world—have to a great extent been held in check by the emergence of modern societies with the concepts of democracy and equality at their core. The realm of fate has to some degree been narrowed through collective social endeavour. In the fifty years since Crick wrote *In Defence of Politics* there has been a 17 per cent increase in life expectancy worldwide and this increase has been most spectacular in the poorer nations of Asia where it has reached 20 per cent. 'The world's a much better place today than it was in 1990, or even in 1970', the United Nations *Human Development Report* for 2010 concludes, 'over the past 20 years many people around the world have experienced dramatic improvements in key aspects of their lives . . . they are healthier, more educated, wealthier and have more power to appoint and hold their leaders accountable than ever before'. This report also highlights a positive relationship between democratic politics and human development and it is a disappointment that some commentators appear so reluctant to acknowledge good news. Democratic politics is by no means perfect but let us not deny its benefits and achievements. There is, however, a certain irony to the manner in which population growth, an ageing population, and obesity have so rapidly evolved as social problems. This is a point that encourages us to explore the emergence of contemporary social anxieties.

Liquid Fear

Zygmunt Bauman is not only someone who has written widely on the existence of drivers of social anxiety in a changing world but he is also someone whose personal history makes him particularly well placed to contribute to a defence of democratic politics. Bauman was born into a poor Jewish family in Poland in 1925. When he was 14 his family fled the Nazi occupation of Poland and went to live in the Soviet Union during Stalin's regime. The outbreak of the Second World War saw him join the exiled Polish Army and although wounded he was able to participate in the Red Army's liberation of Berlin in May 1945. In 1948, at the Warsaw Academy of Social Sciences, Bauman met his wife and lifelong companion, Janina, who as an inhabitant of the Warsaw ghetto had narrowly avoided deportation to the Nazi death camps by spending several years living in hiding. During the

1950s and 1960s Bauman established his academic career and remained a loyal, but increasingly critical, member of the Communist Party. In March 1968, however, he was forced to flee Poland for the second time after being accused by the Communist Party of corrupting the Polish youth by allowing students to publish critical letters. First he took his wife and children to Israel, via a refugee camp in Austria, and then on to Australia and Canada before finally arriving in England and a post at the University of Leeds.

Bauman has therefore been a victim of totalitarianism, in the form of both Nazism and later Communist anti-Semitism, which Crick sought to warn against. As Bauman admitted in his inaugural lecture in 1972, 'In the professional life of a sociologist his most intimate, private biography is inextricably entangled with the biography of his discipline; one thing the sociologist cannot transcend in his quest for objectivity is his own, intimate and subjective encounter-with-the-world'. Bauman's own 'encounter-with-the-world' was shaped by the politics of fear and exclusion and with a concern for those similarly marginalized, hurt, or excluded. His writing has therefore attempted to understand the world anew, particularly in relation to the effect of social transformation on individual lives and the emergence of new forms of insecurity, uncertainty, and fear. For Bauman we live in a world that lives from one day to another, managing successive crises and struggling to brace itself for new ones but never quite knowing where it is going or why. At the heart of Bauman's work lies a plea for a belief in collective endeavour. In his *In Search of Politics* (1999) Bauman returns to Sigmund Freud's argument in *Civilization and its Discontents* (1930) that 'civilization' (Western modern civilization) was a trade-off in which one cherished value (individual freedom) is exchanged for another (a degree of security). This trade-off has been *reversed*, Bauman argues, as security, delivered through collective engagement and support, has been sacrificed in order to maximize individual liberty and freedom within a market environment. The erosion of public support for politics was a symptom of this altered relationship. Bauman's 'search for politics' can therefore be interpreted as a defence of politics as he seeks to expose the frailties of mass consumerism ('the accumulation of junk and more junk') and explain the existence of ambient insecurities ('gnawing existential mistrust') which leads him to focus on the issue of liquidity in relation to both broad social trends but also more specifically in relation to social fears and the creation of what I term 'false fears'.

In *Liquid Modernity* (2000) Bauman sought to connect the existence of widespread social anxieties in many advanced liberal democracies with the concurrent pattern of human achievements and the eradication of many of the 'old' risks. His explanation rests on the notion of a transition from 'solid' to 'liquid' modernity, which has created a new and unprecedented setting for individual life pursuits, confronting individuals with a series of challenges and issues never before encountered. Social forms and institutions that once provided individuals with a sense of anchorage or 'solidity', such as tight family units, integrated communities, and stable careers, have altered in a way that forces individuals to splice together a series of short-term projects or transient relationships in a way that allows them to inject meaning and value into their lives. Such fragmented and increasingly mobile lives require individuals to be flexible, adaptable, and willing to abandon commitments and loyalties when new opportunities arise. The liquidity or fluidity of modern life therefore demands that individuals live their lives under conditions of endemic uncertainty, flux, and conflict and our sense of certainty and our grasp of change have become weaker so we have become more susceptible to scaremongering, moral panics, fear-driven marketing, and crisis inflation. Bauman returned to these themes in *Liquid Fear* (2006) in order to argue that contemporary fears arose not simply due to a prevailing sense of fatality but more due to a sense that the dangers besetting us are to some degree elusive, vague, ethereal, or quite simply different.

Bauman's arguments resonate with two strands of research and writing that help us to contextualize both the political implications of liquidity and its very practical implications. The link between liquidity, mobility, collective sentiment, and political attitudes is possibly best represented in Robert Putnam's influential book *Bowling Alone* (2000). This described the decline in social capital amongst the American public and explained this with reference to a variety of factors including changing employment patterns and the individualization of leisure time (personal computers, television, gaming, etc.). Putnam's core thesis echoes that of Crick by suggesting that a strong and vibrant democracy depends upon the existence of an educated and engaged citizenry. Whereas Putnam is concerned with the bigger picture and utilizes mass surveys and data banks, a second strand of literature adopts a more applied approach that emphasizes the social and psychological effects of short-term working. Ivor Southwood's *Non-Stop Inertia* (2011) provides a very personal account of the psychological and social impacts of what he terms the 'normalisation of insecurity' across a range of work sectors that has fostered not only a 'sink or swim' individualism but also a constant sense of insecurity, a perpetual sense of crisis, and the endless circulation of anxieties. An overwhelming sense of precariousness created by the monotonous unpredictability of intermittent work and the unstitching of the social fabric of modern societies also forms the focus of Guy Standing's *The Precariate* (2011). Taken together, the work of Southwood and Standing help us trace the changing emotional landscape in general, and the position of the 'unanchored worker' in particular, in a way that chimes directly with Bauman's more theoretical focus on liquidity. The concept of 'liquid fear' therefore provides a first step in terms of helping us understand the *politics of crisis* because it points to the existence of social vulnerabilities that can be exploited. It also points to the need to explore the manner in which the risks that confront modern societies have altered in recent decades. Put simply, Bauman's focus on liquidity forces us to engage with the concept of the risk society.

World at Risk

The link between Ulrich Beck and Zygmunt Bauman takes the form of their shared focus on social order and social change. Both scholars examine the manner in which traditional institutions and structures have been replaced to some degree by a primary focus on individualism, consumerism, and free markets but whereas Bauman's contribution to these debates focuses on liquidity, Beck's concerns the emergence of a 'risk society' in which 'hazards and insecurities induced and introduced by modernisation itself' have undermined public faith in politics and politicians. At the heart of Beck's 'risk society' is therefore a distinction between 'old' and 'new' risks. 'Old' (or 'natural') risks relate to the traditional risks faced by developing societies and include such elements as poverty, dangerous animals, disease, and natural disasters. These risks are therefore relatively tangible, observable, geographically specific, and offer a degree of actuarial certainty in the sense that they can be assessed and insured against. The 'new' or manufactured risks, by contrast, are the product of human activity and represent the unintended consequences of social and scientific progress. These 'new' risks (embryology, nanotechnology, artificial intelligence, computer

viruses, pollution, over-population, resource depletion, nuclear incidents, bio-terrorism, etc.) are complex, unpredictable, mobile, and frequently difficult to observe. Despite this Beck remains an optimist. As
'new' risks are generally the product of human activity and ingenuity
it is, Beck argues, possible for societies to assess the levels of risk and
engage in a process of 'reflexive modernization', in which the concepts of sustainability and the precautionary principle are deployed in
order to decrease or manage levels of risk.

The distinction between 'new' and 'old' risks provides a very simply
way of beginning to understand the politics of fear, and particularly
the link between the *politics of crisis* and the *crisis of politics*. The distinction paints a deeper and richer picture of the changing nature of politics and how this impacts upon both the public and politicians in terms
of managing uncertainty and competing demands. In order to use this
distinction as a form of stepping-stone to reflect *back* on the existence
of ambient insecurities and *forward* to the challenges of replacing pessimism with optimism, the rest of this section focuses on the following
themes: optimism; what we might term 'visibility'; rationality; certainty; and fear, because of the manner in which they contribute to a
broader defence of politics against crisis.

One of the main symptoms of clinical depression is the inability to
remember any happy times or personal achievements and as a result
even the most successful person can come to believe that their life has
been racked by failure and disappointment and that this situation will
never change. This pattern of undoubted achievements wrapped in a
sense of failure appears strangely familiar to those who study politics.
In a 'world at risk', to use the title of Beck's 2009 book, in which scare
stories and narratives of crises dominate every media outlet, it can
become easy to lose a sense of perspective and history. Indeed the history of collective social endeavour realized through democratic politics has made life far less risky than it was even half a century ago but
we forget our achievements and are rarely encouraged to reflect upon
them.

During the twentieth century, for example, it is estimated that smallpox killed between three and five hundred million people. In the early
1950s an estimated fifty million cases of smallpox occurred in the world
each year and as recently as 1967, when the World Health Organization launched an intensified plan to eradicate smallpox, the 'ancient
scourge' still threatened 60 per cent of the world's population, killed

every fourth victim, scarred or blinded most survivors, and eluded any form of treatment. Less than a decade and a half later the World Health Organization was able to announce the official eradication of the disease. The reason for highlighting this fact is not to deny the existence of other global diseases, like Hepatitis or HIV, but simply to underline the point that, despite the economic crisis, life does continue to get better for most of the world. As Gardner concludes in his book *Risk*, after reviewing a range of fears that seem to underpin modern social anxieties: 'there's never been a better time to be alive'. The trouble with being human these days does not appear to have its roots in the existence of traditional threats or in the fact that we have failed so badly in the past but in a lack of collective confidence combined with the rather ethereal nature of modern risks. Our lack of *optimism* therefore appears linked to the issue of *visibility*.

The work of Bauman and Beck each in its own way highlights the manner in which the roots of contemporary fears and insecurities lie in very different issues to the concerns that threatened societies in the past. The 'new' risks each share a certain elusiveness that serves to create further anxiety. In a sense life was much easier when the threats we faced were nature-based, visible, and obvious; they had teeth or erupted on our bodies in the form of raging sores and boils. 'New' risks generally lack that sense of tangibility and immediacy that can be harnessed to produce a significant collective response. They also tend to have a mobile character that frequently creates distinct sets of winners and losers in terms of the costs and benefits of development. This issue of visibility takes us to a central element of the *politics of crisis*: the public cannot grasp the significance of certain 'new' risks (or they find them simply easier to ignore) because they are too abstract and not dramatic enough in terms of affecting directly *their* day-to-day lives. The danger of this situation, however, is that by the time the symptoms of the problem become readily apparent it may actually be too late to address the central causes. This, in turn, forces us to reflect more closely on the nature of collective action, and particularly the distribution of profit and pain, by shifting our lens to the topic of *rationality*.

The opaque link between cause and effect that is a feature of many 'new' risks creates basic collective action problems. These are problems concerning the provision or maintenance of public goods that demand the collaboration of several people, groups, tribes, societies, or nations. Take, for example, Garret Hardin's well-known example of a piece of common land on which herders can graze their animals. The land is a finite resource that can be destroyed through over-grazing but the allocation of costs and benefits is unequal. The herder who continues to add additional animals to his herd receives all the proceeds for each additional animal whereas the costs of this behaviour are borne by all those who have a right to use the pasture. The 'tragedy of the commons' for Hardin is therefore the likelihood of over-exploitation by 'free riders' who refuse to put the common good before their own interests. The topic of population growth provides a more contemporary twist to Hardin's argument: when a couple decide to have a large family, the negative impact of that decision in environmental terms is. not immediately obvious and the resource costs of that decision will arguably be borne by society as a whole rather than by the couple. The global financial crisis that began in late 2007 provides another example of how, as Joseph Stiglitz has argued, a system that socializes losses but privatizes gains is doomed to mismanage risks. The issues of rationality and choice flow into a closely related feature of the debate concerning 'new' risks: the *quest for certainty*.

The voluminous literature on risk that has emerged in recent years generally begins with a journey back to the Enlightenment project and the questioning of traditional institutions, customs, and morals and a strong belief in rationality and scientific progress. The aim of this project was to create a progressive and civilized society based upon the taming of nature and fate. The 'Age of Reason', however, has to some extent been defeated by the emergence of 'new' risks that defy our capacity to deliver a degree of certainty. The global financial crisis and the Fukushima disaster both provide stark insights into the nature of modern crises. Despite the clear differences between the two events, they are unmistakably linked by a common theme: a failure to master risk. Moreover, as Nassim Nicholas Taleb emphasizes in *The Black Swan* (2010), one of the paradoxes of human development is that crises and disasters generally produce great leaps forward in terms of scientific and technical progress. There is even a saying in the airline industry that engineers learn more from one crash than from a hundred thousand successful flights. And yet one of the challenges of 'new' risks is that they seem to frustrate the Enlightenment's quest for certainty and understanding that to a large extent still structures modern expectations. This is due to the simple fact that they depend upon complex chains of relationships (some technological, economic, personal, political, etc.), along which any severe disruption may lead to unpredictably catastrophic events.

Real life is simply unpredictable and, as the forecasts of the International Panel on Climate Change (IPCC) demonstrate, even 'experts' struggle to predict the likely implications of Beck's 'new' risks with any precision. This is reflected most graphically in relation to the 'war on terror'. As Walter Laqueur's *The New Terrorism* (1999), Mikkel Vedby Rasmussen's *The Risk Society at War* (2006), Peter Neuman's *Old and New Terrorism* (2009), and Christopher Coker's *War in an Age of Risk* (2009) demonstrate through both theory and practice, the 'war on terror' epitomizes Bauman's notion of 'liquid fear'. The literature on 'new terrorism' reveals the simple fact that politicians must frequently make decisions on the basis of imperfect information and contested opinions. There are no simple answers to complex questions; no 'black' or 'white' options but a frequently blurred and messy acknowledgement that a catastrophic risk *may* exist. It is in exactly these situations that politicians must make decisions based upon instinct, feelings, and a form of statecraft that might more accurately be called 'soulcraft'.

Acknowledging that politicians are frequently forced to make major decisions on the basis of 'gut instinct' rather than unequivocal evidence might be taken as sufficient explanation in itself as to why 'new' risks provide such fuel in terms of anxiety and fear. I want to go beyond this, however, to illuminate very clearly how 'new' risks relate to the *politics of crisis* and how (in turn) this explains the *crisis of politics*. In order to do this I want to make a number of very simple arguments:

1. The liquid and mobile quality of 'new' risks, combined with the lack of any expert consensus, makes them more amenable to scaremongering.

2. Certain social groups will exploit these risks for self-interested reasons. Molehills will always be turned into mountains.

3. This creates a constant climate of instability and crisis that reinforces the 'bad faith model of politics', in which politics is constantly viewed as failing, or at the very least is unable to deliver social stability.

4. The social amplification of risk and the politics of fear constantly expand the range of issues and concerns that 'mere politics' is expected to resolve.

5. Life is risky. This is inevitable. Expecting politics to insulate the public from every conceivable accident, disaster, or 'Act of God' is simply ensuring that it is destined to disappoint.

6. If we expected a little less, and gave a little more, we could replace the 'politics of pessimism' with a more balanced and optimistic account of why politics matters.

The uncertainty surrounding 'new' risks allows them to be manipulated to create fear and anxiety in ways that were simply not possible in relation to many 'old' risks that were easier for the public to understand and observe. The *politics of crisis* is therefore frequently based not on the existence of any significant risk but on the creation of a widespread *perception* that a danger exists (there is often a lot of smoke but very little fire). The *politics of crisis* is analogous to a labelling game, in which certain actors will seek to label certain events as crises in order to place and maintain an issue on the political agenda or exert pressure on the government. New enemies are constantly created and quickly develop into social concerns of epidemic proportions— radical Muslims, feral teenagers, computer hackers, rogue scientists, or just simply strangers—as interest groups, business, and opposition parties feed the media salacious speculation, which is then presented to the public as fact.

Philip Jenkins's *Intimate Enemies* (1992) and Jeffrey Victor's *Satanic Panic* (1993), for example, both focus on the moral panic surrounding Satanic ritual abuse in the United States and Britain during the late 1980s. Their research reveals how specific interest groups fed the media sensationalist stories that were then presented to the public as factual information irrespective of the lack of hard evidence underlying the claims. In *Flat Earth News* (2008) Nick Davies similarly exposes the role of the media in creating fear of imminent social collapse over the 'Millennium Bug', which led governments around the world to unnecessarily spend millions of pounds of public money. Philip Alcabes's *Dread* (2009) provides a number of more recent examples of exactly the same phenomena. This includes the manner in which the actions of just one scientist were quickly inflated into an incident of epidemic proportions. In September 2001 letters containing Anthrax spores were sent to several media organizations and the offices of two American senators, killing five people and infecting seventeen others. The incident was rapidly amplified into an epidemic of national proportions and an industry fuelled by fears created a climate of crisis and anxiety that far outweighed the scale of the initial threat. Since then the American government has spent over twenty billion dollars protecting the public from bio-terrorism even though, as Alcabes notes, 'such a problem never existed'.

The *politics of crisis* is therefore inflationary. It feeds on inflated fears about what is unknown, undesirable, or misunderstood. Fear and imagination help drive the crisis narratives as much as and frequently more than fact. Specific incidents will be magnified into *systemic* crises. The fact that a sense of fear, dread, and panic appears to pervade modern life matters, however, because once virtually everything is perceived to be in more or less unending crisis, we lose our capacity to discriminate between the day-to-day ebb and flow of politics and those issues that really demand our collective attention. This creates a constant climate of instability, insecurity, and political failure that reinforces a 'bad faith model of politics', in which politicians and political processes are constantly viewed as failing. It also matters because the definition and articulation of an increasing range of issues as crises increases the expectations gap between what the public demand and what politics can supply. Politics cannot assume responsibility for or control every facet of life. Natural disasters will happen; accidents will occur; things will go wrong—but by criticizing politicians for failing to control an ever-expanding range of issues we create a system that is destined to disappoint. When faced with a moral panic or media feeding frenzy it is very hard for politicians to refuse to intervene in some manner (even if the actual roots of the problem or the best way to respond is far from clear); and yet constantly responding to pseudo-crises or media crises reduces the time and energy that politicians have for focusing on the more mundane issues of delivering public services or adopting a long-term approach to the challenges of governing.

The irony of this situation is that very few 'disaffected democrats', especially amongst the younger generation, who now appear so willing to turn their back on 'mere politics', have any direct experience of a *real* crisis (invasion, drought, famine, war, etc.) due to the security and stability provided to them by democratic politics. It is as if our demands can never be sated.

The *crisis of politics* tells us more about the *politics of crisis* (i.e. the abuse and manipulation of social anxieties by those who have something to gain by promoting the politics of fear) than it does about the actual failure of politics. It is a strange quirk of fate that in our socially, technically, and medically advanced societies a veritable industry of fear has emerged with the intention of maintaining a climate of crisis and anxiety. We act like puppets on a string, forced to dance to the tune of modern-day weather-makers who send a succession of storms and crises to darken our days. Politics and governing has always been a tough business but in recent decades we seem to have lost our sense of confidence and scale, and in its place have created a storm in which wave after wave of crises crash upon the shore of politics. When the storm is raging the capacity of politicians is put to the test to the extent that they frequently fear they will never get to calmer waters and dry land. Even in those rare moments of calm, politicians instinctively know that it can only be a question of time before a new crisis is organized. Governing in a constant state of crisis management is exhausting, distracting, and ultimately only beneficial to those who have an interest in whipping up the storm.

The metaphor of a storm and crashing waves provides an opportunity for me to reverse my argument and through this to ask some rather awkward questions about both the limits of politics and of human nature. These questions ultimately take us back to the very heart of Bernard Crick's arguments in his original *Defence* regarding the frailties of democracy and the dangers of authoritarianism.

Storms of my Grandchildren

There is a storm on the horizon. Its consequences will be far-reaching and some call it the 'crisis of crises' but we appear unable or unwilling to face up to the challenge. We are possibly even too selfish to pay the price we know will have to be paid or too willing to blame our politicians for weaknesses that are actually systemic. Climate change is not a false fear, and even if it was, the challenges of global population growth still demand attention. It is a 'new' risk that poses a collective action problem on a global scale. To deny the existence of this crisis is a dangerous game to play. It is also a game that exposes the inner contradictions of democratic politics and has encouraged some to argue in favour of more authoritarian forms of politics. Indeed, the 'authoritarian alternative' is resurfacing amongst debates concerning the failure of politics and the nature of the climate-change challenge. In fifty years' time, when someone comes to consider writing the centennial edition of Crick's *Defence*, it will be climate change that dictates whether the case for democracy can still be made. There are those who would dispute my position and argue that climate change is a myth. They may turn out to be correct (I really hope they are) but if they're wrong and we have missed the chance to act then a future generation will find it hard to forgive us. My concern is that many eminent scholars have already concluded that democratic politics has failed and that we are too late, while others suggest we have just a decade or two to avert certain catastrophe.

John Leslie's *The End of the World* (1996), Martin Rees's *Our Final Hour* (2003), Jared Diamond's *Collapse* (2004), Elizabeth Kolbert's *Field Notes from a Catastrophe* (2006), and Clive Hamilton's *Requiem for a Species* (2010), to name just a few key books, each in their own way reveal how it will be a supreme test for democratically elected governments to show the leadership, resolve, and sacrifice to address the climate-change challenge. Leaders are generally forged in such times of crisis. Due to the very manner in which crises destabilize established forms of governance, they create opportunities for change, learning, and adaptation. My connection with the work of Beck and Bauman emanates from a shared belief that cultivating a less fearful existence can only be secured by taking responsibility for this challenge. We must have the strength to face up to fundamental questions that cannot be side-stepped about the limits to growth and development, the role of politicians and the state, the frailty of markets, the nature of justice, and the responsibilities of communities and individuals. If we are to make the bold act of hoping possible, we must not turn our backs on democratic politics but once again accept that democracy and freedom are not synonymous and that the public can be a selfish master to serve.

As a political scientist and not an environmental scientist I must tread carefully as I attempt to navigate the political ecology that surrounds the politics of climate change. However, a simple account of the latest report from the International Panel on Climate Change (and a host of other respected international scientific bodies) would read: 'The Earth is warming, the ice is melting, snow cover is rising and thinning, sea temperatures are rising, species are migrating or dying... Without far-reaching and immediate reforms to cut global carbon dioxide emissions the remainder of this century could be dominated by resource wars, the flooding of coastal cities, mass migration, famine in the developing world, more episodes of extreme and violent weather in the developed world.' When I read the scientific reports and their predictions for the future I am reminded of Thomas Hobbes's *Leviathan* (1651) and his description of the 'state of nature': 'solitary, poor, nasty, brutish and short . . . war of all against all'. I do not believe this to be our fate. Although William Ophuls has already written a *Requiem for Modern Politics* (1998) I hold more positive views about human nature and human capacity, but when all is said and done, the core challenge is not climate change but too many people, demanding too much.

The root issue is therefore global population growth and public expectations, not simply climate change. The global population is currently estimated at 7 billion and projections expect this figure to reach 9 billion by the middle of the twenty-first century (some studies suggest that the world's population may not stabilize until it has reached 12 billion). Population growth on this scale is unprecedented in human history. The debate about when food supplies would outstrip demand dates back to Thomas Malthus's prediction at the end of the eighteenth century that population growth would outrun food supply by the middle of the nineteenth century. Paul Ehrlich returned to this argument in *The Population Bomb* (1968) to predict famine in the 1970s and 1980s. Scientific and technological developments, however, averted crisis as the development of high-yielding varieties of cereals and grain alongside the intensive use of pesticides and fertilizers allowed food production to keep pace with population growth.

Whether food production will be able to keep pace with demand when faced with an increase in oil prices and drier climates is, however, uncertain. Professor John Beddington, the British government's chief scientist, has predicted the emergence of what he called a 'perfect storm' by 2030 as food shortages, water scarcity, and insufficient energy resources threaten to unleash unrest, cross-border conflicts, and mass migration. The notion of a 'perfect storm' is an arresting, almost biblical analogy and the threat of rising sea levels provides a rather ironic link to Bauman's emphasis on *liquid fears*. Sadly, what is arguably most interesting about the topic of climate change is that it appears to have hardly registered in the Western imagination and as a result the political response to this issue has been weak. Although the international community has acknowledged that a serious problem exists *in principle*, the outcome of various United Nations organized meetings has revealed a severe rhetoric–reality gap to the extent that it is debatable whether a developed 'politics of climate change' actually exists.

Climate change and population growth both highlight the existence of what we can for simplicity label the 'energy gap'. More and more people are demanding an increasingly energy-intensive lifestyle (global energy consumption is expected to double by 2050) but scientists are telling us with increasing urgency that we have over-exploited finite resources and that we risk becoming locked into an inevitable struggle for diminishing resources. The main political response has so far been a mixture of denial combined with attempts to *increase supply* (by identifying new oil reserves, burning more coal, growing biomass crops, and building new nuclear reactors). The gulf, however, cannot be bridged by simply *increasing supply* and must at some point involve a focus on *reducing demand* in the sense of weaning the public in advanced industrialized countries off their high-consumption lifestyles. But the Achilles heel of any form of governance that relies on popular support is most obvious when it comes to the need to make decisions that are likely to be unpopular with the public. It is for exactly this reason that an increasing number of commentators are making the case *against* democratic politics and instead returning to Plato's arguments in favour of philosopher kings.

As William Ophuls's *Ecology and the Politics of Scarcity* (1977) and Garret Hardin's *Managing the Commons* (1979) illustrate, the notion of the 'authoritarian alternative' based around depoliticizing politics in order to allow an insulated class of ecological mandarins to make decisions in the public interest has existed for some years and draws its inspiration from Plato's *The Republic*. The failure of many countries to achieve even modest carbon emission reduction targets (in 2009 fossil fuel CO_2 emissions stood at 9.28 billion metric tonnes, the second highest level in human history and 37 per cent higher than 1990, the Kyoto reference year), combined with rapid industrial development in countries like China, India, and Brazil, have led several observers to reconsider whether democratic politics is able to meet the climate-change challenge. 'We should not be blind to the possibility that an authoritarian meritocracy might have advantages in world crisis management compared to the present democratic mediocracy', David Shearman and Joseph Smith suggest in *The Climate Change Challenge and the Failure of Democracy* (2008). 'Today it is debatable whether we can wait for democratic reform, bit by bit, election by election, and decade by decade.' This sense of frustration stems from the belief that democratic politics is simply too glacial in terms of its capacity to react and evolve. The need for discussion, compromise, and a consensus around the lowest common denominator may be positive characteristics in relation to day-to-day policy-making but when viewed against the demands of addressing climate change this mode of governing is viewed as too slow, cumbersome, and prone to self-interested veto points. Steve Schneider's *A Patient from Hell* (2005), for example, reveals the manner in which the findings of peer-reviewed scientific research are watered down during the IPCC's internal review process in order to satisfy the national representatives of oil-producing countries.

As the previous chapter's focus on the 'logic of discipline' emphasized, the electoral cycle produces short-term pressures, even temptations, which are hard for politicians who rely on popular support to resist. Short-term benefits ('Jobs now', 'low taxes', 'cheap flights', etc.) will generally trump long-term sustainability, and global social-attitude surveys reveal that politicians do not have a monopoly on short-termism and self-interest. Tony Blair's frank admission in January 2007 that 'I'm still waiting for the first politician who's actually running for office who's going to come out and say that people should not fly—and they're not. It's like telling people you should not drive anywhere' provides a simple illustration of why Shearman and Smith suggest 'perhaps the really big decisions that are vital to the future of humanity are best imposed'. The evidence for the failure of democracy to respond to the challenge of climate change is therefore powerful. Decades of scientific warnings and environmental campaigns have resulted, at best, in a modest form of green-washing in which cars suddenly become 'environmentally friendly' and coal becomes 'clean'. Such Orwellian double-speak would not have surprised Crick but it leaves us with the thorny challenge of how to defend democratic politics against the climate change challenge and explains why an increasing number of commentators are reluctantly coming to the conclusion that the 'authoritarian alternative' may have something to offer.

My response is, not unsurprisingly, couched within the case for democracy and rests on two simple claims: firstly, the authoritarian alternative has nothing to offer; and, secondly, the answer to the climate change challenge is, if anything, *more* democracy not less. More, however, of a different kind of democracy (not more of the same), because we should not confuse politics as it has been practised in the past with how it might function in the future. Nor should we underestimate the force of public pressure to deliver change. My argument is not anti-capitalist, anti-American, or even deep-environmentalist but simply a claim that we must as a global society live within our means because the gap between what we demand and what the Earth can supply has been stretched to breaking point. There is no evidence to support the theory that authoritarian politics would or could deliver a more sustainable way of life. The available evidence suggests that democratic states generally do better than their authoritarian counterparts when it comes to environmental protection (and power-sharing consensual democracies, like the Netherlands and Switzerland, also out-perform power-hoarding majoritarian democracies, like the United Kingdom and New Zealand). What then is needed in order for democracy to meet the challenge of climate change?

My answer rests on three arguments that each in its own way sits within the other, and takes us from a specific focus on politicians, through to a focus on the responsibilities of the public and then to a broader critique of the contemporary nature of liberal democracy. The arguments can be summarized as:

1. The need for a more muscular and honest form of democratic politics;

2. An emphasis on the public being part of the problem and part of the cure; and

3. The need to view politics as a counterweight to the market and not the basis of the market.

Some might say that politics is already too muscular, too tribal, and too adversarial. In many ways they are correct, but in making this point I am really going back to my previous attempt to sketch out the contours of a more honest account of politics. The first pillar of this account is that democratic politics revolves around putting collective interests above individual wants and desires. The second pillar is that a stable democracy must impose some form of limits on public engagement in politics and resist the insatiable growth of public demands. The third is that politics, and therefore politicians, cannot satisfy every person all of the time (since it lacks the resources and because many individuals or groups seek to put self-interest before the public interest). But the nature of democratic competition creates what we have called a 'governing paradox', in which the need to garner and sustain popular support grates against the need sometimes to deny the public, reject demands, or make unpopular decisions. To date, politicians have generally taken the path of least resistance when it comes to the climate-change challenge and have engaged in a game of mass delusion, in which we all kid ourselves that we are facing up to the challenge of climate change through various green-washed 'feel good' policies that slake our guilt but do little to address the problem.

Politicians have, in effect, been too weak. A governing philosophy of 'not in my term of office' has trumped the need for action and inflated rhetoric has veiled the need to take tough choices. Politicians urgently need to rediscover their moral nerve and capacity to speak with the authority and weight of their predecessors. At the heart of this rediscovery must be the acceptance that the first business of government is to govern, which may at times call for the deliberate endurance of unpopularity. The time has come for politicians to be a little brave and accept that there are limits to growth and that patterns of consumption and lifestyles need to change. There is no need for us to turn our backs on democracy, accept authoritarian rule, or return to living in caves but there is a need for us to accept the fact that democracy brings with it responsibilities as well as rights (limits as well as freedoms). The public will have to shout less and listen more and politicians will have to set out a clear agenda for change and then see that programme through in the face of public disquiet. We must therefore carve out a democratic path between the 'authoritarian alternative' and the 'business as usual' approach that we are currently on, and in order to do this we might usefully return not to Plato's faith in philosophers and an enlightened elite but to Jean-Jacques Rousseau's faith in the social contract.

We are all part of a collective community that comes together through the democratic process to agree certain rules and limits. If some individuals or social groups lapse into self-interested or what Rousseau calls 'egoist' behaviour then it is legitimate for the state, as the ultimate expression of the 'general will', to force them to abide by the rules. The problem in recent years is that our politics has become obsessed with the protection of *human rights* to the detriment of any focus on *human responsibilities* across a range of dimensions (e.g. to the planet, to other species, or to future generations). We cannot avoid the fact that some policies will have to have a hard edge to them, many will be unpopular and actively resisted, and sometimes achieving change will demand both carrots *and* sticks. I am well aware that to advocate a more muscular form of politics is unlikely to be popular, but addressing the challenges of climate change was never going to be easy. There are no technological solutions, silver bullets, quick fixes, or magic potions for this problem. I am also aware that Rousseau has been derided as the inventor of pseudo-democratic dictatorships but I prefer to see him as a realistic democrat, realistic in the sense that he accepted that governing was never going to be easy and that free riders would always exist. He never promoted one 'exclusive truth' and nor was his ideal, the all-embracing state, often considered the key feature of totalitarianism. He wanted citizens to have real control over their political affairs but was also willing to accept that sometimes the public could be a selfish master to serve. He was therefore willing to view the public as being both part of the problem *and* part of the cure.

One of the core aims of this book is to defend the achievements of politics and the behaviour of politicians by explaining the nature of the challenges and pressures they face. My argument is that many of those 'disaffected democrats' would behave in exactly the same way as the politicians they loathe with such intensity if they were placed in their position. It is too easy to carp from the sidelines and blame those politicians who provide so easy a target when in fact you are simply individualizing guilt in order to contribute to the myth of collective innocence. Don't hide behind a childish distinction between 'them' and 'us', because to deny your own capacity is cowardice dressed up as ignorance. Franklin Roosevelt's warning that the public should 'never forget that government is ourselves and not an alien power over us' remains valid today. The ultimate rulers of any democracy are not the President or Prime Minister, not the secretaries of state or members of parliament, but the public and voters. The bizarre beauty of the climate-change challenge therefore stems not just from the way in which it quite brutally exposes the weakness of our political system but also from the manner in which it can only be resolved through collective measures. In other words, the great beauty of climate change is the manner in which it 'whisks us up in a whirlwind and throws us down against . . . ourselves', as Alastair McIntosh concludes in *Hell and High Water* (2008). The politics of climate change revolves around a campaign not for abundance but for austerity; a campaign for less not more; and it therefore forces us to reflect upon our deepest assumptions about what adds value and worth to our lives.

This is a critical point. For too long 'politics' has been defined as involving politicians, formal political processes, and political institutions like legislatures and parties. This narrow definition has excluded the fact that the public is part and parcel of 'politics' and must play an active role. There are no spectators in this game. This might sound obvious but if we are honest about why there is no developed or coherent politics of climate change, we cannot simply blame 'big business' or 'selfish politicians' but must accept our own responsibility for placing short-term benefits before long-term sustainability. Although achieving a dramatic reduction in carbon emissions is undoubtedly difficult, it *is* economically and technically possible. One of the reasons that politicians engage in spin and blame games, however, is because the public are themselves generally guilty of double-speak when it comes to climate change. The public demands that politicians address the issue but only as long as it does not reduce their capacity to, for example, drive their large cars or enjoy cheap air travel.

A great deal of the environmental literature is imbued with anti-political sentiment and an unquestioned belief in the 'bad faith model of politics' that overlooks the role and capacity of the public. The role of big business in promoting the position and visibility of climate-change sceptics has been well documented, as have the donations that have been made by oil companies to politicians who are likely to block reform. But it is also true that the public's approach to mass consumption also makes them complicit in a system that displays little appetite for far-reaching change. My aim in making this point is simply to emphasize that politicians and political parties are, like markets and private businesses, incredibly sensitive to public opinion and public pressure. A more aggressive approach to the challenges of climate change would undoubtedly stem from an upsurge in public concern and public demand that measures be taken. But the position of the public on climate change remains ambivalent and racked by double-think.

Politicians therefore operate at the cutting edge of the public's expectations and demands. They represent the collective projections of what we are in denial of and carry the brunt of our compartmentalized thinking. Politicians are therefore under huge pressure to create and hide behind a veil of ambiguity, through the use of sleight of hand or smoke and mirrors, when it comes to environmental reporting, as a means of bridging conflicting interests, values, and demands. Let me put this slightly differently: politicians lie, obfuscate, and engage in 'green-washing' not because they are stupid but because, unconsciously, we—the electorate—set them up for it. The trouble is that in a democracy we tend to get the politics that reflects who we are. The question this leaves us with is how to create a citizenry that takes the politics of climate change seriously and as a result empowers their elected politicians to introduce meaningful decisions? The answer to this question takes us back to the emphasis on political literacy and active citizenship that formed the focus of the second half of Crick's career. The public is not stupid, lazy, or selfish. Larry King's comment in 2008 that 'nobody cares about fifty years from now' ignores the fact that people do care about their children and grandchildren. The real problem is that individuals are constantly bombarded with sensational-ist claims and counterclaims about the existence and risks of climate change.

Just as I have argued that it is closer to the truth to suggest that the public do not understand politics than to claim that they 'hate' politics, it is also closer to the truth to suggest that the public do not under-stand the science and implications of climate change rather than that they don't care about it. There is a severe knowledge gap between scientific data and public understanding. Although it is difficult to make predictions about the future consequences of climate change with complete precision, there is now a general consensus within the scientific community about the general direction of travel and what needs to be done. Public education and the democratization of infor-mation therefore form the foundation of a coherent response to the challenges of climate change and there are numerous reference points that support this optimistic account of human behaviour. Over twenty years ago Elinor Ostrom explored the nature of collective action prob-lems in her book *Governing the Commons* and discovered that locally active small-scale businesses were able to reach decisions that were not 'just for profit' but were frequently driven by an instinctual preference for sustainability and mutual cooperation. More recently, experiments with deliberative forms of democratic engagement have illustrated that information, discussion, and deliberation among participants generally induces a 'green shift'. In *When the People Speak* (2009), for example, James Fishkin trumpets the deliberative polls held on green issues in the United States that resulted in a commitment to greater investment in renewable energy and conservation. The effect of having to debate an issue in public therefore tends, as Jon Elster has argued in his work on 'the civilizing force of hypocrisy', to replace the language of self-interest with the language of reason.

To focus on the need for politicians to be more vigorous and on the need for the public to take responsibility for their own complicity in the challenges we face is not enough. Oil has allowed a standard of living for the Western world that was incomprehensible two generations ago. It has lifted our expectation levels far beyond what is necessary and to the point that items that were until fairly recently viewed as luxuries—cars, phones, foreign travel, etc.—are now viewed as basic necessities of modern life. They are not. This was a feature of modern life noted by the Labour intellectual Tony Crosland four decades ago when he noted that 'what one generation sees as a luxury, the next sees as a necessity'. Dealing with the challenge of climate change therefore demands that we accept that, as Richard Heinberg (2008) put it, *The Party's Over* in terms of the availability of cheap oil. Instead of viewing this as a threat that will inevitably lead to a decline in our standard of living, a more optimistic response to the 'peak oil' dilemma is to view it as an opportunity to *change* our way of living that can only come from building a more authentic set of social and political relationships.

In order to nurture a shift from 'the politics of pessimism' to 'the politics of optimism' and dare to hope for a more positive future for our children, it is necessary not to focus solely on the respective roles of the governors and the governed but also to reflect on the nature of that relationship in terms of how 'success' and 'failure' are defined. At the moment, our definition of success is measured in terms of economic growth but there is an urgent need to disentangle the concept of democracy from the nature of modern capitalism. There is a strange assumption that political freedoms and economic freedoms are for some reason different sides of the same coin, that market freedoms that produce economic growth are somehow the necessary condition and breeding ground for political democracy, and (conversely) that democratic politics is the sole frame in which economic success can effectively be pursued and achieved. The great danger of self-evident truths, however, is that they are frequently wrong. The 'economic miracles' of Chile, South Korea, Singapore, Taiwan, and currently China were not forged in the crucible of democratic politics but through various forms of dictatorship and bureaucratic authoritarianism.

The source of our difficulties vis-à-vis climate change does not lie simply in the nature of democracy per se but in the particular form of thin or hollow democratic politics that has evolved in recent decades. It is a form of faux democracy modelled around consumption, individualism, and materialism that is ultimately both unsustainable and unsatisfying. Democracy could be consistent with a system that promoted environmental sustainability but the real challenge is to displace the dominance of the current emphasis on economic growth at all costs. The problem in trying to displace the dominance of the market is that we have become entangled in an economic system based on the production of both false fears and false needs, which hollows out our collective potential. We know the price of everything but seem to have forgotten the value of everything that matters in life. This is not intended as an argument against the market or against capitalism but simply in favour of a less excessive way of life.

Above a fairly modest income level there is no relationship between happiness and income. There is no more than transient gratification in a consumerism driven by envy and wealth accumulation. Why do we find this lesson so hard to accept? Alexis de Tocqueville recognized this condition in his *Democracy in America* back in 1835 when he wrote that 'Americans were often restless in the midst of their prosperity . . . wanting ever more and suffering when they saw someone else with assets they lacked'. Today we label this condition 'affluenza' and chart its social impact in terms of rising debt, anxiety, stress, guilt, and depression. Breaking this cycle of consumerism and daring to speak a new language of hope and optimism therefore demands that we return to Crick's notion of democracy as a counterweight to the market as opposed to *the basis* of the market. Speaking a new language of hope must also bring with it an acknowledgement of the limits of markets in the sense that they risk 'devouring their own moral capital', as William Olphus eloquently wrote in his *Requiem for Modern Politics*. This notion of moral capital as a form of social glue that binds society together resonates with Bauman's emphasis on liquidity and also Robert Putman's work on the declining levels of social capital. If the only social cohesion offered by faux democracy is little more than superficial consumerism, there is little wonder that politics has become ephemeral and tenuous to so many.

Chasing happiness through shopping as a consumer-citizen in a marketplace democracy may reflect the 'triumph' of liberal democracy but it is ultimately unsatisfying both individually and socially. Every storm, as we all know, has a silver lining and in this case one of the benefits of the global financial crisis has been the manner in which it created a debate about the boundaries between politics and the economy that was simply not possible in recent decades. Challenging the 'grow-or-perish' ideology of total capitalism was, until the financial crisis, defined as the act of a lunatic, idealist, or revolutionary (and frequently all three). Today, by contrast, a debate exists not about 'the end of capitalism' but about taming global capitalism and exploring the ways in which markets can deliver sustainable solutions. Sustainable solutions will undoubtedly involve some individuals, communities, and countries contributing more than others; the process will be messy, often laboured, dull, untidy, muddled, and occasionally dirty, and in a classic example of closing a gap from above and below, the developed world must pay the highest price while also supporting the developing world to industrialize sustainably. The climate-change challenge therefore provides us with an opportunity to develop a sense of global citizenship and new cosmopolitan institutions with the capacity to forge new relationships based around the politics of the free rather than the politics of fear.

Politics of Fear

If democracy and freedom were the defining concepts of the twentieth century, risk and fear look certain to take their place in the twenty-first century. Despite all our achievements, a sense of hopelessness and fatalism seems to have descended upon modern life to the point where the notion of 'crisis' appears almost a cultural metaphor for contemporary politics. Challenges, threats, and urgent questions undoubtedly need to be addressed but there is first a need to regain our sense of collective self-confidence and our belief in our capacity to shape the future as we have done in the past. Too many of us are scared of life; too willing to shrug our shoulders and shake our heads; too many willing to blame others instead of stepping into the arena ourselves. The world would suddenly become a far better place if we could just get a grip on our destructive delusions and instead face up to the issues that really demand our attention. Like it or not, the truth about climate crisis is an inconvenient truth (to borrow a phrase) that means we are going to have to change the way we live our lives. My point is that this may not necessarily be a bad thing. Prosperity without growth is possible but it will demand that we view prosperity in more than simply financial or material terms. Although rediscovering the art of living wisely may well deliver some relief from the trials and tribulations of modern life, this chapter needs to be brought to a close so that we can focus on the most heinous offenders when it comes to manipulating the public, creating false fears and false wants, and promoting unrealistic expectations. So finally I should like to make three brief points.

Firstly, if politics is in crisis, it seems to have been so for some time. *The Crisis of Democracy*, for example, was the title of the final report of the trilateral commission into political disaffection in Western Europe, the United States, and Japan in the 1970s. Making this point is not to deny the importance of taking political disengagement seriously but it is to suggest that in a 24/7 'real time' media world the 'crisis of politics' may originate more in the scaremongering strategies of specific actors and social groups (i.e. 'the politics of crises') than in the actual failure of democracy. It could also be said that the term 'crisis' is in danger of becoming overused in the sense that it has been so broadly applied in recent years that it has lost its meaning in a world obsessed with hyperbole. Classic books like Samuel Prince's *Catastrophe and Social Change* (1920), Pitirim Sorokin's *Man and Society in Calamity* (1942), and Lewis Coser's *The Functions of Social Conflict* (1956) certainly placed the bar far higher than we do today in terms of defining a crisis. We need to regain a tighter grasp of what constitutes a crisis, disaster, or catastrophe because we have slipped into a climate of constant instability that reinforces an unjustified sense of failure.

Many readers may respond by suggesting that by writing of the dangers of climate change, dangers that inevitably remain contested in terms of cause and effect, I too have inevitably contributed to an attitude of pessimism, dread, and foreboding towards the future. But to suggest this would be to miss the central claim I have tried to make in this chapter. My argument is simply that most of the concerns that occupy the minds of the public in the developed world are false fears that generally stem from the social amplification of risks that are simply negligible for the average man or woman. In the second decade of the twenty-first century your chances of experiencing a violent death are lower than at any previous point in history. At the very same time we appear almost in a state of denial about the most pressing and very real storms on the horizon. My intention is not therefore to cultivate an attitude of pessimism, dread, and foreboding but quite the opposite: it is to cultivate a sense of belief and optimism that climate change is not an insurmountable challenge but may in fact be perceived as a positive opportunity. 'The harder the conflict', as Thomas Paine stressed in *The Crisis* (1776), 'the more glorious the triumph'. However, as Natan Sharansky notes in his *Case for Democracy* (2004),

Those who seek to move the Earth must first, as Archimedes explained, have a place to stand. Moral clarity provides us with a place to stand, a reference point from where to lever our talents, ideas and energies to create a better world. Without moral clarity, without a reference point, those same talents, ideas, and energies are just as likely to do harm as good. (p. xviii)

In many ways this book, this defence of politics, is all about providing that moral clarity and those reference points. Sharansky sculpts his writing around 'free societies' and 'fear societies', the former generally inculcating modern democratic values and assumptions, the latter being forged around tyranny, persecution, and pain. Having spent nine years as a Soviet political prisoner in a Siberian forced labour camp, Sharansky is particularly well qualified to write in favour of freedom not tyranny, democracy not dictatorship, and the rule of law not the rule of the secret police. Although his *Case for Democracy* is quite different from this *Defence of Politics*, in the sense that his focus is on the transition *to* democracy while this book is focusing on the contradictions *of* democracy and the dangers of post-political or post-democratic governance, his emphasis on the difference between a 'free society' and a 'fear society' provides an obvious connection and vantage point from which to restate my own concerns. In essence, 'free societies' are becoming 'fear societies'—'fear societies' not in the physical, personal, terrifying sense that Sharansky meant but in the more elusive and vague sense that underpins Bauman's focus on 'liquid fears' and Beck's focus on 'new risks'. Although the origins of the fear are quite different, both leave us exhausted and unable to draw upon our achievements as the source of a sense of optimism about the future.

My final point focuses on the issues of exhaustion and achievements. As this chapter has illustrated, in recent decades the logic of the market and the logic of discipline have conspired to promote a dangerous brand of anti-political gutter populism. The 'authoritarian alternative' is one variant of this anti-political line of reasoning that reveals a feature of democratic regimes that is often overlooked—innate fragility. All political philosophies contain a number of contradictions and in this regard democracy is no different; and yet I am, like Crick, willing to defend democracy as a civilizing and largely honourable endeavour and willing to warn you that anyone who claims they can rule beyond the *polis* is either a God or a beast. The increasingly loud voices of those who seek to resurrect arguments in favour of an enlightened dictator or philosopher king serve to remind us that democracy is a fragile creature that should never be taken for granted. Moreover, fragility, be it emotional, economic, or political, tends to reflect the existence of some kind of exhaustion. This is most powerfully illustrated in Jared Diamond's *Collapse* (2006), which charts the historical demise of a number of societies and in doing so exposes a very clear link between fragility and exhaustion—not exhaustion in the sense of physical tiredness but exhaustion in relation to social understanding. Societies therefore become exhausted when their people become so used to the rights, privileges, and material prosperity endowed by their civilization that they no longer value them sufficiently to defend, maintain, or build upon them. The history of democracy can therefore be told as the story of successive efforts to keep both the purpose and its pursuit alive, after the disappearance or achievement of its original ambitions.

The notion of telling a story to keep alive the original aims and the continuing achievements of democratic politics brings me to the topic of my final defence and in turning my attention to the media I make no apology for my lack of restraint and inability to talk in anything but fairly harsh terms. If we really want to understand how the public are misled, abused, and exploited, it is to journalism and the media, not just to politicians and politics, that we should turn. To return to the focus of this chapter as a link to the next, the phrase 'Crisis, what crisis?' has gone down in political folklore as Jim Callaghan's response to a question about the Winter of Discontent that played a major role in bringing down the Labour government in 1979. Although the phrase reinforced a popular feeling that the government had lost touch with the country, the Prime Minister never actually said it: it was a creation by a journalist working for a British tabloid newspaper, *The Sun*. If the facts were rarely allowed to get in the way of a good story thirty years ago, the pressure on journalists to deliver 'breaking news' today creates a powerful tendency towards 'crisis inflation', in which even the smallest issue can be rapidly amplified into an example of *systemic* failure. It is for exactly this reason that the next chapter seeks to defend politics from the *media*.

6

A DEFENCE OF POLITICS
AGAINST THE MEDIA

In despising politicians and in reducing the amount of space given to democratic debate the media have made their worst mistake. Journalists confuse being subservient to politicians (which no media can allow themselves to be) with being subservient to democratic politics. The media have not come up with a better idea than democratic politics, and they do not claim to have officially done so: but in many ways, explicitly and implicitly, they act as if they have. The media have claimed the right to judge and condemn; more, they have decided—without being clear about the decision—that politics is a dirty game, played by devious people who tell an essentially false narrative about the world and thus deceive the people. This has not been the only, but it has been the increasingly dominant, narrative that the media have constructed about politics over the past decade or so... it remains dominant.

John Lloyd, *What the Media Are Doing to Our Politics* (2004)

There is an argument here that needs addressing—that we in the media are undermining faith in the very democratic institutions we claim to be holding to account and undermining the capacity of our society to have a rational debate about the choices we should make. There is undoubtedly a real challenge to those of us interested in politics to reach out to those who are least interested.

Nick Robinson, *A Troubled Marriage* (2006)

Our confidence is low and our self-belief is shaken. Most of all, we feel weak, at points almost listless. The future once so firmly in our grip, seems to have broken loose in search of new masters. Read much of our media, and that's how it is: malaise, decline, impotence, challenges unmet, promises unfulfilled... The role of the media in modern democracy is an issue every senior politician I know believes is ripe for debate. Yet it is virtually undebated, because the media on the whole resent the debate and inflict harm on those who attempt to engage in it.

Tony Blair, *A Journey* (2010)

'Our Republic and its press will rise and fall together,' Joseph Pulitzer wrote in the *North American Review* in 1904. 'A cynical, mercenary, demagogic press will produce in time a people as base as itself.' For Pulitzer the role of the media was twofold: first, to expose political corruption and incompetence and secondly to provide the public with the information they needed to understand and play an active role in politics. My concern is that a century later the media has become increasingly cynical, mercenary, and demagogic to the point at which it no longer supports democratic politics but actively undermines it. The problem of integrity in modern politics is not therefore simply about politicians or their officials. It is a problem that reflects broader changes in the nature of society and particularly in relation to those intermediary bodies, like the church, trade unions, families, etc., that have traditionally played a role in cultivating political literacy and understanding. The role of these intermediate institutions was the focus of a book that was published alongside Crick's *Defence* in 1962—Anthony Sampson's *Anatomy of Britain*. Almost fifty years later in his final book, *Who Runs this Place?* (2004), Sampson concluded that a common pattern could be observed based around the general decline in the power and influence of all the intermediate institutions apart from the media. What Edmund Burke famously described as the fourth estate had become, according to Sampson, increasingly aggressive, assertive, and moralizing, to the extent that it now had an unmatched ability to make or break reputations. Such conclusions are by no means exclusive to Britain. Robert Putman's work on the decline of social capital and the growing influence of the media in the United States, for example, adopts a different methodological approach and style of writing while painting a very similar picture.

My concern about the growth and contemporary role of the media takes us back to the notion of a gap—let us call it for the sake of brevity the knowledge gap—and the question of how citizens acquire the information they need to make sense of the world, to become active and engaged with other citizens, and to have their opinions and assumptions positively challenged. In this context my argument is simple: at a point in history when the public need more information about the challenges of governing and the respective successes *and* failures of those they elect, the media is providing them with less and less. A growing emphasis on profit and market share and the absence of a media culture that permits meaningful democracy has deprived the public of the information they need to act as responsible citizens. Worse than that, the media is providing a daily diet of lies, exaggeration, and misrepresentation about politics in order to further the interests of journalists, editors, and shareholders rather than the public interest. Sound-bites and isolated incidents used inaccurately are the norm, as are the constant nourishment of a culture of contempt, the juvenile view that everyone involved in public life is motivated solely by self-interest and ego, combined with the impudence to deny they have had any role in bringing about the resulting decline in public confidence. Some might argue that this has always been the case and it is true that Crick's original *Defence* emphasized the manner in which 'the people are ground down in fear by constant news (half-real or wholly invented) of conspiracies against the nation and the party'. A flourishing and independent media is generally viewed as a hallmark of a stable and functioning democracy and many countries around the world are held back by the power of authoritarian regimes to control or suppress the media. It is, however, simply too easy and naive to view an independent media as without doubt a 'good thing'. My argument is that a cynical and sleaze-driven media that is focused on selling newspapers or advertising space above all else can be as, if not more, destructive to democratic politics than the suppression of the media would be.

My concern is that although the relationship between politicians and the public is generally and inevitably mediated through the media as a lens, the media distorts the public's view of politics in a way that can only generate cynicism, fear, and despair. In turning my attention to the media I make no apology for my lack of restraint and for my inability to talk in anything but fairly harsh terms because I have lost count of the number of times journalists have misquoted me, or I have been offered large sums of money to add my name to articles written elsewhere. As Michael White, himself an experienced and respected journalist, admitted in January 2011, 'the media . . . has slipped into the lazy heresy that politics is an organized conspiracy against the public interest . . . the boot is more often on the other foot'. Many journalists, producers, and writers seem to exist in a parallel universe quite separate from the real world, in which hard and difficult decisions must be taken. It is easy to sit at your desk and mock those who must decide whether to send troops to a war zone, if the risks of a terrorist threat merit the imposition of restrictions on civil liberties, or whether to redistribute resources from the sick to the homeless (or vice versa) when you yourself have never had to make a major decision, justify it to the public, and then live with the consequences.

If we really want to understand how the public are misled, abused, and exploited, how 'false wants' and 'false fears' are created, and why the 'expectations gap' appears so difficult to close, then it is to journalists and the media, not just to politicians and politics, that I think we need to turn. The media generally claims it is in the business of protecting the public but all too often they abuse their role and position by adopting a shallow and essentially destructive view of politics and politicians. This is an argument that the media dislikes because it strikes at the heart of their power and role in a modern society but it is an argument that can no longer be ignored. Many media professionals privately admit their concerns about the changing nature of their profession, the decline in standards and serious content, and the long-term consequences in terms of public trust and engagement, but few are willing to stand up and be counted. Politicians who question the role and power of the media are immediately condemned for either having something to hide or seeking to shift the blame for their own mistakes. By contrast, politicians who attempt to develop a mature relationship with the media are caricatured as being obsessed by 'spin' and media manipulation, as if they had no incentive to seek to ensure that their message or explanation for a decision might travel, relatively undamaged, to the public. If the public truly 'hates' politics, as many scholars have argued, my impression is that this reflects the fact that the public's main source of political information flows from a media industry that peddles the lazy and cynical assumption that all politicians are liars, rogues, and cheats. This is therefore a chapter about the demonization of politicians and politics, couched within an argument that the real demons may in fact be the people creating the news rather than the people featuring in it.

This is a chapter that promotes the simple argument that if we are to defend politics, we must strike down this naive view that allows the media to present themselves as heroic fighters constantly protecting the gullible public against manipulative politicians. In order to make this argument this chapter is structured around four simple questions:

1. What is the media, in terms of newspapers and current affairs television, doing to our politics?

2. What is political satire and comedy doing to our politics?

3. Will the 'digital democracy' based around the 'new media' really save us?

4. How might the concept of 'civic journalism' help us replace the 'politics of pessimism' with a new 'politics of optimism'?,

In order to respond to these questions this chapter is divided into four sections. The first section focuses on the recent evolution of the 'old media' and on a decline in editorial and journalistic standards that has become increasingly clear across the advanced world in recent decades. The simple argument is really that in the scramble for markets most newspaper editors and producers of current affairs programming appear to have forgotten the critical difference between 'the public interest' and 'what interests the public'. This is not an argument in favour of staid and sober reporting or dull documentaries but it is one that emphasizes proportionality and professional responsibilities to the public. The problem, however, with focusing on the 'old' media is that it overlooks a significant demographic trend in which the majority of young people now tune in to alternative programming (specifically late-night chat shows, political comedy, and satire) in order to educate themselves politically. It is for exactly this reason that the second section adopts a more original focus by tracing the evolution of political comedy and satire and arguing that it is possible to identify a shift away from the more traditional forms of comedy and satire that used wit and humour as a form of *constructive* social criticism towards a more aggressive, cynical, anti-political, and ultimately destructive mode of democratic engagement. This is a shift that some comedians have themselves expressed concern about. In 2011, for example, Eddie Izzard encouraged his fellow comedians to be aware of their own capacity for spreading and reinforcing political cynicism, 'Comedy is easy to use like a stiletto to take things apart, it is always about taking things down. In politics I like building things.'

The idea that newspapers or even the mockery offered by comedians on late-night chat shows actually matters in the twenty-first century could be viewed as a slightly quaint but ultimately dated approach to understanding the role of the media. There has been a great deal of speculation and debate about the internet's potential to facilitate greater political engagement and understanding, particularly amongst younger citizens. It is for exactly this reason that the third section focuses on whether web-based platforms are delivering the dialogue and debate that was once found in the 'old' media or if the internet is simply reinforcing and perpetuating an ultimately thin and destructive interpretation of the 'bad faith model of politics'. Having examined how the emergence of 'digital natives' is generally encouraging people to talk to other like-minded individuals, rather than forging links between people who hold different views and opinions, the final section focuses on the responsibilities of the public vis-à-vis modern journalism. It suggests that the concept of 'civic journalism' may offer a bridge through which the media can rediscover its public role and values and the public can be aided to become informed citizens.

This chapter's focus on the media therefore allows us to develop our understanding of a range of issues and themes that have been discussed in previous chapters. If we want to understand the creation of an 'expectations gap' and the existence of a 'perceptions gap' (the focus of Chapter 2), it is only through acknowledging the role of the media that a full account will be delivered. If we want to understand how market pressures (the focus of Chapter 3) can alter relationships and lead to the promotion of both 'false wants' and 'false fears' then the recent history of the media provides a cutting case study. If we want to understand what life is really like for politicians, why they behave in the manner they do, and particularly why it is possible to identify a trend towards the depoliticization of decision-making (the focus of Chapter 4) then it is to the media that we must look. The media have for too long acted as invisible political actors and one of the main intentions of this chapter is to *politicize* the role of the media by highlighting its increasingly shallow, divisive, and destructive qualities. It is exactly these qualities that provide a connection with the politics of fear, the creation of 'new' risks, and the theme of crisis inflation that were discussed in the previous chapter (Chapter 5). The politics of fear *is* the politics of the media, due to an almost uncontested belief that 'only bad news sells', combined with the fact that journalistic success is measured in the number of political scalps that a story delivers. In this context the truth frequently melts away and Bauman's notion of 'liquidity' re-emerges as a valuable shorthand phrase that captures the modern media's approach to facts and information. Stripped down to its simplest form this is therefore a chapter about a profession that has become more akin to a blood sport with politicians and other prominent figures as its victims, a profession obsessed with witch-hunts and the demonization of politicians.

What the Media are Doing to Our Politics

Such is the extent of information and access that is now available that I am often reminded of Stevie Smith's poem 'Not Waving But Drowning' (1957) when trying to plough through the official documents, reports, and files of information that are now routinely made available to the public. The poem tells the unfortunate tale of a man who begins to drown while swimming in the sea. The man waves for help but the onlookers on the beach simply presume that as he has always been such a success in life he cannot be in trouble but is simply waving at them: 'Nobody heard him, the dead man . . . not waving but drowning.' With this in mind there is a certain irony in the fact that, just when we have more information about political processes and why certain decisions have been made, when the light of public scrutiny has been shone into almost every corner of public governance, levels of public trust in politics appears to have almost collapsed. The gap that has emerged between the governors and the governed arguably hinges on a critical but rarely discussed distinction between *knowledge* and *information*. We live in a time when many of us are information-rich yet knowledge-poor in the sense that we have more access to raw data about why policies succeed and fail and a much closer (some would say too close) relationship with our politicians but little understanding of the (messy) nature of politics or the (limited) ambitions of democracy. If it is the job of the lonely scholar to synthesize this glut of information into a coherent analysis, it is equally the job of the journalists to review this information in order to distil it down into an accessible form for public consumption. The presentation of information within a balanced account of the issue is therefore a hallmark of good journalism. At least it was.

To understand how the situation has changed it is necessary to return to John Stuart Mill's essay of 1859, *On Liberty*, which is often given by journalists as both a justification and foundation for their profession. 'Complete liberty of contradicting and disproving our opinion', Mill argued, 'is the very condition which justifies us in assuming its truth for purposes of action; and on no other terms can a being with human faculties have any rational assurance of being right'. The role of the media is, so the argument goes, to provide the public space in which contesting positions and arguments can be made and in which the claims of office-holders can be either verified or challenged. Yet it is almost impossible to reconcile Mill's emphasis on accuracy, balance, and pluralism with the approach of the modern media. Indeed it would be closer to the truth to suggest that across those large parts of the world where political disaffection is rife the media no longer acts as a positive check on the behaviour of politicians or the outcome of policies but has become little more than an establishment dedicated to a theatrical mistrust of individual politicians, a cultivated indifference to the real-life intricacies of policy-making, and a refusal to accept that media power brings with it responsibilities.

It is a curious paradox of modern times that the information explosion that has occurred in relation to politics, combined with the media explosion created by 24/7 news, digital television, and on-line newspapers, has generally led to a decline in the standard of journalism—a decline in the sense of less healthy debate, less coverage of competing arguments, less considered and evidence-based reporting, and less information on which the public can make an informed decision about the behaviour of its elected politicians or whether politics is failing. The modern mainstream media has therefore altered radically in a way that offers 'more of less'. More scandal, deceit and sensationalism; less knowledge about anything that really matters; the modern media is trapped in a professional hole, in which it believes that 'only bad news sells'. This, in turn, projects a deeply distorted picture of politics onto the public that affects public attitudes. This 'media malaise' argument is supported by a wealth of evidence and scholarship. As far back as the 1960s Kurt and Gladys Lang argued that television's style in chronicling political events could affect the fundamental orientation of the voter towards their government. The media, they suggested, could stir up disenchantment and distrust due to their emphasis on crisis and conflict in lieu of clarifying normal decision-making processes. The influence of the media was, the Langs argued, at its highest in relation to the 'inadvertent audience', who watched the news and current affairs programmes but lacked any real interest in politics. During the 1970s the link between media cynicism and public attitudes became clearer as Michael Robinson's term 'videomalaise' was introduced to describe how the media fed political cynicism and social mistrust. Throughout the subsequent decades more evidence of a link between the media's commitment to the 'bad faith model of politics' and the erosion of public support for politics accumulated.

Thomas Patterson's award-winning *Out of Order* (1993), for example, began from an explicit belief that 'Politics in America is practised by a governing class whose members, within the limits of human behaviour, mean more or less what they say and more or less keep the promises they make', and then sought to compare this 'good faith model of politics' with the dominant approach of the media. He discovered a shift from descriptive to interpretive reporting, a trend towards portraying politics and politicians in increasingly critical and unfavourable terms, and linked these developments to rising levels of political mistrust in the United States. A subtle yet important shift in the nature of political coverage that Patterson identified related to the imposition of an increasingly restricted interpretation of political behaviour that defined politics narrowly, as little more than a series of strategies for getting and keeping power. As a result the media would define any policy, decision, or announcement as a self-interested act for the benefit of the individual or party, thereby ignoring any implicit social or economic benefits.

In *Breaking the News: How the Media Undermine American Democracy* (1996) James Fallows argued that a relentless focus on scandal, spectacle, and the 'game' of politics was driving citizens away from politics and making it harder for even the most committed politicians to do an effective job, and at the same time was gradually eroding our collective ability to assess what was happening in the world and decide how to respond. These concerns culminated in Joseph Cappella and Kathleen Jamieson's *Spiral of Cynicism* (1997), which set out in great detail how the strategic frames employed by the media damaged public trust in politicians and government. From Deborah Tanner's *The Argument Culture* (1998) through to Robert McChesney and John Nichols's *The Death and Life of American Journalism* (2010) there exists a great body of work that examines the political implications of the media in terms of social capital, public trust, tabloid culture, journalistic styles, and—most importantly—the media not *reporting* the news but actually *creating* the news through a process of fabrication, manipulation, and framing.*
From Canada to New Zealand and from the United Kingdom to

---

* With Putnam's *Bowling Alone* (2000), Patricia Moy and Michael Pfau's *With Malice to All?*, Thomas Patterson's *Vanishing Voters* (2003), Kathleen Hall and Paul Waldman's *The Press Effect* (2004), John Lloyd's *What the Media are Doing to our Politics* (2004), Nick Davies's *Flat Earth News* (2008), and Francois Debrix's *Tabloid Terror* (2008) providing stepping stones in between.

Japan, research in recent decades has voiced concern over the link between an overwhelmingly negative approach to politics in the media and its impact on public understanding and trust. For those who are interested in politics and take a keen interest by watching the news or regularly reading newspapers, the role of the media may well deliver positive reinforcement effects, as Pippa Norris argued in *A Virtuous Circle* (2000) and less convincingly in *Democratic Deficits* (2011), but for most 'disaffected democrats' the media creates and perpetuates a very pessimistic and gloomy view of public life.

Why? Why has the role of the media apparently shifted from acting as a positive 'watchdog' operating in the public interest to inform the public, root out corruption, and hold politicians to account to behaving like an 'attack dog' focused largely on delivering scandal, sleaze, and forced resignations? The simple answer is that the emergence of 24/7 rolling news, combined with an ever-increasing number of television channels, radio stations, magazines, and newspapers have created an insatiable demand for stories. This has created a 'journalists' dilemma' that is analogous to the 'governing paradox' that was discussed in previous chapters. Whereas the latter focuses on how to reconcile the need to make unpopular decisions with the politician's need to retain public support, the journalists' dilemma focuses attention on the journalist's need to deliver a story that will attract large audiences while also maintaining high professional standards. In a congested and increasingly competitive marketplace journalists, editors, and producers are implicitly and explicitly encouraged to emphasize failure instead of success, conflict instead of compromise, and targets missed rather than targets achieved. Few issues are addressed in any real depth or in a way that engages with large audiences—talking *points* (and usually the same one across all outlets), rather than *issues* of social concern, dominate. Sound-bites, by their very nature, are the opposite of balanced reporting and comment. The result is a retreat away from in-depth current affairs towards 'infotainment' based upon the identification or creation of conflict, scandal, personal character assassination, unsubstantiated allegations, and rumours dressed up as fact. The reality of the modern media's approach to politics was laid bare in 2007 when the journalist and broadcaster Jeremy Paxman used the MacTaggart Lecture to suggest that journalists were increasingly betraying 'the people [they] ought to be serving'. More specifically, he highlighted the existence of a powerful pressure towards 'expectation inflation'. He confessed that on some days as the main presenter of *Newsnight* if he was truly honest he would have started the programme by stating in no uncertain terms, 'Not much has happened today, I'd go to bed if I were you'. However in the current climate the media 'chatterati' could not, he argued, accept such truisms. 'The story needs to be kept moving, constantly hyped . . . in this context even the slightest development is fallen upon as if it were a press release announcing the second coming'. If there is not a story, one will have to be invented; hence the rise of celebrity culture and reality television.

My point here is not to deny the existence of problems with our political system but simply to emphasize the corrosive influence of constant negative media reporting on public confidence in politics. I am bemoaning the decline in journalistic substance, seriousness, and sense of proportion that has been identified across the world. In many ways this is an incredibly easy argument to make in the wake of the phone-hacking scandal that engulfed News Corp in July 2011 but it is not an argument that relates to just one organization. It is a systemic problem and challenge for the media and there are very few journalists, editors, or producers who, when talking in private, will not admit to holding serious concerns about the general direction of their profession. Sustaining or increasing market share generally involves being more anti-government, more anti-politics, more aggressive, more polemically extreme, more rhetorically bitter and savagely dismissive. The approach of the media to politics is couched more and more in the language of extremes—there is little room in modern political coverage for shades of grey. Politics is portrayed as an arena forged upon binary distinctions—saints and sinners, triumphs and disasters, saviour to failure, hero to zero, chumps and champs, knights and knaves. As a result, issues become strangely depoliticized within public discourse as the more interesting shades of grey that provoke debate and offer real options are rarely exposed. Indeed the larger narrative or higher purpose is gone. With very few exceptions, the media refuses to engage in the complexity of modern life and has turned its back on many of the social functions that 'news' was until recently expected to perform (providing both sides of a story, allowing politicians to explain why a certain decision has been made, offering information in an accessible form, etc.).

Critics may accuse me of nostalgia but it is quite clear that the division between news and comment has been eroded: the reporter or interviewer is free to suggest, or even impose, their own explanation or implicit judgement. All stories are fixed into an existing narrative that politicians are not to be trusted and the approach of the interviewer is generally infused with a mixture of disapproval, contempt, mockery, intrusion, and hectoring. Politicians, it seems, are regarded as being for the use of the medium—a commodity to be spent—to be used and abused. There is a lack of any kind of respect for achievement or status. There is no feeling for what is private in life. The audience is invited to judge the performance not the issues. The reality of life for most politicians is that it is impossible to cultivate a mature and balanced discussion about any issue with the public through the media because anything they say, any personal viewpoint expressed, any misjudged comment, any glimpse of being willing to stray from the party line will be seized upon and used as the basis of a destructive story. Most of the politicians I have ever worked with, in the UK and abroad, would like to be more frank, more honest with the public but the simple fact is that they can't because when they do so they are generally slaughtered by the media. Politicians are constrained, defensive, and ambiguous for the simple reason that they know that the media offers little space for mature balanced discussion but is focused on generating scandal, dissent, or confusion. Politicians understand that the role of an interview is to embarrass, expose, and humiliate and as a result they have developed their own self-preservation mechanisms (media training, media managers, sticking to the script, refusing to make definitive statements, etc.) but both sides assume bad faith. For politicians the stakes are too high. An admission, even a minor one, will be treated as a scandal or evidence that the government is close to collapse.

There is, however, a much bigger picture that we need to acknowledge that provides a link between this section's focus on the changing political economy of the media and this book's broader focus on the nature of democratic politics. Put very simply, it is just too easy for the media to denigrate 'mere politics' due to the fact that it cannot please everyone all of the time, it 'cannot make every sad heart glad'. Politics will, as I have stressed throughout this book, often produce messy and tangled outcomes that are difficult to understand. Some issues will have to be kept secret and politicians will from time to time have to renege upon their promises and authorize practises they would in a perfect world not tolerate. It is simply too easy for journalists to ignore the realities of life, pretend that invidious decisions did not need to be taken, or carp from the sidelines. Democratic politics is a cruel and worldly profession. It is not, however, as grubby as journalism (and I take heart from the fact that opinion polls consistently reveal that if there is one profession the public trusts less than politicians it is journalists).

If there is a common theme running throughout this book it is a focus on rebuilding authentic political relationships and I want to return to this theme in the final section of this chapter by emphasizing the concept of 'civic journalism'. My concern, however, at this stage of the chapter is that the focus of my target in terms of defending politics has been simply too obvious. To highlight a decline in both the quality and quantity of political journalism on the TV, radio, and in newspapers, to emphasize the manner in which increased competition between media outlets has led to a focus on sensationalism and scandal, and to suggest a link between the belief that 'only bad news sells', and link this to the broader social decline in public confidence about democratic politics, is simply to bring to the fore a debate that has been simmering for some time. Moreover, it is possible to argue that conventional forms of news and current affairs outputs are simply less relevant than they used to be, and this is particularly true amongst those sections of the community that have become most disillusioned with conventional politics. If we are truly to understand the relationship between the media and political disaffection we need to be more innovative. It is for exactly this reason that the next section focuses on political comedy and satire.

Satire, Lies, and Politics

Does hope lie in humour? Aristophanes, Aristotle, and even Machiavelli understood the advantages of incorporating humour into political commentary and in this section I want to examine the role played by political comedy and satire in either widening or closing the gap that has emerged between the governors and the governed. Many would say that it is impossible to talk of political comedy *and* satire in one breadth as to do so encompasses too broad a range of medias and genres, but my aim here is simply to cultivate a debate about the role and power of a hitherto largely invisible set of political actors (writers, comedians, producers, etc.). My intention is to contribute to a more complete understanding of the dynamics that underpin popular attitudes to formal politics and my argument is that a subtle shift in the nature of political comedy and satire has taken place in recent years from using wit and sarcasm as an element of constructive social criticism towards a use of comedy as an element of toxic, destructive 'attack politics', which perpetuates a shallow and misleading view of politics. At the core of this shift is a transition within comedy and satire from an emphasis on healthy scepticism to almost pure cynicism.

Although this focus on comedy and satire may form a rather unexpected topic for a book which seeks to defend politics, it is a focus that I am sure Bernard Crick would have welcomed. His biography of George Orwell rejoiced in the use of allegory and symbolism that Orwell's satirical novels, like *Animal Farm* (1945) and *Nineteen Eighty-Four* (1949), employed to convey political warnings concerning indifference, ignorance, and greed. For both Orwell and Crick, humour and satire could be used not only as a tool of healthy political criticism but also as a form of political education. Half a century later, however, technological development has changed the dominant forms of political comedy and satire from the twentieth century's attachment to novels, poems, dramas, short stories, magazines, and novellas to the dominance of late-night comedy shows, satirical political series, or stand-up comedy in the twenty-first century. To enter the contemporary world of political comedy and satire is therefore to enter the world of *The Daily Show* and *The Colbert Report* in the United States, *Have I Got News for You* and *Mock the Week* in the United Kingdom and *This Hour has 22 Minutes* in Canada. It is also to enter a world that matters more than ever for four simple reasons:

1. Research suggests that younger people are increasingly tuning in to late-night comedy as their main source of political information.

2. Research also suggests that an increasing number of television viewers cannot easily distinguish between entertainment and fictional dramatizations, on the one hand, and news or current affairs programmes, on the other (meaning the former significantly effects how they think about 'real' politics).

3. Opinion polls reveal that young people trust comedians and talk-show hosts far more than politicians to tell the truth and accurately represent issues.

4. The dominant message emanating from political comedy and satire is an increasingly aggressive form of the 'bad faith model of politics'.

The question I want to throw at you is therefore: is kicking the life out of politics and politicians really that funny or do comedians and writers need to spend more time thinking about their social responsibilities and less time thinking about how to get cheap laughs? Jon Stewart, presenter of *The Daily Show*, might with justice respond that his programme 'is comedy, not even pretending to be information', but a lot of viewers don't seem to understand this. The whole point of political comedy and satire, as I am sure Stewart understands, is to convey a point, argument, or message, and the bottom line is that it has become one that almost exclusively promotes distrust and the abuse of those in politics. In March 2006 Michael Kalin used his column in the *Boston Globe* to explain 'Why Jon Stewart isn't funny' in the following terms:

> The ascension of Stewart and *The Daily Show* into the public eye is no laughing matter. Stewart's daily dose of political parody characterized by asinine alliteration leads to a 'holier than thou' attitude towards our national leaders. People who possess the wit, intelligence, and self-awareness of viewers of *The Daily Show* would never choose to enter the political fray full of buffoons and idiots.

It is possible to suggest that the nature and style of political comedy and satire has changed in three interrelated ways over recent decades. Firstly the subtleties of the genre have been lost. *Yes, Minister*, for example, provided a sympathetic and some would say accurate portrayal of the complexities of governing. The multi-award-winning *The Thick of It*, by contrast, which is often described as the twenty-first century's answer to *Yes, Minister*, presents a far more aggressive characterization of all politicians as spin-obsessed incompetents. If the intention of traditional satire was to make you think while making you laugh, the new genre of political satire seems more intent on simply harpooning its targets right through the heart.

Moreover (and secondly) the line between fiction and non-fiction is today blurred in the sense that a great deal of modern political satire and drama aspires to a level of authenticity that can often leave the viewer confused. The recent growth of 'drama documentaries' provides a case in point as these programmes reconstruct real events, depict real people, and are based on journalistic research but at the same time include scenes that are either based on guesswork or are artificially exaggerated in order to make them more dramatic. The boundary between representation and reality is further blurred by the use of digital technology (blending archive footage with new material) and the appearance of retired politicians or officials to add authenticity. In 2008, for example, the current affairs programme *Newsnight* commissioned a series of eight short dramas about the decision-making process in the run-up to the invasion of Iraq. Although these dramas (collectively entitled *10 Days to War*) were shown immediately before *Newsnight* with the intention of maintaining a clear barrier between drama and news, the gap between fiction and non-fiction was ultimately blurred by the manner in which the drama set the agenda for discussions conducted between relevant politicians and officials in the news programme itself.

The final change concerns a shift from policies and ideological positions to a focus on individuals and what has been termed a shift from satire to 'snark'. In his book *Snark: It's Mean, it's Personal and it's Destroying our Conversation* (2010) David Denby illustrates the emergence of a form of humour that aims to reinforce pre-existing prejudices (through a combination of personal, low, teasing, rug-pulling, finger-pointing, snide, obvious, and knowing sneering, etc.) rather than developing substantive critiques. A vast body of scholarship on modern comedy and satire from Iceland to Israel charts the manner in which comedy now tends to focus on the physical flaws and personal failings of politicians rather than their achievements or long-term commitment to social causes. It reveals a focus on the trivial rather than issues that are central to political affairs, and it approaches politics with a high degree of negativism that frames almost all politicians as selfish, incapable, and corrupt. Moreover, where issues of substance are raised, the challenges are defined not by way of the natural complexities of modern democratic governance but simply as a function of the absurdity and incompetence of political elites.

I can already hear the massed ranks of comedians and dramatists screaming 'That academic bore needs to get a life . . . it's just a joke!' and yet my concern is that this shift from healthy scepticism to destructive cynicism is actually exerting a real-world effect in terms of either sustaining or fuelling political cynicism. Although proving this link in hard terms is incredibly difficult, persuasion models from the discipline of social psychology reveal how the constant repetition of clear messages, in contexts that reinforce the credibility of those messages, tend to change attitudes. Comedians are seen as credible and programmes like *The Daily Show*, *The Colbert Report*, and *Saturday Night Live* provide softened echoes of hard news content but usually with an anti-political barb. Jay Leno may well promote a view of comedians and writers as thermometers rather than thermostats of public opinion about politics by arguing that 'we reinforce what people already believe', but studies suggest that comedy and satire may well have a more influential and darker edge. Three brief arguments support this point.

Firstly, research shows that individuals who watch large amounts of late-night comedy and satire tend to have over-inflated perceptions of their own levels of political knowledge and understanding. The focus on trivial issues and personal mockery unsurprisingly delivers relatively little in terms of broad political literacy and yet, largely as a result of the negative tone of the genre, individuals then tend to blame this lack of understanding not on themselves but on those evil politicians who run the system. The second reason why political comedy and satire may exert more influence than many comedians seem to acknowledge is due to what psychologists call the 'sleeper effect'. Because they know it is 'only a joke' an audience's motivation to scrutinize and challenge the underlying message is reduced, which in turn may actually allow it to exert more of an influence, especially when reinforced by complementary messages from the media. Finally, watching political comedy shows and satire has in some studies been demonstrated to be associated with lower levels of trust in politics and higher levels of cynicism, which, taken together, detract from democratic discourse and overall interaction.

To suggest that writers, comedians, or satirists have real political power is by no means new. Aristophanes' powers of political ridicule were feared and acknowledged to the extent that Plato singled out his play *The Clouds* as contributing to the trial and execution of Socrates. My aim in this section has been to expose this power as part of a broader account of the position of the media as a largely invisible political actor that arguably wields great power with very little responsibility. In *From Art to Politics* (1995) Maurice Edelman explored the link between comedy and public attitudes and suggested that because only a very small proportion of the public has any direct involvement in politics or with politicians, fiction supplied a substitute form of knowledge that was unchallenged by personal familiarity. 'Art is', he argued, 'the fountainhead from which political discourse, beliefs about politics and consequent actions ultimately spring.' For many people the jokes they hear comedians telling and what they hear on the late-night talk show is their main, if not their only, source of information about politics. What this very brief foray into the sphere of political comedy and satire suggests, however, is that the critique of politics has changed its force and nature in recent politicians.

To regard the media in all years, which in turn points to a narrowing of the ideas available to the public about their its forms, both conventional political and current affairs programming and less conventional political humour and satire, in purely negative terms is clearly to overlook the positive democratic role that is being played by some outlets. It is possible that political comedy and satire could foster political engagement by building a sense of community amongst viewers and making politics more enjoyable. This is exactly what happened in October 2010 when thousands marched through Washington, DC to attend a mass rally organized by the Comedy Central team of Jon Stewart and Stephen Colbert under the banner of 'March for Sanity'. Linked rallies were also held in over twenty American cities. Stewart described the aim of the event as being to allow the mass public to express their voice in order to promote reasoned discussion and end the 'partisan hockey' whereby the more extreme voices of American politics dominated debates and engaged in shallow forms of demonization that simply alienated most of the public. Maybe hope does lie in humour after all, but there was a subtle irony in the manner in which, despite Stewart's insistence to the contrary, most news coverage across America portrayed the rally as nothing more than a 'spoof' event that was designed to mock Al Sharpton's 'Reclaim the Dream' rally that had been held a couple of months earlier. Whatever the underlying aims of the 'March for Sanity' rally were, the simple fact is that events of this kind, alongside more constructive forms of behaviour, represent very much the exception rather than the rule and therefore do little to unveil the need to rediscover a form of civic journalism and, dare I suggest, even a new genre of civic humour. Now, however, I want to set these issues aside for fear that I may be focusing on the 'old' media too much and the 'new' media too little.

The Myth of Digital Democracy

During the final decades of the twentieth century a range of books trumpeted the great potential of the Internet to reshape democracy. 'To the extent that democracy needs saving', Tracy Westen argued in

National Civic Renewal, 'the new generation of interactive digital communications technologies has arrived—just in time to help'. Howard
Rheingold, an early and influential advocate of the democratic potential of the Internet, used the pages of the *Whole Earth Review* to suggest
it would become 'the great equalizer' due to the manner in which it
would shift 'the balance of power between citizens and power barons';
while in *The Electronic Republic* (1996) Lawrence Grossman similarly
created transformative expectations by suggesting it would 'extend
government decision-making from the few in the centre of power to
the many on the outside who may wish to participate'. The Internet
would for these campaigners not just supplement conventional politics
but lead to a paradigm shift in the nature and process of governing as
technological developments would allow citizens to reclaim control
over public affairs. Political participation would become more convenient, information more readily available and accessible, public deliberation involving large numbers of people would become easier. This
would, in turn, cultivate greater social understanding of competing
viewpoints and on-line voting would facilitate a deeper and more
direct form of democracy. Digital democracy would, therefore, offer a
way of closing the expectations gap and help in forging a more mature
and realistic debate about both the failures and successes of democratic
politics. A decade or so later I am left wondering what happened, what
went so wrong. Although there is a clear link between access to the
Internet and the drive towards democratization, as clearly seen in the
Arab Spring, in those long-standing Western democracies the internet's influence is, on the whole, destructive.

Far from fostering democratic values or active citizenship, cyber-
space has emerged not as a public arena dedicated to the common
good but as a fragmented landscape of shrill and sectional demands,
united by the simple belief that politicians are venal, stupid, and men-
dacious. The history of digital democracy is littered with great hopes,
dashed expectations, and broken promises. We remain information
rich, yet knowledge poor, which is a great shame because digital
democracy promised so much (but has delivered so little). This sober
and pessimistic argument is reinforced in a more recent body of writing that has charted the Internet's role as a mediator between the governors and the governed. Books including Vincent Mosco's *The Digital
Sublime* (2004), Matthew Hindman's *The Myth of Digital Democracy*
(2008), and Stephen Coleman and Jay Blumler's *The Internet and*

Democratic Citizenship (2009) all point to a legacy of dashed expectations and the evolution of an impoverished relationship between the public and politicians. In order to explain what has happened and why politics needs defending from the Internet it is necessary to briefly explore five interrelated questions:

1. What does the evidence reveal about who is using the Internet?
2. What kinds of groups and collective activities does the Internet appear to promote?
3. What kind of citizenship does the Internet appear to promote?
4. What does the evolution of the Internet suggest about its future potential for making democracy work?
5. What does the politics of the Internet tell us about the nature of democratic engagement more broadly?

In terms of who use the Internet for harvesting political information or engaging in *political activity*, the evidence is clear: it is generally only that small section of the public who have always been politically engaged and active. On-line activity therefore tends to mirror off-line activity and there is little evidence that the Internet has allowed the previously disengaged to reconnect. What is more, research suggests that contrary to closing the knowledge gap, the Internet has actually widened this gap, creating what could be called a 'fatter' model of democratic elitism rather than a broader, flatter model of vibrant mass politics. Put slightly differently, the Internet may have delivered a political world that is denser, wider, and possibly more inclusive and pluralistic but only to a minority of people who were already engaged. There is no doubt that the Internet has transformed the nature of social communication. Tweeting offers news faster than any other source, blogging allows everyone to voice their opinions, SMSs can organize events, and 500 million people across 190 countries are signed up to Facebook. But for the vast majority of people the Internet has very little if anything to do with politics. As Hindman's *The Myth of Digital Democracy* reveals, traffic to political websites is not only sparse, with about one-tenth of 1 per cent of all web traffic (compared to the 10 per cent of traffic that goes to porn sites) but is also highly concentrated in a small number of very popular sites that generally reinforce rather than challenge existing opinions (on-line self-segregation ensures that 95 per cent of blog readers only ever read material that reflects their own ideological position). Although this may provide a case of what Michael Schudson (resonating with Keane's work on 'monitory democracy' that was discussed earlier) calls 'monitorial citizenship' in his *The Good Citizen* (1999), nevertheless the breadth and depth of this virtual democracy hardly points towards a democratic renaissance. If anything, it points in the opposite direction and towards the perpetuation of the vaunted 'crisis of democracy' that is concerning so many people.

This is because, to move to the focus of our second question, the Internet has proved better at cultivating deep pools of social capital amongst like-minded individuals but has fared far worse in terms of building social bridges between those groups. This is a critical point because many of the vaunted advantages of the onset of a digital democracy, like increasing access to government information and forging new lines of democratic accountability, were actually secondary dimensions of the Internet's core promise to develop and promote those democratic values that are necessary for an active and engaged form of citizenship. A virtual public sphere could, it was argued, connect disparate individuals (politically, geographically, etc.) and foster dialogue and deliberation about key social challenges. On-line discussions would force citizens to encounter alternative perspectives, articulate their goals and priorities in ways that appeal to others, sharpen their sense of the realistic options and necessary trade-offs, abandon support for indefensible positions, and develop mutual respect that allows groups to coexist and cooperate when they disagree. In a sense, then, the Internet's connectivity would inject 'the civilizing force of hypocrisy' back into public debates.

In reality, the nature and structure of the Internet has done the opposite. As Cass Sunstein argues in his *Republic.Com 2.0* (2009), it has allowed people to pick and choose sites in a way that reduces engagement with alternative viewpoints and reinforces partisanship. The result is a shift towards well-organized 'smart mobs', 'information cocoons', and 'echo chambers', wherein users avoid the news and opinions that they simply do not want to hear. Balkanized groups tend to move towards the views of their most radical members. Members of such groups do not understand other perspectives or learn how to relate to people who are different. Beliefs (even completely false ones) are therefore reinforced rather than challenged. Not realizing that most thoughtful citizens do not agree with them, on-line group members generally assume that the government is either failing or corrupt when it takes contrary positions. The result is a form of political activity, practised by a comparatively small section of the public, that is increasingly shrill and aggressive in its approach to politics and politicians while also being increasingly unrealistic about what politics can and should deliver. The Internet has therefore provided a voice and a platform for an increasing range of sectional demands but not one attuned to cultivating or promoting any conception of the common general good.

As a result, just at the historical moment when we need a richer relationship between politics and politicians in order to confront the shared challenges we face, the Internet has delivered an arguably more impoverished relationship than we have ever had because of its failure to build social bonds *across* and *between* competing groups. This insular form of attitude reinforcement breeds a dangerous form of detachment, in which those who use the Internet as a political forum are rarely challenged to consider alternative viewpoints or how the common good might make compromise necessary. 'Digital natives' tend to fall into a naive view that the general public shares their own view of the world and as a result politics is failing. As a further consequence, crude libertarian, anti-political, and anti-establishment values flourish and manifest themselves in a worldview that appears dedicated to maintaining the population in a perpetual state of self-righteous rage. Peter Riddell's *In Defence of Politicians* (2011) takes this argument further by characterizing the essence of much on-line politics as,

hate-filled rants, invariably anonymous since their cowardly authors are unwilling to share their identities... many are offensive and contemptuous of anyone with whom they disagree, which means most politicians are invariably regarded as venal and useless. There is seldom even the slightest hint of any understanding of the complexities of government, or that politicians are trying their best, however mistaken they may be. (p. 32)

This tension between the fragmented nature of the Internet and the collective emphasis of politics forces us to step back a little and reflect upon our third question's focus on the topic of citizenship. In this regard it is possible to argue that the Internet has evolved to offer a very thin model of individually orientated on-line politics— 'thin' in the sense that it focuses on the opportunities afforded to individuals to have *their* particular interests realized through the 'new' media. It therefore offers a narrow liberal-individualistic model of consumer-citizenship which understands the web as primarily facilitating the effective transmission of viewpoints between individuals and representative decision-making processes. This liberal-individualistic approach is founded on the view of individuals as rational, self-seeking, instrumental actors and redefines citizenship away from an emphasis on collective political engagement towards citizenship as an individualized economic activity. This intensified focus on the consumer-citizen model of democracy helps explain the failure of the Internet to live up to the high expectations that were originally promulgated about its capacity to revitalize politics.

Works like Nicholas Negroponte's *Being Digital* (1995), James Bohman's *Public Deliberation* (1996), and Wayne Rash's *Politics on the Net* (1997) anticipated the emergence of a deeper and richer form of democratic citizenship that has in reality simply not emerged, due to the gradual colonization of the Internet by profit-driven market actors. The link between the issue of citizenship and the evolution of the Internet is therefore that the Internet initially emerged very much as an open access 'common good' facility. It was therefore imbued with a focus on educating, reflecting, arguing, challenging, learning, deliberating, contributing, and to some degree radicalizing as part of a broader commitment to democratic citizenship. However, the Internet's political vibrancy, energy, and potential has since the turn of the millennium been tempered through a well-documented and gradual colonization of the web by a small number of dominant media companies. This rapid commercialization of the Internet not only reduced the promise of the web as a levelling medium but has also squeezed out the more radical or questioning political voices. Far from democratizing politics, the Internet is increasingly allowing a small number of elites to control the flow of web traffic through their control of the dominant search engines. Google, Yahoo! and Microsoft handle 95 per cent of all search requests. This capacity to control the main gateways into the net, as Alex Halavais's *Search Engine Society* (2008) illustrates, provides a handful of private companies with the capacity not only to shape how political material on the web is accessed and presented but also to funnel traffic to popular, 'mainstream', and frequently pay-per-view sites (the top ten websites receive 25 per cent of all web traffic). As Robert Chesney first argued over a decade ago in *Rich Media, Poor Democracy* (1999), 'The only thing certain at present is that the eventual course of the Internet will be determined by where the most money can be made, regardless of social and political implications'.

This section has provided a rather gloomy account of the role of the Internet vis-à-vis politics. Its argument has not been that the Internet offers no democratic potential or that it is not used as a constructive tool of democratic participation and engagement by some sections of the community but that at the broadest level the great hopes for a digitally inspired democratic renaissance have not been fulfilled. In many ways the evolution of the Internet has mirrored that of the 'old' media in terms of a narrowing of news output, a preference for comment over information, and a clear drift towards what I would term 'junk journalism'.

And yet in some strange way I am quite glad that the predictions of a digital democracy have proved mythical. To me the promise of digital democracy and on-line engagement appeared not simply to be an excuse for laziness but, more importantly, it completely overlooked the central and defining essence of *democratic* politics. Politics revolves around building relationships, forging trust and emotional connections that can never be built through tapping a keyboard or adopting a disembodied telepresence. Politics is a face-to-face human activity and the danger of on-line engagement is that it could supplant off-line participation in those social groups that so often make a real difference to people's lives. If Robert Putnam hates the television for its impact on social capital, I similarly loathe the Internet for its impact on the lives and attitudes of the younger generation. Virtual communities are dead communities and I don't want to be bowling alone in a network society.

This rather strong line of argument takes us back to this book's focus on honest politics and the need to understand the challenges of democratic politics, especially as the public becomes more diverse and the world more interconnected. Democratic politics is a hard, dirty, and tiring game. It is a worldly art in which we must all make tough choices and balance our rights as an individual against our responsibilities as a citizen. The problem with the Internet is that it makes it all appear so easy. Web-based interest groups and paypal offer a new form of cheque-book citizenship in which individuals are nominally members of social groups but never actually attend meetings or participate in face-to-face activities. Moreover, the great democratic potential of the Internet tended to be implicitly based around the issue of convenience and the naive assumption that, if we could only make voting, accessing government publications, or expressing an opinion easier, then vast sections of the public would suddenly re-engage. The problem with this focus on convenience is that politics is rarely convenient. It is by its very nature inconvenient because it hinges on reconciling conflicting opinions and demands while also responding to a succession of unexpected incidents, challenges, and risks. Is it possible that digital democracy failed because it simply tried to make politics too easy by suggesting that individuals could fulfil the requirements of an active and responsible citizen without ever having to leave the comfort of their own home or be exposed to unsolicited, diverse, and occasionally unwelcome views? Does the Internet simply make it too easy to 'exit' from on-line debates and discussions when the tone of the debate forces you to start questioning your own political opinions and judgement?

Liars! Cheaters! Evildoers!

The first line of Janet Malcolm's influential book *The Journalist and the Murderer* (1990) reads, 'Every journalist who is not too stupid or too full of himself to notice what is going on knows that what he does is morally indefensible'. Although I cannot compete with the power or wisdom of this sentence, I can draw strength from it to conclude that if a key indicator of the health of a democracy is the state of its journalism and the standard of its media, I cannot help but feel we are in trouble. There may well be a problem of integrity in modern politics but I have no doubt there is an even bigger problem of integrity within the modern media. Don't let the media fool you into believing that they are the 'good guys', who protect you from the predatory politicians. Of course, like a magician who reveals the secrets of his profession, I am not supposed to reveal the secrets of political journalism and many have warned me that a settling of scores will undoubtedly take place at some point in the future. 'They'll get you. You know that don't you?' the senior civil servant whispered in my ear at a function in the Royal Automobile Club. 'They will hate it and at some point will exact their revenge.' It will be instructive to see if her warning proves correct (and please feel free to rush to my defence should the media at some point descend on me like a feral beast in one of their frequent feeding frenzies). For now, however, let me conclude this chapter by forging a link between the media's demonization of politicians and the broader 'politics of pessimism' that this book seeks to challenge before reflecting on how the media might play a more constructive role that contributes to a 'politics of optimism'.

To talk of demonization is to make an inevitable link with Stanley Cohen's *Folk Devils and Moral Panics* (1980). Cohen was interested in why societies appeared to be subject, every now and then, to periods of moral panic in which a person or group of persons emerges to become defined as a threat to societal values and interests. At the centre of the moral panic is the 'folk devil', who became an object of fear or contempt and provided the focus of a citizen backlash and some form of external intervention: 'visible reminders of what we should not be', Cohen emphasized, '... unambiguously unfavourable symbols'. Rightly or wrongly, the folk devil is therefore seen as the source of the societal threat and a full-scale *demonology* takes place by which the members of a new 'evil' category are placed in the 'gallery of contemporary folk devils'. Politicians were explicitly defined by Cohen as one element of the 'moral barricade of right-thinking people' who identified deviant social groups in the late 1960s. Fifty years since Crick penned his *Defence* and thirty years since Cohen published *Folk Devils*, it is possible to argue that politicians have crossed the moral barricade and have now themselves become the focus of a moral panic and of media-led demonization. As Tom de Luca and John Buell argue in *Liars! Cheaters! Evildoers! Demonization and the End of Civil Debate in American Politics* (2005) the general shift from a debate over policies in the media to a focus on personalities and private lives may represent a form of politics but ultimately the public and democracy is the loser.

Recent events also place the issue of demonization in sharp relief. The attempted assassination of Congresswoman Gabrielle Giffords in January 2011 led to a far-reaching debate concerning the use of violent language and imagery in politics. Groups on the far left and right of the political spectrum have in recent years made the demonization of politicians, frequently in a very aggressive and personalized format, their priority. 'We shouldn't demonize the government, its employees or its elected officials,' Bill Clinton told the American public in the aftermath of the shooting of Giffords. 'We can disagree with them but we ought to remember after the Oklahoma bombing, the difference between disagreement and demonization.' Clinton's sentiment echoes from a very different perspective the argument of the Dutch politician Pym Fortuyn in April 2002. 'The government and the media has demonized me personally,' Fortuyn argued on live national television, 'and if something were to happen to me then they will be partly responsible, and they can't just walk away and say "I'm not the one committing this attack". They helped to create the climate, this atmosphere. It needs to stop.' Two weeks later he was murdered.

The media offers great potential for enhancing democratic mobilization, engagement, and literacy but it also has a destructive quality that must somehow be kept in check. My fear is that we may have fallen for the romantic view of journalists and the media as heroic and beleaguered champions defending democracy when we should in fact stop glorifying those who make their reputation from being constantly cynical about politics and politicians. The problem with cynicism is that it is ultimately a fatalistic creed: it feeds disengagement because it tells us that in the end selfishness and mendacity will triumph, so why bother? Most politicians are not liars, cheats, evildoers, or demons. Nor are they angels or superheroes. Many politicians are in fact quite normal and generally fairly boring. This is because politics itself is generally boring, which in turn explains the challenge it presents to the modern media. To make it interesting enough to attract and sustain viewers, listeners, or readers it has to be 'sexed up' through the addition of scandal, deceit, and lies at every turn. My focus on the humdrum and dull—Max Weber's 'slow boring through hard wood'—and on the media's shift towards the sensationalist presentation of politics as a toxic brand does, however, leave me with a slight concern that I might be shooting the messenger. At the very least, to focus attention on the media risks overlooking the argument that I have attempted to make in earlier chapters: that if politics is failing, we are all to some degree complicit.

Any defence of politics against the media inevitably raises questions about the role of the public and the type of society in which we wish to live. Individuals make decisions about the choice, style, and content of the news with which they engage, and the behaviour of the market suggests that the public's appetite for sensationalist journalism is voracious. Scapegoating politicians or the media might make everyone else feel self-righteous, but it is also ugly. Blanket condemnation is too easy without stepping back still further and asking: from where is the demand coming? The truth is that the public often gets both the politicians and the media it deserves.

If the relationship between the media and the public is in need of repair, this can only come from change on both sides of the relationship.

In terms of supply the public must take seriously their responsibilities to be informed citizens, rather than passive consumers of gossip and tittle-tattle. As Alexis de Tocqueville emphasized in the 1830s, citizenship brings with it the obligation to cultivate 'habits of the heart' that allow you to look beyond yourself and appreciate your position as one element of the bigger picture. At the same time, however, it is the duty of the media to provide the information and knowledge through which citizens can engage in robust debates about the common good and the fate of our collective destiny. The public need to know about public affairs if they are to play an active and considered role in public life.

This obligation on the media is encapsulated in the concept of 'civic journalism' that in many ways takes us right back to the views of Joseph Pulitzer that opened this chapter. This is a form of journalism that would not seek to feed on speculative stories that owe little to reality; would not amplify specific incidents into systemic failings; would not focus on those ambitions that were not achieved rather than the majority that were; and although civic journalism would have to be 'right' (i.e. correct in terms of factual content) it would not need to be right *now*, in terms of being the first to break a story. Civic journalism would not set out to cultivate a more optimistic view of politics but it would at least provide a more balanced and considered account of why politics matters.

'What has surprised you most about life as the President of the United States?' a young student asked Barack Obama on the eve of the 2010 mid-term elections. 'I've been surprised', the President replied, 'by how the news-cycle is focused on what happens *this minute*. Sometimes it's difficult to keep everybody focused on the long term. The things that are really going to matter in terms of America's success twenty years from now, when we look back, are not the things that are being talked about on television on any given day.' The essence of civic journalism would revolve around the intellectual strength to offer fresh ideas in place of tired assumptions while also having some level of emotional sympathy for those who do at least have the courage to step into the political arena. With this in mind it is possible to shift our focus from defending politics from its various foes towards a more optimistic account that allows us to speak in praise of politics.

7

IN PRAISE OF POLITICS

Politics may be a messy, mundane, inconclusive, tangled business, far removed from the passion for certainty and the fascination for world-shaking quests which afflict the totalitarian intellectual; but it does, at least, even in the worst of political circumstances, give a man some choice in what role to play, some variety of corporate experience and some ability to call his soul his own.

Bernard Crick, *In Defence of Politics* (1962)

If we understood politics rather better, we would expect less of it. Consequently, we would be surprised and dismayed rather less often by its repeated failures to live up to our over-inflated and unrealistic expectations.

Colin Hay, *Why We Hate Politics* (2007)

The current economic downturn is only one aspect of a much more fundamental crisis. At its heart lies a fatal mismatch between public expectations and political rhetoric on the one hand, and the realities of tightening resource constraints, destructive climate change and the mechanics of global capitalism on the other. We now live in a society where everyone believes that they have a divine right to ever-rising living standards: that we have finally reached the sunlit uplands of ever-increasing consumption, and if the good times come to an end, our leaders must be to blame.

David Marquand, *The Scapegoat* (2010)

'We are all in the gutter,' Oscar Wilde once wrote, 'but some of us are looking up at the stars.' Why is it that this quote floats into my mind as I end this book? Could it be that the notion of a 'gutter' captures something about the messy and sometimes dirty rough-and-tumble of everyday politics while those who participate, those who dare to step into the arena, do so due to a sense of optimism and a belief in the capacity of 'mere politics' to make life better and are therefore 'looking up at the stars'? However, I cannot speak in praise of politics through the metaphor of a gutter because to do so would be to sail too close to the language and assumptions that have mistakenly brought politics into such disrepute. Eleanor Roosevelt's suggestion that 'It is better to light a candle than curse the darkness' appears a simpler and more accurate statement of the essence of this book. Making the case for politics is certainly difficult in the current climate. Even when you explain to the public that things will go wrong and that mistakes will be made, it is very hard to get across a sense that this is part of life and simply the result of the difficulties of the decision-making process, an accident, or even simply bad luck rather than some political conspiracy. Nevertheless, I have tried to write boldly and clearly with the aim of restoring a degree of confidence in the virtues of democratic politics as a great and civilizing human activity. I have tried to swim against the tide of popular opinion and I hope you feel I have at least been able to tread water, and have not drowned in my attempt to adopt what some might view as a brave (others a foolhardy) position. But as Bernard Crick emphasized in his original *Defence*, 'Only free men stick their necks out'.

You might think that I have stuck my neck out too far and for rather too long and that now the time has come for me to pull it back in and let everybody else have their say. I beg, however, that you allow me just a little more time to reflect upon how my defence of politics against *itself*, against the *market*, against *denial*, against *crises*, and against the *media* are each united by a common theme that allows me to speak out *in praise* of politics. If asked by the weary, fatigued, or bored to state succinctly in three short paragraphs what message this chapter seeks to implant in the mind of the reader I would respond as follows.

The simple fact is that what we obtain too cheaply we tend to esteem too lightly and my concern is that too many disaffected democrats take what politics delivers for granted. 'Politics' is not some strange activity conducted by 'them' rather than 'us'. The fruits of democracy are best seen through the lens of 'everyday politics'; in the schools and the hospitals, in the roads and the trains, in the courts and the shops, in community groups and social protests, in bars and sports clubs, in work and play, and most of all in the freedom to question and challenge.

From the nursery to the nursing home 'everyday' politics improves people's lives.

Those who have always lived in liberty do not appreciate the enormous power of the freedom that earlier generations fought for. Hundred of millions of people reap the benefits of freedom and stability but have no memory of life without democracy. For those lucky enough to live without the scars of lost generations, without the fear of brutal oppression, and for those who have never tasted their own blood at the hands of oppressors, let me warn you: never turn your backs on politics. Beware of those who promise you a pain-free future or the elimination of risk, and take a breath before you pour scorn on those who have at least dared to step into the arena. Politics is, at base, a moral activity and therefore a lack of trust in the capacity of political institutions, political processes, and politicians reflects a much deeper lack of faith in ourselves and in each other. This is because the nature of politics defines the nature of any society. Democratic politics therefore matters because it underpins *free* societies and not *fear* societies. It is not perfect. As I have commented previously, it cannot make 'every sad heart glad' but it can and does deliver stable societies that uphold certain values; it delivers certain public goods and protects the vulnerable and needy but does so in ways where the power of politicians ultimately and very directly depends on the popular will. Winners will win and losers will lose but at least the losers always get to state their case and then live to fight another day. If a crisis exists it is not that politics is failing but that we have lost our moral nerve and self-belief in the capacity of politics to foster positive change. The crisis of politics is therefore, at root, a crisis of confidence.

Democracy revolves around the possibility of collective decision-making about collective action for the common good but we have allowed it to become redefined as the freedom of individuals to pursue their own selfish interests and decide upon their own actions. The real failing of politics is therefore the manner in which it has cultivated societies in which everyone believes that they have a divine right to ever-rising living standards irrespective of their own personal endeavour, and if life fails to deliver then it must be those loathsome politicians who are to blame. No politician has the magic to satisfy *a world* of greater expectations, and the world does not have the resources to satisfy those expectations. Demonizing politicians might contribute to the myth of collective innocence but at the end of the day we are all complicit. As Eric Joyce, himself a politician, had the cheek to suggest,

What if it were the case that our democratic system does not systematically and dysfunctionally send just the scum of the earth to Westminster [or Washington, Canberra, Berlin, Paris, Rome or any other capital city]? What, instead, if it were true that many people were living lies and using politicians as a means of exorcising their own demons of guilt and frustration; politicians the vessel for their own imperfections?

We are all part of the problem and part of the cure, and our future will be defined by whether we reconnect to the power of genuine democratic politics in order to manage the transition from an Age of Abundance to an Age of Austerity or whether we continue as political infants until the challenges on the horizon are directly upon us. Individual responses to collective problems will always fail and only politics (and therefore politicians) can navigate the challenges that lie ahead. We are not therefore in 'end times' but we are in a time when we need fewer people carping and heckling from the sidelines and more people debating, learning, engaging, voting, and standing for office.

In this regard I hope to have at least provided some food for thought that may help you nourish a more positive and constructive approach to politics. The rest of this chapter is dedicated to fleshing out these points in just a little more detail. For those too tired or too full to take any more nourishment, I thank you for your time and hope that you do not think ill of me for what I have sought to say within these pages. For those with the space for just a little more food for thought let me conclude this book by seeking to engage with four simple questions.

1. Are we witnessing the death or end of politics?

No, we are witnessing the beginning of a new stage.

2. Does the public really 'hate' politics?

No, they just don't sufficiently understand it.

3. Why does politics matter?

Because it defines the very nature of our lives and society.

4. How should we regard those politicians who step into the arena?

With healthy scepticism and civilized respect.

As you can see I could not resist setting out my simple answer after each question and the rest of this chapter is dedicated to explaining and justifying these responses in a little more detail as part of a broader attempt to cultivate a more engaged and optimistic political future. Most importantly, what these four questions combine to offer is a focus on the future of democratic politics, and specifically about the need to ensure that our forms of political understanding and engagement evolve and mature in line with the challenges that will shape the twenty-first century. With this in mind let me reassure you that we are not living in end times. In fact, the most exciting stage of democratic history is just beginning.

Living in the End Times

It is possible that you never see more clearly what life is, or what you have in your life, until it is over. It is for this reason that an encounter with a dead creature can teach you so much. You can scrutinize its shape and form, you can touch and feel and smell, but what you really sense is what is missing, what has gone—life. To talk about the 'death' of politics, however, is surely misleading. Politics will exist whether it is defended or not. Politics is us. It is all human interaction. And yet we cannot ignore the existence of a widespread sense of concern that *democratic* politics is somehow failing and that politicians are not to be trusted. As a result the present age has been declared anti-political, post-political, and even unpolitical. There is, as Andrew Gamble writes in *Politics and Fate*, 'an urge to discredit and disparage politics and as faith in politics declines, so concern with and involvement in politics, decrease. The space for politics is shrinking, and with it the possibility to imagine or to realise any serious alternative to our present condition. This it seems is our fate.'

There is without doubt a wealth of literature on 'endism' in all its forms ('the end of politics', 'end of authority', 'end of history', etc.), and much of it highlights important social, economic, or political trends in the starkest of terms. Slavoj Žižek's *Living in the End Times* (2010), for example, talks of the 'forthcoming apocalypse' and draws upon Elisabeth Kübler-Ross's *On Death and Dying* (1969) to sketch out the history and future of liberal democracy and global capitalism. The four horsemen of this coming apocalypse that Žižek identifies (ecological crisis, economic imbalances, the biogenetic revolution, and increasing social divisions) have surfaced at various points during this book. For Žižek, our situation can therefore be defined as one of terminal decline in which our collective response to these challenges corresponds to the stages of grief (i.e. denial, anger, bargaining, depression, withdrawal, and acceptance). To talk of depression and withdrawal is to revisit the dark cloud of fatalism and despondency that undermines public distrust and disengagement from politics (discussed in Chapter 1). Fate and our future have acquired an unfortunate association with death, destruction, and impotence that for some reason completely overlooks the massive achievements of democratic politics during the twentieth century. Almost all our achievements come from the simple act of democratic political leadership amplified coherently by the many. This applies not just to the great or appalling acts but to the numerous mundane things that keep society running (waste disposal systems, electricity grids, sewerage systems, etc.). Nonetheless, we seem almost blinded to the evidence that collectively *we can* address major challenges and are instead trapped within the politics of fear. The outcome is a dangerous cocktail of fatalism, pessimism, and denial.

We are not living in end times. Our fate remains firmly in our hands. We are, however, living in a historical phase in which certain challenges cannot be ignored and where opportunities for positive new beginnings abound. The real danger is that we allow our modern pessimism and belief in the 'bad faith model of politics' to cloud our judgement about what we have and what we might be. In many ways the current pessimism about politics unmasks the fact that there are limits to the benefits of individualism and consumerism and therefore poses a need to construct a more meaningful way of living together; to rediscover 'the art of living', and by doing so move our conception of citizens back from consumers to instigators of social change. This thought brings us back to Žižek's work. He too ultimately rejects the notion that politics is somehow ending, but instead suggests that liberal–representative democratic politics (i.e. democracy as we know it) will not be able to deal with the four horsemen he identifies. His final stage of 'acceptance', where 'the subject no longer perceives the situation as a threat, but as a chance of a new beginning' is *exactly* the point at which we now stand and through which we can realign our social values and forge a more optimistic account of politics. So before we abandon ourselves to the inevitability of the apocalypse, let us dare to consider a different alternative based upon a new set of values. Let us have the confidence and self-belief in our capacity to shape the future through collective action.

The Italian author and politician Ignazio Silone was right when he wrote that although theories and policies can form the basis of a political platform, 'only a system of values can construct a culture, a civilization, a new way of living together'. A new 'politics of optimism' must therefore accept that the quality of modern life is determined not just by what we do or can accumulate for ourselves but how we interact with others, how we treat our friends, and how we engage with those we do not like. As has already been stressed, politics is *everyday politics*. It exists for most people not through the news, on the internet, or in Parliament but through the thousand-and-one encounters and transactions that shape each day of our lives (at the doctors, at our work, in our schools, on public transport, etc.). The great irony of the relentless pace of globalization, technology, and all the other factors that have changed the nature of political rule in the last fifty years is that they have arguably made us more reliant on each other, not less, if we are to lead successful and, most of all, happy lives. We need one another and we need to work together because it is only through a recommitment to and a deepening of *democratic* politics, as opposed to an individualized form of market-based *life* politics, that we will be able to enjoy the future.

This is an argument that can be traced back within the contours of John Keane's wonderful work *The Life and Death of Politics* by simply acknowledging the truth of William Morris's famous statement in *A Dream of John Ball* (1888) that 'fellowship is heaven, and lack of fellowship is hell; fellowship is life, and lack of fellowship is death'. To employ the language of 'heaven and hell' or 'black or white' risks injecting a false sense of clarity into political affairs, which by their very nature tend to be blurred and partial. As previous chapters have illustrated, politics should rarely be corralled into two simple and mutually opposing parts (public/private, good/bad, right/wrong, hero/zero, black/white, etc.) because to do so overlooks the various shades of grey that give politics its richness and that present real options around which everyone can to some degree agree. It is for exactly this reason that the golden thread running throughout each chapter of this book has been a focus on the need for proportionality and balance.

My defence of politics against *itself* was not therefore an attempt to dull the existence of great expectations but purely to suggest that if we understood politics a little better, particularly in relation to its internal contradictions and tensions, we might expect a little less of it. We might also understand that politics delivers *rights* and *responsibilities* and from this reflect just a little on whether we have all become a little too good at taking and demanding but possibly less good at giving and offering. 'Politics' does not simply involve the conduct and decisions of politicians but also creates a set of expectations regarding the behaviour and decisions of the public. This focus on shifting the balance also underpinned the defence of politics against the *market*. The reduction of everything to a financial value or a market-like relationship has arguably sharpened our sense of entitlement while dulling our sense of belonging to a broader political community. The Logic of the Market and the Logic of the State pull in quite different directions and although this can sometimes create a degree of creative tension, it also risks undermining the collective ethos, those social values on which so much depends. The question is not therefore focused on the market *or* the state but simply how we come to an appropriate balance and face up to fundamental questions that cannot be avoided, about the role and limits of governments and markets. These are questions about the respective responsibilities of individuals, communities, and the state that need to be tackled in order to make the case for renewal and a reformed public realm for the coming decades.

The issue of balance also informs the politics of *denial*. It is completely acceptable and appropriate that politicians may on occasion wish to draw upon the expertise, knowledge, and legitimacy of various types of expert. The problem occurs when the scale of that involvement becomes disproportionate to the extent that politicians no longer appear responsible for anything and as a result the public feels there is no point in voting or engaging more broadly. The politics of *crises* similarly emphasizes the need to retain a sense of scale and proportion. Crises will occur from time to time and fear can sometimes act as a positive social force against complacency or denial. Yet we have somehow (at least arguably) reached a situation where everything is defined as a crisis and as a result *free societies* have become *fear societies* (at exactly the point when *fear societies* in North Africa and the Middle East are fighting to become *free societies*). Most people in the developed world have never been so prosperous, safe, or educated and yet they feel fearful, let down, and disengaged. Everything certainly appears upside down and inside out. There is no need for me to return to my defence of politics against the *media* apart from saying that we urgently need to reflect upon what the belief that 'only bad news sells' is doing to our politics. Returning to this book's focus on *supply* and *demand* in relation to politics, it is also necessary to ponder upon the social responsibilities, not just of those who supply a constant flow of junk journalism but also those who demand and pay to consume sensational and salacious stories.

We are not therefore living in *end times* but we are living in *changing times*, changing in the sense that politics over the short to medium term will be focused on managing decline. In this sense the global financial crisis, the problems of the euro and the general economic downturn form specific parts of a much broader challenge posed by the mismatch between political promises and public expectations at one extreme, and the realities of diminishing resources, over-population, and destructive climate change, on the other. The future of politics therefore rests on the politics of public expectations and the need for politicians to focus on managing demand as well as supply. The 'politics of optimism' that I seek to encourage, however, does not revolve around the politics of low expectations or seek to restrict politicians to the lowest rungs on the ladder of social ambition, but it does seek to replace blind faith or ignorance with defiant optimism and understanding. Only a God or a beast would claim to be able to satisfy a world of ever greater expectations, but democratic politics does provide a way of managing the transition in a way that presents a civilized future and prevents society descending into a set of warring tribes.

For now, however, it is necessary to conclude this section by simply stating that the great value of democratic politics lies in its capacity for change and renewal. How politics has operated in the past should not be confused with how it might operate in the future and it is almost undoubtedly true that one consequence of the 'bad faith model of politics' has been that 'politics' and politicians have to some degree become too apologetic, too feeble, too doubtful, and lacking a sense of mission. In this regard, the challenges that lie on the horizon present great opportunities in the sense of acting as unifying forces around which we can all agree. Fear might therefore offer a sense of social cohesion against a common threat. As Ulrich Beck argues, 'In an age where trust and faith in God, class, nation and progress have largely disappeared, humanity's common fear has proved the last—ambivalent—resource for making new bonds.' Maybe the existence of fear can provide grounds for optimism, but what do you do if a free society is simply not fearful enough or lacks the self-belief to respond? Highlighting the positives and minimizing the negatives will only be achieved if we can rebuild a sense of self-belief and self-confidence. The twenty-first century will reward those who lead from the front; those who can harness public support for far-reaching change; those who can bridge boundaries, reject common assumptions, and think anew; and those who are optimistic and open-minded instead of those who appear to have already conceded defeat. We can either forge change or have change forced upon us. In shifting from 'the politics of pessimism' to 'the politics of optimism' the problem is not so much our situation or the clouds on the horizon but ourselves. Rachel Carson captured this dilemma in the same year that Crick published his *Defence* when she wrote in her book *Silent Spring* that 'The human race is challenged more than ever before to demonstrate our mastery, not over nature but of ourselves'. It is in order to engage with this dilemma that the next section reflects on why our relationship with politics remains so ambivalent.

Why We Hate Politics

Just as we are not living in 'end times' so too do I believe that we do not 'hate' politics. It would be closer to the truth to suggest that the public no longer understands politics or how it affects their lives and it might also be true to suggest that people generally and understandably tend to react against any individual or organization that attempts to tell them what to do. The fact that politics is founded, as discussed previously, on the basis of *externalized rationing*, in which we all sacrifice a degree of our freedom and income for the benefits we accrue from public services and for the chance to live in a free society, obviously provides ample opportunities for individuals and groups to complain and criticize. Our aim here must be to set out a way of helping the public to understand politics better and shift the popular debate away from the failure of politics and politicians and more towards the mastery of ourselves.

We have travelled far and wide to get to this point and so it may be worth revisiting just a few of the key arguments or themes we have encountered on this journey. The simple argument of this book has

been that the balance between the methods of *attack* (plentiful, aggressive, multi-dimensional, popular, etc.) and *defence* (limited, passive, static,
highly unfashionable, etc.) have become out of kilter. Politicians (and
this *is* their fault) have generally adopted the tools and strategies of a
crude form of 'attack politics' that alienates vast sections of the public.
Few politicians appear to have the moral strength to consider whether
winning an election is really worth it if the price of achieving a victory
is that all you inherit is a desert. Perhaps the next generation of politicians will think more carefully about the nature of political competition and how they win power so that they have something to inherit
and build upon when they get there. We cannot, however, be too hard
on politicians. The expectations that people now have of politicians
and the political process, particularly in a world where ideological loyalties and religious beliefs have waned, have increased massively. In the
days when we believed that there were, to use an old legal phrase 'Acts
of God' (i.e. things that were wholly out of human control), the expectations we laid on the shoulders of decision-makers were lower. We
knew and accepted in some sense that the capacity of man and woman
was limited. But we now place on the politicians themselves those
expectations that we once passed on to the supernatural and we refuse
to believe that these are beyond our control. This means that we now
have completely unrealistic expectations of politicians and when they
fail we blame them for things that are as completely beyond their control as beyond ours.

A braver man might go further and dare to suggest that our political
capacity and energies are being exhausted by the emergence of a culture of expectation or what might more accurately be labelled a malevolent sense of entitlement amongst sections of the public. Individualism
combined with celebrity culture and a host of other factors appear to
have convinced some people that there is no sense in working hard or
saving today in order to secure a better future, due to a false expectation
that politics will somehow create a perfect society and a better life for
all. That is not how politics works. Democratic politics will only (can
only) deliver social benefits in proportion to the degree of support it
receives from the public, not simply in terms of financial support but
also public support in terms of people engaging, questioning, volunteering, standing, and so on. To some extent, therefore, the public gets
the politics and politicians it deserves. By this I mean that if politicians
are not realistic or truthful about the raising of expectations, and in the

claims they make about what is possible, it is quite difficult for the public not to vote for the ones that promise the most *unless* the public themselves are exercising a little bit of realism and scepticism, based upon some understanding of politics.

Political literacy and understanding and not hatred therefore sits at the centre of any debate about revitalizing politics, explaining how democratic politics works or why it matters and how we might cultivate a deeper and more optimistic approach to politics. The key to promoting the public understanding of politics takes us back to the theme of 'everyday politics' that we have already discussed. Politics is messy and it sometimes fails and it often does not work out exactly as you hoped it would because politics is just the same as any other human activity. There is no special political skill, no special political person or class, and no special political morality. It is all a matter of people struggling with different issues just like it is in a family, a small business, or a local sports team, in fact in any other walk of life. The issues may be bigger and the consequences greater and potentially more dangerous but when all is said and done the nature of the decisions that politicians face are exactly the same as the nature of other decisions that individuals or groups face throughout their lives. As the US historian and social commentator Garry Wills writes in his *A Necessary Evil* (1999),

Like any human institution—like the family, or the university or the labor union—governments fail and become dysfunctional or destructive at times. Even the best of governments will show on occasion most of the faults that governments are accused of—becoming wasteful, inefficient, impersonal, rigid, secretive, oppressive. But when marriages fail, we do not think it is because marriage is an evil in itself. Government is a necessary good, not a necessary evil; and what is evil in it cannot be identified and eliminated from the good if the very existence of the good is being denied at every level. (p. 297)

If you can get this simple message across and explain that formal politics is in many ways like family politics or community politics then the gap in terms of social understanding tends to close very quickly. As a result it is perfectly possible to imagine an approach to politics that is skilful in not inflating public expectations, which does not take that dangerous extra step to outbid opponents, and which does not drive up the public's expectations far beyond what is reasonable. The public would, however, need to reciprocate this offer of good faith by defying Mencken's belief that the public will always admire 'the most daring liars' while detesting violently 'those who try to tell them the truth'. This adage brings us neatly to our second theme and an opportunity to look more closely not at politicians but at ourselves. Indeed, the antithesis to any defence of politics that seeks to promote the collective above the individual would have to be Wolff's *In Defence of Anarchism* (discussed above). A respectable anarchist would by definition have to see the role of the state as inevitably reducing freedom and treating individuals as little more than children. Maybe it is possible, however, to defend the unpardonable sin of paternalism on the basis that we might 'hate' politics exactly because, like children, we resent being told what to do?

As Alain de Botton ponders in *Citizen Ethics in a Time of Crisis* (2010), we could ask whether a lack of freedom remains the principal problem of communal life in advanced liberal democracies. 'In the chaos of the liberal free market, we tend to lack not so much freedom, as the chance to use it well. We lack guidance, self-understanding, self-control, direction … Being left alone to ruin our lives as we please is not a liberty worth revering.' Libertarians of whatever hue would generally argue that any suggestion by the state about how we should live our lives or spend our money can only be an unwelcome distraction from our own free capacity. The sense of this position is surely undermined to at least some degree, however, by the evidence of double-think amongst the public. Even Žižek's *Living in the End Times* is rooted on the very first page in an acceptance that 'The people wanted to have their cake and eat it: they wanted capitalist democratic freedom and material abundance but without paying the full price'. Could it be that on occasion we actually need and secretly want a well-timed nudge, push, or shove, as long as it moves us along a road we know we really need to travel? If this is true, it is possible that we need to revisit certain baseline assumptions and not define the role of the state as an inherently intrusive and undesirable one. To make this point is not to trumpet the heavy hand of the state or attempt to promote some modern version of the enlightened dictator but it is to inject a little balance into the debate about the relationship between the individual and society. Is it possible that we 'hate' politics simply because, unlike those unfeasibly self-contained, sane, and reasonable grown-ups that we are assumed to be by liberal politicians, most of us are still more like disturbed children (or political infants)? As Alain de Botton notes,

We may in many situations long to be encouraged to behave as we would hope to. We may want outsiders who can help us to stay close to the commitments we revere but lose sight of. We may benefit from having witnesses who can shame us away from indulging our anger, narcissism, sadism, envy, laziness or despair. Freedom worthy of illustrious associations should not mean being left alone to destroy ourselves. It should be compatible with being admonished, guided and even on rare occasions restricted and so helped to become who we hope to be.

The notion of 'becoming who we hope to be' takes us back to the theme of finding a new way of living together that is sustained through a set of authentic political relationships. The ugly truth is that the need for environmental sanity, if not in the face of climate change then in the face of over-population, will challenge the culture of consumption. These challenges will deliver near and present examples of what Joseph Schumpeter labelled 'gales of creative destruction' in his *Capitalism, Socialism and Democracy* (1942), and only creative optimism will see us through. This is because the Age of Abundance will pass whatever we do. Indeed it will probably pass a lot more quickly than seemed likely just a decade or so ago, and managing the transition will demand not simply a new moral compass but a new moral economy in which what gives our lives meaning is recast. What we might label 'the politics of decline', by which I mean the transition to a more sustainable lifestyle, should not be defined as a threat or a 'bad' thing but might more positively be viewed as an opportunity not to *reduce* our standards of living but to *change* our standards of living in a way that provides depth and meaning. This, in itself, forces us to remake the case for democracy and set out exactly why politics matters.

Why Politics Matters

At around ten o'clock at night on 16 December 2010 a young man named Mohamed Bouazizi borrowed 200 dollars in order to buy fruit and vegetables to sell the next day. With his nickname of 'Basboosa', Mohamed Bouazizi was well known and liked within the small Tunisian town of Sidi Bouzid. His father had died when he was 3 and he had worked since he was 10 to support his mother and five siblings in a country that was rife with poverty and corruption. At about 10.30 the next morning the police began harassing Basboosa as he sold his wares from a wheelbarrow in the streets. He did not have enough money to pay the police the bribes they demanded and this led to him being abused, beaten, and spat upon by local officials and the police, and his wares eventually tipped into the gutter. The local governor refused to listen to his complaint or even meet with him and so, worn down and exhausted by the daily struggle to live within an authoritarian society, Basboosa poured petrol all over his body and set himself alight. That was the spark that lit a series of protests and revolutions across North Africa and the Middle East. It is also a spark that chimes with Eleanor Roosevelt's comment about lighting a candle and cursing the darkness.

Democratic politics matters, despite all its imperfections, because it will not tolerate persecution, torment, or oppression. It sheds light where otherwise darkness would fall. Politics matters because it is founded on compromise, it protects certain rights and freedoms, and it ensures that the politicians are dependent upon the public, rather than the public being dependent on the politicians. Fundamentalism—be it religious, environmental, economic, biological, or cultural—is therefore incompatible with any form of democratic politics simply due to the fact that it represents a refusal of dialogue in a world whose peace depends upon it. However convinced men or women are about the rightness of their party or cause, they must compromise its claims to the needs of some electoral and legal framework, at least in so far as the only way of removing it from power does not have to become a revolution. The brinkmanship and partisan posturing in August 2011 concerning the Congressional approval of the US federal budget provides an illustration of the capacity of democratic politics and its institutions to bridge a great range of opinions and demands. The process may not have been very pretty and, as the President admitted publicly as he finally signed the budget in the Oval Office, 'As with any compromise, the outcome is far from satisfying'. Yet the simple fact is that political compromises are the price that has to be paid for liberty and stability. Let us not delude ourselves that we are not paying a price but let us summon reasons to remember why it is normally worth paying. If all boats are burnt, if assertions are made categorically, as in a totalitarian party, then the pace of the advance can only be intensified and made desperate. Politics is to be praised, like science, for always retaining a line of retreat and for allowing you to make contact with others with whom you may wish to share your thoughts, your hopes, your dreams, and even your anger.

So democratic politics is founded on an acceptance of difference and a belief in conciliation. Where authoritarian regimes state 'you are wrong and I am right', democratic regimes, by contrast, will say, 'I believe in one thing, you believe in another but let's just acknowledge our differences, learn from each other and rub along as best we can'. And politics certainly does *rub along* in the sense that it produces tensions and gridlocks, it can be slow and frustrating, it tends to grate and grind and it is inevitably a messy and worldly art. But there is no end to the praises that can be sung for politics. As Crick wrote in his original *Defence*,

in politics, not in economics, is found the creative dialectic of opposites: for politics is a bold prudence, a diverse unity, and armed conciliation, a natural artifice, a creative compromise, and a serious game on which free civilization depends; it is a reforming conserver, a sceptical believer, and a pluralistic moralist; it has a lively sobriety, a complex timidity, an untidy elegance, a rough civility, and an everlasting immediacy; it is conflict become discussion; and it sets us a human task on a human scale. Politics deserves much praise simply because politics is a preoccupation of free men and women and its existence is a test of freedom. The praise of free men is worth having, for it is the only praise which is either free from servility or condescension.

Politics then is civilizing. It rescues mankind from the morbid dilemmas in which the state is always seen as a ship threatened by a hostile environment of cruel seas and enables us, instead, to see the state as a city settled on the firm and fertile ground of mother earth. It can offer us no guarantees against storms encroaching from the sea but it can offer us something worth defending in times of emergency or amid threats of disaster.

Politics, then, is a way of ruling divided societies without undue violence. This is both to assert, historically, that there are some societies at least which contain a variety of different interests and differing moral viewpoints and to assert, ethically, that conciliation is at least to be preferred to coercion among normal people. But let us claim more than these minimum grounds: politics is not just a necessary evil; it is a necessary good. It matters, as I have already stressed, because it is all about making difficult decisions about thorny issues, or the distribution of limited resources with inadequate information and then about trying to win support for them. Promoting the public understanding of politics in this manner may also demand that we attempt to remove some of the magic or glamour that surrounds formal politics. Politicians are no better or worse than the rest of us, in fact they are just the same as the rest of us. It is therefore not necessary to get too precious about politics. There is no need for everyone to be actively engaged in politics, or become expert in the nature of modern governance. Politicians will always provoke cheap mockery from spectators but they should not take these things to heart. Successful politicians must learn how to swallow insults and learn from their mistakes. Politics can withstand a lot of apathy and when the normally apathetic person suddenly becomes greatly interested in political questions, it is often a sign of danger.

There is, however, a need to achieve a sense of balance or proportionality amongst those who are politically active. Democratic politics is a voluntary and collective activity and people should be encouraged to join in (by voting, participating, volunteering, observing or generally cultivating some level of political understanding) but if individuals do not, they have to some extent given up on their right to criticize it. Politics is not a spectator sport. It is not a game you can decide to play or not. It is, however, a game that demands a continuous civic conversation about how we live together and what we want to accomplish. There is nothing democratic politics cannot achieve, but shaping our future and replacing the 'politics of pessimism' with 'a politics of optimism' will require that we all start facing up to our civic responsibilities. Let me state just one more time that *if* politics is failing, we are all to some degree complicit. The former politician Tony Wright captured this sentiment in the 2009 *Political Quarterly* Annual Lecture when he reflected on the theme of 'doing politics differently' and what would be involved.

Politicians could play it straight. Journalists could play it fair. Interest groups could say who is to have less if they are to have more. Governments could promise less and perform more. Intellectuals could abandon their 'mechanical snigger'. Social scientists could start writing in good plain English. The blogosphere could exchange rant for reason. Electors could decide to become critical citizens.

Revitalizing politics, building a set of authentic political relationships and forging a more optimistic view of the future therefore depends on us all taking responsibility for the depth and nature of democratic politics in the twenty-first century. In fact what we need is a new public service bargain that creates a balanced set of incentives *and* sanctions for those who dare to step into the arena.

The Man [and Woman] in the Arena

'A writer's life is a highly vulnerable, almost naked activity,' Harold Pinter told the audience when he collected his Nobel Prize in December 2005. He went on to note that 'We don't have to weep about that. The writer makes his choice and is stuck with it. But it is true to say that you are open to all the winds, some of them icy indeed.' I expect that chill winds may blow in my direction when this book is published but that is simply the price I will have to pay for trying to say something different and for trying to make the case for something I believe in. If I have failed to make the reader think, if I have wasted your time and failed to convince you that if placed in their position you might act just as politicians do, then I can only apologise. My only response would be to say that it is better to try and fail than never to try at all or, just like Boris Pasternak's eponymous character in *Doctor Zhivago* (1958), 'I don't like people who have never fallen or stumbled. Their virtue is lifeless and it isn't much of value. Life hasn't revealed its beauty to them.' I may well have fallen and stumbled along the way but I hope to have revealed just a little of the beauty of 'mere politics' to you.

It is important to note, however, that I am not, have not, and never will be 'an academic' in the traditional sense of the term. This is both a blessing and a curse—a curse in the sense that leaving school at 16 without any qualifications has left me with a pathological frailty about the quality and standard of my work, a gift in the sense that when I write, my thoughts lie not with academic conventions or established modes of scholarly enquiry but simply with a desire to paint the world as I see it and to help people understand the realities of governing in the twenty-first century. If I have fallen and stumbled at various points, it might also reflect the fact, just as Crick's original *In Defence of Politics* was written 'in one deep breath at a particular time' so was this book. As noted before, the basic outline of this book was conceived and for the most part written during a single long train journey from Exeter to Sheffield.

This book is not finished. It remains to some degree, like democratic politics, a work in progress to be challenged, refined, developed, and critiqued. Nevertheless, the time has now arrived to draw it to a close and let other people take forward the debate I have attempted to ignite. So let me bring this book full circle and conclude by returning to the analogy of a storm and tying it to the notion of a new public service bargain.

Away from the bear pit of the legislature or television studio, political life is focused on the maintenance of a system in which ideas, conflicts, and interests are openly articulated and peacefully resolved. It is rarely glamorous or easy, it is often dull and messy, and it is generally not a profession full of liars, cheats, and scoundrels (every profession has its bad apples and politics is no different). It is, however, an increasingly hard and brutal business. It is not for the faint-hearted and although this has always been the case there has been a step-change in recent years in relation to the intensity of the pressures, the brutality of the criticisms, the personalized nature of the attacks, and the arbitrary targeting by the media. The storm that to some extent inevitably encircles democratic politics has for a range of reasons become more intense and toxic. My concern is that we are hollowing out the incentives that need to exist to attract the best people from all walks of life to get involved and stand for office. A process of demonization has occurred that can only end in a situation where 'normal' people feel inclined to walk away, leaving only the manically ambitious, socially privileged, or simply weird in their stead. In a sense we risk creating a self-fulfilling prophecy that politicians are 'all the same' exactly because of the climate we have created. This narrowing of the talent pool from which politicians are increasingly drawn is directly attributable to the sheer force of the storm that is constantly breaking upon the shores of politics. Politicians must operate with an almost perpetual swirl of scandal and intrigue breaking around their heads. Many good people currently brave the storm in the hope of making a positive difference to their community, city, or country but someone with a life, a family, interests beyond politics, the ability to do other things, can feel deeply inclined to stick to them and leave the political storm to itself.

We need to calm the storm. 'Attack politics' benefits only the sellers of expensive advertising space and certainly not the public. The real question with which this book leaves us is: how does politics need to evolve and mature for the modern world? This is a subject of profound importance to all countries no matter at what stage they are in terms of democratic progress. The problems we face in the twenty-first century cannot be solved by thinking the way we did when we created many of these same problems in the twentieth century. As a result we need to rethink the way we make decisions and relate to each other and the way in which we conduct our politics. The sooner we have this debate and have it in a sensible and educated and reasonably generous spirit, the better. It is *the* issue of our times. The twenty-first century is going to change dramatically in its geopolitics with the rise of major new power centres in the world, not all of which will be democracies. If we want to protect our democratic freedoms and play a role in which we shape the future, rather than being tossed about in a storm that will take us who knows where, we need to be able to show that we are able to redefine what politics means to us in a meaningful way. Ultimately what matters is the moral ambience, the background on which public life is conducted and carried forward, but the 'bad faith model of politics' provides a very poor canvas for us to draw upon.

As such, there is an urgent need to decide how democracy is going to change as a result of all the other changes that are going on around us. With this debate in mind I want to acknowledge my great debt to Bernard Crick and end this book by going back not fifty years to his *Defence* but almost exactly a hundred years to a speech delivered with both anger and passion by Teddy Roosevelt in April 1910. 'The Man in the Arena' remains the most authoritative rebuke ever given to those who carp from the sidelines about the failure of politics.

It is not the critic who counts; not the man who points out how the strong man stumbles, or where the doer of deeds could have done them better. The credit belongs to the man who is actually in the arena, whose face is marred by dust and sweat and blood; who strives valiantly; who errs, who comes short again and again, because there is no effort without error and shortcoming; but who does actually strive to do the deeds; who knows great enthusiasms, the great devotions; who spends himself in a worthy cause.

It is in this spirit that I urge readers to reject the bland fatalism that has for too long blinded us to the merits of democratic politics and in future dare to sing out in its defence.

MORE FOOD FOR THOUGHT

7 *In Praise of Politics*
   Living in the End Times   Slavoj Žižek (2010)
   Why We Hate Politics   Colin Hay (2007)
   Why Politics Matters   Gerry Stoker (2006)
   The Man [and Woman] in the Arena   Teddy Roosevelt (1910)

INDEX

Index